Small States in World Politics

Thanks so much
for your visit!

Jeanne

Small States in World Politics

Explaining Foreign Policy Behavior

edited by
Jeanne A. K. Hey

BOULDER
LONDON

Published in the United States of America in 2003 by
Lynne Rienner Publishers, Inc.
1800 30th Street, Boulder, Colorado 80301
www.rienner.com

and in the United Kingdom by
Lynne Rienner Publishers, Inc.
3 Henrietta Street, Covent Garden, London WC2E 8LU

Library of Congress Cataloging-in-Publication Data
Small states in world politics : explaining foreign policy behavior /
Jeanne A. K. Hey, editor.
p. cm.
Includes bibliographical references and index.
ISBN 1-55587-920-9 (alk. paper)—ISBN 1-55587-943-8 (pbk. : alk. paper)
1. International relations. 2. States, Small. I. Hey, Jeanne A. K.
JZ1316 .S45 2003
327.1'01—dc21 2002031722

British Cataloguing in Publication Data
A Cataloguing in Publication record for this book
is available from the British Library.

Printed and bound in the United States of America

The paper used in this publication meets the requirements
of the American National Standard for Permanence of
Paper for Printed Library Materials Z39.48-1984.

5 4 3 2 1

For Jackson and Owen—
May you live in a world
that is healthy and safe for all children

Contents

Acknowledgments

This project was born in a turret office in the Chateau de Differdange in southwestern Luxembourg. I would therefore like to begin by thanking Ekkehard Stiller, Maisy Dumont, and the faculty and staff of the Miami University Dolibois European Center (MUDEC). Conversations with MUDEC faculty, especially Monique Kieffer Kinsch, Guy De Muyser, and Emil Haag, proved immensely important in helping me to form my thoughts and questions about small states in general, and about Luxembourg specifically. Ekkie Stiller was particularly helpful in connecting me with politicians in Luxembourg.

I also extend a heartfelt thanks to all the contributors to this volume, including those whose chapters do not appear in the final version. The book has assumed different forms over the many months. Contributors were gracious in managing the many changes and requests put to them. This is truly a collaborative and collective effort, though I certainly accept all responsibility for any deficiencies in the volume. Lynne Rienner not only responded with enthusiasm and generosity to my original proposal, but she was also key in suggesting contributor names. Bridget Julian was always available, helpful, and sympathetic, while at the same time maintaining a high standard of quality. Her understanding during a difficult time was especially important for me. I could not ask for a more ideal editor.

In Oxford, Heather Moore, Oliver Funk, and Olexiy Kalinichenko helped in preparing the list of references. Dorothy Pierson receives my most ardent appreciation for her work in transcribing my editing notes of the final chapters. Lots of ink from my side and software problems with the various chapters made this an arduous task. As always, Dotti performed it perfectly and with a smile that (almost!) never faded. My appreciation goes to Ryan Barilleaux, chair of Miami University's Department of Political Science, who provided very helpful advice.

Throughout the project I could always count on praise, encouragement, and suggestions from my husband, Thomas Klak. His academic expertise far exceeds my own and he stands as a constant source of inspiration and support. Our son Jackson spent many hours in preschool while I worked on this and other projects. Together with Tom, we toured numerous small states in Europe while I was beginning this research. Our son Owen was born during the first year of work on this project. I edited many first drafts with him asleep beside me, or playing on the floor. His infancy and this book are forever etched together in my brain. My children have affected my life in many profound ways, not the least being to put my work into perspective. They always provided me with something more important to do than work. Yet they both have been remarkably generous in sharing me with the office. For both of these things, and because they bring me such joy, learning, and new windows on the world, I dedicate this book to them.

Jeanne A. K. Hey

1

Introducing Small State Foreign Policy

Jeanne A. K. Hey

The international system has undergone fundamental changes in the past fifteen years, with strong implications for small state foreign policy. Small states today enjoy more international prestige and visibility than at any other time in history. In most cases, their physical security is ensured, while the rise of such transnational efforts as the European Union (EU), the Free Trade Agreement of the Americas, and the North Atlantic Treaty Organization (NATO) put them on a legal and diplomatic footing with larger countries. The end of the Cold War means that small states in the third world are no longer pawns in a global competition for superpower status. The Gulf War, the first major global conflict to occur after the collapse of the Soviet bloc, was fought to defend the sovereignty of a tiny state, Kuwait. Luxembourg and Belgium, the smallest members of the European Union, are not only seats of the EU's major institutions, but also active and often influential players within the European bloc. Kofi Annan, the widely popular Secretary-General of the United Nations and now a Nobel peace laureate, is from Ghana, a country that has for years played a role in regional affairs that is greater than its small status would suggest.

That said, many poor small states, no longer able to play the superpowers off one another, have fewer policy options now than at the height of the Cold War. They often find themselves caught between the demands of the international economic power brokers—including the United States, the European Union, the International Monetary Fund (IMF), and the World Bank—which call for fiscal restraint, and those of their own citizens, who are eager to receive the benefits of government spending. Meanwhile, wealthy small states that have pursued regional integration to advance their own goals and influence now find their protected status threatened by the expansion of such regional institutions as the European Union. In this time of both great opportunity and great risk for small states, this book examines small state behavior in the global arena.

Defining Small States

Much of the literature on small states spends a great deal of time on the problem of definition. Yet, despite decades of study, no satisfactory definition has been found (Pace 2000: 107). Baehr (1975: 459) even concluded that the definitional problems were so great as to make the concept of smallness useless as an analytical tool. In contrast, I argue that no strict definition is necessary either to employ "smallness" as an analytical device or to glean findings about foreign policy behavior from it.

Attempts at definitions have included geographical size, population size, and a country's degree of influence in international affairs (Vital 1967; East 1975; Sanders 1989; Von Daniken 1998). A review of the research reveals that scholars have at least three different communities in mind when they speak of "small states": microstates with a population of less than 1 million, such as the former British colonies in the Caribbean (e.g., Clarke and Payne 1987; Braveboy-Wagner 1989; Sanders 1989); small states in the developed world, especially Austria, Belgium, Luxembourg, the Netherlands, and Switzerland (e.g., Goetschel 1998; Katzenstein 1985); and small states in the so-called third world, including former colonies in Africa, Asia, and Latin America, many of which are larger than states in the first two categories. The problem emerging from this threefold typology is that conclusions about foreign policy behavior are typically drawn *within,* rather than *across,* the three types, thereby limiting their applicability to general small state foreign policy theory.

The three types include many countries. Indeed, as Daniel Thurer (1998: 37) points out, "if we look at today's world, we easily discover that it is a world made up of small states." Roderick Pace (2000: 107) similarly notes that the European Union will very soon be dominated by states with populations of less than 10 million. But as Paul Sutton (1987: 7) reminds us, a small population or geographical size does not necessarily coincide with a "small-scale political system." Luxembourg, a tiny state by any definition, has a thriving, competitive parliamentary democracy, a developed bureaucratic structure, and stable constitutional institutions. It thus certainly illustrates Sutton's point. Similarly, small size does not automatically translate into vulnerability in the international arena. Although Israel is a very small state in terms of area, it remains one of the most active and even aggressive actors not only in its region but also on the global stage.

Do such examples mean that all attempts to develop a theory of small state foreign policy are in vain? The authors of this book hold that the answer is no—clearly, individual exceptions to theoretical precepts do not alone invalidate a theory, and as Wilhelm Christmas-Moller (1983: 43) has pointed out, nobody denies the existence of small states. But the question remains: Where do we draw the line between small and nonsmall states? A rigid definition that groups countries by population, geography, or any other quantifiable measure is of little service; researchers will always want to include exceptions to such definitions because they *feel* that the exceptions are small states, despite their non-adherence to strictly defined criteria (Cohen 1987: 209). Instead, we adopt David Vital's position (1971) that a concept—a loosely defined notion of small states that eschews rigid specifications—is preferable to a definition when discussing small states.

For the purposes of this book, then, the concept of a small state is based on the idea of perceptions. That is, if a state's people and institutions generally perceive themselves to be small, or if other states' peoples and institutions perceive that state as small, it shall be so considered. This approach is consistent with those articulated by Robert Rothstein and Robert Keohane, who have pointed out that the psychological dimension should complement any objective criterion by which to define smallness. Rothstein (1968: 29) argued that "a small power is a state which recognizes that it can not obtain security primarily by use of its own capabilities, and that it must rely fundamentally on the aid of others." Keohane (1969: 296) offered a different, but still perception-based, conceptualization: "A small power is a state whose leaders consider that it can never, acting alone or in a small group, make a significant impact on the system." More recently, Laurent Goetschel (1998: 13) wrote that "in traditional political thought . . . 'small' in the context of foreign and security policy meant that such a state was perceived as no danger to neighboring states." In other words, states are deemed small not by any objective definition, but by their perceived role in the international hierarchy. In fact, the research on small states, despite its attempts at formal definitions, is best characterized by an "I know one when I see it" approach to choosing its subjects of inquiry (Hey 1995a).

I would argue that this approach improves on rigid definitions that fail to reach an agreed-on group of small states. It also avoids the intellectual squabbles that invariably arise in reaction to any specific definition of a small state. Indeed, the small state literature has been too bogged down in such arguments. The conceptual approach adopted in this book suggests that we define small states as they themselves and others define them, and in so doing make our research efforts parallel to the world in which small states and others interact.

What Do We Know About Small State Foreign Policy Behavior?

Definitions aside, early research on small states coincided with that on "weak states" and "small powers."[1] The focus was on small states' role within a hierarchical international system, as well as on their relatively limited power capabilities. Vital (1971) spoke of a global "class structure" that deprived small states of the option of using force in the way that larger states could; and there was general agreement that small states would seek out multilateral organizations and alliances to ensure their security and achieve foreign policy goals. Furthermore, small states would seek limited foreign policy objectives and engage in a relatively low number of activities.

Maurice East (1975), however, concluded that small states were in fact more likely than large states to engage in risky behavior. Because small states had fewer diplomatic and information-gathering resources, he contended, they were more likely to become involved in international affairs when the stakes were already high and high-risk action had become necessary. Peter Katzenstein (1985) further complicated the picture by demonstrating that small European states, many with weak military capabilities, outperformed their larger neighbors in policy flexibility and creativity, thus turning on its head the idea that small states were at a permanent disadvantage.

Although the underlying theme of research conducted by Robert Rothstein, David Vital, and Marshall Singer was that small size and weakness did curtail foreign policy options and goals, these authors also noted important exceptions to this general rule. Vital (1967) acknowledged that level of development, geography, importance to great powers, internal stability, and other factors modified a state's foreign policy behavior. Singer (1972) argued that some small states possessed "attractive power," even if they lacked "coercive power," by which he meant that small states could exploit their importance to other countries in ways that enhanced their foreign policy success. Rothstein (1968) studied the impact of various world systems on small states and found that some gave small states more options and security than others. For example, although a bipolar system affords small states maneuverability in that superpowers scramble to win their allegiance, it offers less security to small states than does a "conservative" balance of power, in which great powers are more intent on keeping what they have than on expanding empires.

An examination of more recent research on small state foreign policy behavior, especially covering the years since the end of the Cold War, reveals two impediments to the development of a theoretically coherent subfield within the study of foreign policy analysis. First, too few *comparative* empirical studies of small states exist in the literature in a way that contributes to theory building. And second, the realist paradigm dominant in the study of international relations posits that the "big players" are worthy of the most scholarly attention because they are the shapers of the international system (Waltz 1979)—which essentially relegates research on small states to a subordinate status within political science.

That said, much valuable empirical and theoretical research has been conducted in the area of small state foreign policy. The following review of that literature, seeking to contribute to the development of a unifying theory, focuses on two questions: What common foreign policy behaviors do small states exhibit? What common explanations are provided to account for those behaviors?

Identifying Small State Foreign Policy Behavior

Scholars studying small state foreign policy have identified a multitude of behaviors that small states either do, or are expected to, exhibit.[2] To summarize the most commonly cited behaviors, small states tend to

- exhibit a low level of participation in world affairs
- address a narrow scope of foreign policy issues
- limit their behavior to their immediate geographic arena
- employ diplomatic and economic foreign policy instruments, as opposed to military instruments
- emphasize internationalist principles, international law, and other "morally minded" ideals
- secure multinational agreements and join multinational institutions whenever possible
- choose neutral positions
- rely on superpowers for protection, partnerships, and resources
- aim to cooperate and to avoid conflict with others
- spend a disproportionate amount of foreign policy resources on ensuring physical and political security and survival

This is a comprehensive and serviceable list. The behaviors observed conform with a theoretical approach that sees small states as insecure, limited in foreign policy resources, and seeking to maintain their influence as best they can in a "realist" world in which they are at a disadvantage. Nonetheless, even a casual glance at the list reveals two primary flaws. First, it is too long to be meaningful, that is, to act as a guide for identifying and predicting how small states will act. Second and relatedly, it is self-contradicting. It tells us that small states rely on superpowers for resources and protection, indicating an alliance, but also that they choose neutrality. It claims that small states focus on diplomatic and economic instruments, but that they are consumed with security concerns, the latter suggesting that military alliances and buildups would be paramount.

Does the fact that these numerous and sometimes contradictory behaviors emerge among small states mean that we can generate no theory to capture the essence of small state foreign policy behavior? The answer depends on whether scholars can identify the conditions under which small states choose among the behaviors available to them. Certainly, small states are not unique in responding differently to similar conditions. In my own research, for example, I discovered that one small state, Ecuador, exhibited a wide range of behaviors when confronting the challenges of underdevelopment and small size (Hey 1995b). Those differences in behavior could largely be accounted for by the ideology and preferences of foreign policy makers, as well as by the issue area under consideration. This was not to say that smallness did not influence foreign policy, only that its influence was not uniformly directed.

Explaining Small State Foreign Policy Behavior

Scholars attribute a myriad of causal factors to small state foreign policy behavior. But if there is one piece of conventional wisdom about how best to explain small state behavior, it is that the answer lies at the system level of analysis. That is, because of their relatively weak power base within the international system, small states will act in passive and reactive modes, rather than as proactive agents of international change (Sutton 1987: 20). This is especially true for states with a weak sense of nationhood, such as Belgium and many of the former colonies (Cohen 1987; Zahariadis 1994).

If it were true that the sources of small state behavior were always or even usually found outside domestic borders, we could rejoice in the fact that small state foreign policy theory had found a parsimonious paradigm that has eluded most other areas of international relations research. The problematic reality, however, is that the small state literature abounds with arguments over theory, cases that do not fit the accepted wisdom, and greatly varying conclusions. I suggest that much of the failure to reach conclusions about what best explains small state foreign policy stems from two fundamental problems.

One problem is some scholars' apparent willingness to debunk the conventional wisdom (i.e., the relative dominance of international determinants of small state foreign policy) on the basis of inadequate evidence. Miriam Elman (1995: 187), for example, argues that we should look to domestic institutional choices rather than international determinants to explain small state foreign policy. Domestic institutions, she claims, are more important than international or individual forces because they define the paths of available options open to a government in a foreign policy situation. This may well be true; but Elman provides no reason as to why it would be particularly true for small states as opposed to any others. So the question remains: Even if all states are bound by their institutional structures and histories, are small states relatively more affected by external constraints? Elman's study of the United States during the pre–Civil War period does not answer the question, especially for modern small states at the turn of the twentieth century.

Similarly, David McGraw (1994) contends that ideological differences among New Zealand's political parties explain that country's foreign policy behavior, but he insufficiently controls for other factors. McGraw argues that, although different New Zealand governments behaved similarly on two dimensions of small state foreign policy behavior (frequency of participation in world affairs and propensity for conflict with large powers), they differed markedly in other areas (moral emphasis in foreign policy, emphasis on multilateralism, and degree of focus on economic issues). He explains that New Zealand's Labour Party is more internationalist and idealistic and the National Party is more realist, and that these differences account for foreign policy variations. This is consistent with my findings on Ecuador (Hey 1995b), which show that, on issues within their control and that carry relatively little risk, Ecuadoran governments have followed their ideological leanings. However, behavior is more uniform in Ecuador than in New Zealand on the "high politics" issues of debt and trade, no doubt owing to Ecuador's status as an underdeveloped state, very vulnerable to decisions and events in the international financial community.

Sasha Baillie (1998) differs from many of her peers in arguing that small state influence and behavior vary and are dependent on three factors: a country's particular historical context, its decisionmaking processes and the institutional framework within which it works, and its negotiation behavior. Addressing a specific question—what determines the extent of influence that a small state can have on a supranational organization?—her study of Luxembourg demonstrates that these three factors help to find the answer. While some of Baillie's concepts are international in nature, such as the European Union's rules and institutions, most of her findings focus on the domestic. This is an example of research that goes beyond an examination of single-level variables, but that lacks the comprehensive analysis of systemic variables that is needed to confirm the study's conclusions.

In contrast to these examples of research that undermines the "conventional wisdom," Nikolaos Zahariadis (1994) errs too much in the opposite direction. Zahariadis takes as a given that small states are disproportionately influenced by external factors when compared with more powerful ones. (Katzenstein's 1985 study of small European states subverted that assumption.) He therefore explains Greek animosity to Macedonian independence solely as a function of Yugoslav nationalism, that is, an external variable that shaped foreign policy behavior in the entire region. His account is persuasive and indeed may be correct. But the point remains the same. Because he does not subject his findings to counterexplanations, he is unable to say with much conviction that system-level factors were the most important. These representative examples, I suggest, reflect the fact that the literature on small state foreign policy lacks the kind of paradigm that can guide researchers to generate conclusions that are comparable and cumulative.

A second problem in the current small state literature is its outdated focus on state security. One can understand the emphasis on security in the first decades after World War II, when realism reigned as the dominant theory in foreign policy analysis, but it does not reflect most small states' priorities today. Realism holds that security is the top priority for all states, and that it would be all the more crucial for small states lacking in resources. But foreign policy analysis has evolved significantly in its "second generation" (Neack, Hey, and Haney 1995). It reveals that other factors at the individual, bureaucratic, and state levels very often have at least as much influence on foreign policy behavior as do international security concerns. The small state foreign policy literature should catch up with this theoretical progress and the concurrent changes in the empirical world.

The turn of the century is probably the safest moment in history for small states in terms of their physical security. International law, a more interventionist United Nations, and an almost completed decolonization process have all contributed to small state security. The collapse of the Soviet Union and the dissolution of Yugoslavia have created a host of new small states, all of which now enjoy international legitimacy and relative safety from outside aggression. Admittedly, that process has been bloody, for example, in some former Yugoslav states. But it is interesting to note that the *larger* former Yugoslav republics of Croatia and Bosnia suffered more at the hands of the Serbs than did the smaller states, Slovenia and Macedonia. Slovenia and Macedonia may be able to attribute their relatively peaceful independence to the low numbers of ethnic Serbs in their populations; the point remains, however, that Croatia's and Bosnia's larger size did not protect them from Serb aggression, and Slovenia's and Macedonia's smaller size did not make them more vulnerable to it. Similarly, in the wake of the terrorist attacks of September 11, 2001, it is the United States whose security is most under scrutiny. Smaller states are considered less vulnerable to the primary security threat of twenty-first-century terrorism.

Toward a Conceptual Framework

James Rosenau, hailed as the father of comparative foreign policy,[3] suggested that the explanatory factors needed to account for foreign policy behavior would vary according to three traits: the size, the level of development, and the political system of any given state (1966). He organized his explanatory factors according to five levels of analysis: system (the international system), role (referring roughly to bureaucratic actors), government (the relationships among government actors), society (public opinion, national culture, and other domestic traits), and idiosyncratic (individual). This levels-of-analysis framework remains a powerful starting point from which to examine small state foreign policy behavior, though for our purposes in this book we collapse the role, government, and society levels into one, the state level.

The basic notion underlying Rosenau's inductive approach is that different categories of inputs into the policy process (system, state, individual) will vary in their explanatory potency according to the "type" of state under consideration. "Small" is one of those types. The essential questions about small state foreign policy remain the same as those that Rosenau proposed. To what degree are small states manipulated by the world's system and the actions of others? Conversely, do leaders in small states have the luxury to implement policy as they see fit because they are not viewed as important or threatening to other states? The most unexamined question concerns the state level: What patterns emerge at the domestic level in small states of widely differing political, economic, and historical backgrounds? This last question is especially important because it includes variations in economic development. To date, the literatures on poor state foreign policy and small state foreign policy have not interacted sufficiently.

In this book we draw on Rosenau's inductive approach. The authors of each empirical chapter have responded to a series of questions that were designed to create studies that will, as a group, generate a significant body of research. Each author presents detailed findings about the recent foreign policy behavior of a particular country, seeking to explore the following:

1. At the system level of analysis: What evidence exists that state security is an important factor in small state foreign policy? To what extent is the small state vulnerable to external influences (regional and global)? Is policy determined by factors and actors outside the state?
2. At the state level of analysis: What evidence exists that domestic factors—such as pressure from the population at large, legislative and other governmental bodies, and elite and popular interest groups—influence small state foreign policy? Does the state enjoy a relatively small and cohesive foreign policy bureaucracy that makes policymaking efficient? Is there evidence that bureaucratic politics plays a role? How does the country's level of wealth and development influence policy?
3. At the individual level of analysis: What evidence do you find that individual leaders and their foreign policy advisers influence small state foreign policy? Do individual leaders have relatively more or less autonomy in decisionmaking than they would if working in a larger state?

It is important to point out here that chapter contributors wrote on the foreign policy behavior and period that they felt were most relevant and to which they could best speak. The chapters are therefore not identical in terms of outline or time period under study.

Volume Outline

This book brings together some of the most accomplished scholars in the area of small state foreign policy. They have emphasized empirical content and explanatory rigor in their country chapters, providing a base from which to draw theoretically informed conclusions about small state foreign policy behavior.

The volume includes chapters from a wide array of "small states." Intentionally, it examines small states with differing regional, size, and development profiles. The reader will recall that we posit that, if a state is perceived as small either by its own people or by others, it should be considered a small state. We do not shy away from that definition, purposefully including both states that many observers would perceive as small and those that are in dispute. This diversity will put to test the utility of the perceptual approach to defining small states. Also, a comparative analysis of the chapters will allow the reader to distinguish between the impact of "small" and that of "underdevelopment" on small state foreign policy behavior, as discussed in Chapter 10.

Chapters 2–4 discuss small states in the Americas. Frank Mora writes about Paraguay's post–Cold War and post–Alfredo Stroessner foreign policy. Jacqueline Braveboy-Wagner, who both pioneered and continues to advance the study of Caribbean foreign policy, examines foreign policy in a series of English-speaking Caribbean states. Peter Sanchez considers Panamanian foreign policy since the ouster of General Manuel Noriega.

Moving the empirical focus to the developed states of Europe, in Chapter 5 I look at the foreign policy of Luxembourg, a tiny state, but one that is very wealthy and a founding member of the European Union. In Chapter 6, Paul Luif examines Austria's foreign policy "under stress," referring to the dilemma Austria faces as a traditionally neutral country in an increasingly integrated Europe.

In Chapters 7–9 respectively, Abdoulaye Saine writes on Gambia's foreign policy since the 1994 coup, Curtis Ryan analyzes recent Jordanian foreign policy, and Zachary Abuza looks at the foreign policy of Laos, a country that has been woefully neglected in Western studies of international relations.

In Chapter 10, I conclude by assessing the findings of the case studies in the context of the questions posed above. I identify the special challenges that small states face, draw out the common conclusions and explanatory forces, and hopefully establish the beginnings of a theory of small state foreign policy that can act as a foundation for future research.

Notes

1. See, for example, Vital 1967, 1971; Rothstein 1968, 1977; Keohane 1969; Singer 1972; East 1975; and Katzenstein 1985.

2. Prominent examples of this research include Vayrynen 1983; Espindola 1987; Sutton 1987; Sanders 1989; McGraw 1994; Elman 1995; Baillie 1998; Goetschel 1998; and Pace 2000.

3. Comparative foreign policy is now known more commonly as foreign policy analysis (Neack, Hey, and Haney 1995).

2

Paraguay: From the *Stronato* to the Democratic Transition

Frank O. Mora

An overview of the analyses of Paraguay's foreign policy reveals that variables at all three levels of analysis play a part in accounting for the landlocked state's international behavior. Paraguay's long tradition of personalism and autocratic rule, since before the regime of President Alfredo Stroessner, emphasizes the role of the executive over the legislature and society in foreign policy decisionmaking.[1] Paraguay's strong caudillo heritage exaggerated personal rule, and weak institutionalization has led to the dominance of the executive in all areas of public policy (Lezcano Claude 1989).

Additionally, the path of Paraguay's managed transition *initiated from above*—provoked by a crisis of internal decomposition in the sultanistic regime of Stroessner—allowed many institutional and structural vestiges of the regime to survive and shape the foreign policy (decisionmaking specifically) of Paraguay's incomplete and precarious democracy. Despite democratization, Paraguay's institutions and bureaucracy are still permeated by patrimonial and clientelist networks. The Ministry of Foreign Affairs, like many other organs of the state bureaucracy, lacks the professionalism, modernization, and rationalization needed to become an efficient actor in foreign policy formulation. It remains stranded in the improvisation and institutional deficiency of the previous authoritarian regime. The incompetence of the foreign ministry resulted in a more executive-dominated foreign policy decisionmaking process. As reflected in the analysis of personalism in Latin American small state foreign policy, "weak countries with limited foreign policy bureaucracies provide ample opportunities for individual leaders to leave their mark" (Hey 1998: 112). This is certainly the case with Paraguay. Therefore, because of the structural continuity and immobilism of Paraguay's "protected democracy" and its continuing status as a small, underdeveloped, and dependent state, the determinants that conditioned and shaped Paraguay's foreign policy during the Stroessner era have not changed dramatically in the post–Cold War, postauthoritarian period.

Finally, the systemic or external determinant of small state behavior is also valuable in explaining Paraguayan foreign policy during the authoritarian and democratic regimes, despite a dramatic structural transformation of the international system (i.e., the end of the Cold War). The literature on small state foreign policy, as noted in the introduction to this volume, has emphasized that because of their weak political and economic power base, small states are vulnerable and constrained in their behavior by the structure of the international system. Whether it is the Argentine-Brazil subregional rivalry, the Cold War and U.S. policy, or the globalization of democracy and markets, Paraguay's external behavior (and regime type) is strongly influenced and dependent upon power relations and paradigmatic changes in the international system.

This chapter examines and compares some of the patterns and variations in the foreign policy of Alfredo Stroessner's personalist-authoritarian regime and the two administrations (Andres Rodriguez and Juan Carlos Wasmosy) of the democratization period (1989–1998). It begins with a discussion of Paraguayan politics and foreign policy during the Stroessner era (1954–1989), emphasizing the personalist-authoritarian tradition and international sensitivities and vulnerabilities of this landlocked nation. The specific objectives and determinants of Stroessner's foreign policy are examined within the context of the three explanatory variables discussed above. Next, the chapter will focus on the structural and institutional features of Paraguay's incomplete and precarious transition and its impact on foreign policy. The chapter ends with a discussion and assessment of the potencies of each variable in explaining Paraguayan foreign policy since democratization.

The *Stronato:* Regime and Foreign Policy

Paraguay's small, isolated, and landlocked position in the Southern Cone, between two rival giants, has a tremendous impact on its security and political and economic development (Gonzalez 1990). Paraguay suffered from marginalization, economic underdevelopment, and foreign intervention, particularly after the Triple Alliance War in 1870. In addition to indigenous Guarani culture and Spanish social organization, geographic isolation and dependence reinforced and enhanced the authoritarian, paternalistic, and fatalistic political tradition of Paraguay.

As Joseph Pincus (1968: 6) notes, Paraguay's traditional culture and vulnerable international situation influenced its domestic political system: "Paraguay's increasing struggle to consolidate its independence, defend its frontiers, and integrate national territory into a defensible political unit has created and perpetuated the tradition of strong personal, authoritarian rule and a highly centralized paternalistic administration of the country."

Few observers consider Alfredo Stroessner's patrimonial regime to be an aberration of Paraguayan political history.[2] The only difference is that the *Stronato* was a more sophisticated, modern, and institutionalized form of autocratic rule consistent with the "neosultanistic" type of regime, in which the "binding norms and relations of bureaucratic administration are constantly subverted by personal fiat of the ruler."[3] The centrality and indispensability of Stroessner (personalism) and the emphasis placed on loyalty to *el único lider* by military and party elites enhanced the power of the executive on public policy matters, decimating any professionalism or rationalization of the state administration.

Stroessner skillfully penetrated and seized control of the two most powerful institutions in Paraguay at the time: the Colorado Party and the armed forces.[4] By 1959 Stroessner had purged many Colorados, turning the party into a tool of his power and legitimacy. Stroessner controlled the Colorado Party, which monopolized political power. Concurrently, he penetrated and politicized the armed forces by introducing political criteria for promotions and assignments while requiring that all officers be Colorado members. The armed forces were further neutralized and controlled, as were the Colorado Party and other organizations of society, by a system of corruption (Stroessner believed contraband to be the "price for peace"), graft, and privilege that was dispensed to all loyal government and military officials. It was through an adroit mixture of democratic trappings, repression, and co-optation that Stroessner was able to successfully demobilize and deactivate society, reducing all possibility for political mobilization independent of the state (Simon 1990b).

The regime lacked any ideology other than xenophobic nationalism and virulent anticommunism. Stroessner identified with the West in the Cold War and wasted no time in declaring the regime's full support for the Truman Doctrine. Asunción received political support and legitimacy, and invaluable material support in the form of military aid and economic and financial assistance that helped prop up his regime (Mora 1997). Until the mid-1980s, the international system proved advantageous for the regime and Stroessner effectively manipulated it to serve his interests. For example, Stroessner's strong anticommunist stance and the internalization of U.S. national security doctrine exemplified the desired objective of exploiting the external for domestic political gain. In Paraguay, the doctrine emphasized the use of security and armed forces to counter all internal and external "communist threats"—the lever used by many Latin American dictators to suppress all opposition, while ensuring U.S. political and economic support needed to extend the life of the regime (Yore 1992). External actors such as Brazil and the United States contributed to the regime's longevity, at least until the mid-1980s.

Foreign Policy Determinants: Relations with the United States and Neighbors

Fernando Masi (1991b: 3) characterized Alfredo Stroessner's foreign policy during much of the regime as "benign isolation." This approach consisted of discriminating and diversifying economic and commercial relations with select states, necessary in overcoming Paraguay's geopolitical prisonality (and in strengthening his domestic position), while maintaining a "low profile" in order to minimize criticism and pass unnoticed under the façade of "representative democracy." In other words, the Stroessner regime did not seek an active role in world affairs for fear that it would attract attention, resulting in pressures against his regime. Conveniently, political instability and dictatorship in many of Paraguay's neighbors and U.S. preoccupation with communism in the region diverted attention from Stroessner's repressive but stable regime. President Stroessner, the dominant actor in foreign policy making, took advantage of an ideological and polarized international system that proved propitious for the type of "ideological and praetorian-caudillist" foreign policy that helped him strengthen and consolidate his neopatrimonial regime.[5]

What were Stroessner's principal foreign policy objectives? First, as mentioned above, maintain a low-profile foreign policy to avoid undue attention to the repressive nature of the regime while seeking political and economic support and legitimacy from key allies: Argentina, Brazil, and the United States. Second, enhance but counterbalance political, economic, and commercial ties with the United States and its two powerful neighbors. In addition to attracting much needed capital and aid for development and modernization, this pendulum policy would diminish Paraguay's vulnerabilities. Third, expand trade and contact with regional organizations and ideologically sympathetic or neutral regimes, especially South Korea, Taiwan, South Africa, and Japan. This not only diversified Paraguay's external relations, but also provided alternative funds for development. Fourth, maintain a strong anticommunist stance in regional and global organizations consistent and supportive of the internal objectives of the national security doctrine regime. Finally, support national and regional integration and cooperation arrangements, specifically in the areas of energy and infrastructure projects.[6] In sum, if there is one overriding goal of Paraguay's foreign policy that encapsulates the objectives discussed above, it is that Stroessner sought (with considerable success) to obtain the support of anticommunist external actors needed to sustain the stability of the regime.

An enduring explanatory factor in Paraguay's foreign policy is its geographic and cultural isolation. Paraguay's vulnerable geographic position as a landlocked buffer state between two powerful and menacing neighbors was an overwhelming determinant of Stroessner's foreign policy. In other words, feelings of insecurity and vulnerability caused by geopolitics and defeat in the Triple Alliance War contributed to certain hermetic and nationalist attitudes.

The second central factor of Paraguayan foreign policy was the absolute concentration of power in the hands of the patrimonial ruler. Paraguay's geopolitical and cultural isolation and the concomitant ideological tradition of national chauvinism enhanced the position and power of *el actor único* in the decisionmaking process of foreign policy. As a result of the monopolization and personalization of power, Paraguay's foreign policy was categorically designed and executed by *el actor único*.[7] As with all public policy matters, the legislature, political parties, and society were excluded from any role or participation in Paraguay's international relations; as a result, no interest or expertise developed in the area of foreign policy.[8] Stroessner made both the important and the trivial foreign policy decisions.

Under Stroessner, Paraguay's political system transformed the state and its bureaucracy into a structure where the patrimonial logic, cronyism, and corruption prevailed. The state bureaucratic-administrative apparatus did not distinguish itself as having adopted much of the rational-legal characteristics of a modern Weberian state. All state agencies and organs were penetrated and made into instruments of his power and patronage—devoid of any bureaucratic professionalism or rationality (Chiavenato 1980: 90–110; Diaz de Arce 1986). With respect to foreign policy, Stroessner's authoritarian regime never concerned itself with professionalizing, institutionalizing, or modernizing the principal government bureaucracy in charge of the nation's international relations. The Ministry of Foreign Affairs was never given the capacity or responsibility for formulating and implementing a coherent foreign policy based on specific national interests. According to one analyst, "the structure of the Paraguayan foreign service (during the Stroessner period) followed many of the rules and requirements of the nation's diplomacy in the previous century . . . there is still no true Paraguayan career diplomatic corps as in Brazil, the United States, etc." (Ceuppens 1971: 207). It is not that Stroessner's Paraguay lacked a law governing the foreign service and ministry; Law 219 of 1970 established the diplomatic and consular service, and Executive Decree 5817 of 1984 established the organic structure and internal regulations of the Ministry of Foreign Affairs.[9] In reality, the ministry and its personnel lacked any of the structure and professionalism the law sought to establish on paper. Stroessner turned the ministry into an institution of patronage where sycophants and cronies were given key positions at the expense of meritocracy and professionalism. As a result of the foreign ministry's incompetence and lack of institutionalization, the charge of formulating and executing foreign policy shifted (by design) to the president and his close advisers in the Palace of Lopez (Simon 1988: 214–215).

The third important factor of Paraguayan foreign policy was the Cold War and Stroessner's relationship with the United States.[10] Stroessner seized and internalized the opportunity offered by the Cold War to align his regime and foreign policy closely with the United States. Once again, foreign policy and security were not defined by a set of national interests or priorities, but by the prerogatives and interests of Stroessner and his regime. Stroessner and his close advisers, particularly Foreign Minister Raul Sapena Pastor (1956–1976), understood that Washington's economic and diplomatic support could be counted on if Paraguay became a fearless defender of U.S. containment policy. Upon assuming power, Stroessner's regime immediately identified with the West and adopted U.S. national security doctrine (Yore 1992). Stroessner became a vociferous anticommunist, following the U.S. position on all matters in return for aid and legitimacy (Estigarribia and Simon 1987: 20; Abente 1988). In defining the principal components of Paraguayan foreign policy, Stroessner (1977: 211) stated:

> In international policy, in general, the Government of Paraguay gives decided support to the United States of America, as leader of the free world in its fight against international communism, and we share with this great nation the ideals of justice, peace, rights and liberty, in order that the world in which we live can be more secure and have more collective and individual guarantees.

In addition to consistently voting with the United States at the United Nations and the Organization of American States (OAS), Stroessner offered, as he said during a meeting with President Dwight Eisenhower in 1956, "Paraguayans and land" (Miranda 1987: 45). In 1965 Asunción supported and offered troops to the U.S. intervention in the Dominican Republic, and in 1968 offered to provide the United States with troops to fight in Vietnam (Hoyer 1975: 296). In terms of "land," in 1955 Defense Minister Herminio Morinigo told State Department officials that the Stroessner government would sign an agreement permitting the United States to build an air force base in Paraguay for the continent's defense (Miranda 1987: 72).

In return for this almost unconditional support, the United States provided exactly what Stroessner had hoped for to strengthen and consolidate his repressive regime: aid and legitimacy. In addition to public and diplomatic pronouncements of support, which translated into legitimacy, Stroessner wanted the United States to express its appreciation by offering material rewards in the form of economic aid, technical assistance, loans, grants, foreign investments, military security assistance, and trade concessions. He needed economic and financial assistance to fund infrastructure projects designed to prop up his regime. Through effective propaganda, U.S.-financed projects were transformed into government-delivered progress. Finally, U.S. aid greased the wheel of the vast network of patronage and corruption by which Stroessner retained the loyalty of the military and Colorado Party officials: the pillars of his patrimonial kleptocracy.

In the critical years of the regime's consolidation (1954–1961), the total U.S. aid package plus loans via U.S.-controlled international banking institutions reached $53.2 million, an average of more than $6 million a year. This is a considerable amount when one considers that the total Paraguayan state budget for 1959 was $21 million (Abente 1988: 83). Aid increased during the Alliance for Progress, partly as a product of, but also in response to, the activity of small guerrilla groups in the late 1950s and 1960s. The regime exaggerated the influence of communists and Fidel Castro in the financing and organizing of these guerrilla groups in order to raise U.S. fears, and consequently U.S. funds.

In the period from 1962 to 1966, the Stroessner regime received $46.5 million in economic and military aid, which, when combined with soft loans from U.S. private banking institutions and international lending institutions, reached $77.9 million. The relationship, as such, continued until 1976 as the United States proceeded to provide close to $200 million in bilateral economic and military aid to Paraguay—with loans, the total amount reached over $288 million (Roett and Sacks 1991: 148; Yopo 1991: 63).[11] Once again, relations with the United States were important because of implications for the longevity of the regime. As Andrew Nickson (1993: 607) concludes, "relations between the Stroessner regime and successive US administrations became extremely close and contributed much to the consolidation of the regime"—the key objective of Stroessner's foreign policy.

Finally, Paraguay's two powerful neighbors and their long-standing influence on the nation's politics and economic development were the fourth determinant of Stroessner's foreign policy. Paraguay remained vulnerable to the geopolitical rivalry between Argentina and Brazil (Kelly and Whigham 1990). Since the end of the Triple Alliance War, Argentina and Brazil had competed for influence in Paraguay, often supporting one party or politician (or general) in elections, civil conflicts, or factional infighting. Politics in Paraguay became almost the responsibility of Argentina and Brazil, which believed that every domestic issue had strategic importance to their respective interests. However, between 1904 and the 1960s, Argentina was the dominant actor, largely because of Asunción's overwhelming economic dependence on Buenos Aires. In the 1950s, 90 percent of Paraguayan exports were shipped through Buenos Aires and nearly 40 percent of Paraguay's trade was with Argentina. Moreover, Argentine investors had controlling interests in Paraguay's key industries, specifically livestock and agriculture (Baer and Birch 1987).

By the time Stroessner assumed power in 1954, some of his predecessors had already initiated a pendular foreign policy in which Asunción played one regional hegemon against the other in order to enhance Paraguay's autonomy while obtaining economic and political support from Buenos Aires and Brasilia (see Birch 1988; Lezcano 1990). However, Stroessner moved the pendulum clearly toward Brazil. More than just reducing Argentina's economic stranglehold, Stroessner was concerned with protecting his regime from Argentine political meddling, which he believed was the greatest external threat to his plans for complete control of the Paraguayan political system (Seiferheld and De Tone 1988: 65). Broader ties with Brazil would translate into economic advantages for the nation and political support for Stroessner. Brazil was more than willing to take advantage of Stroessner's preferences for closer military and economic ties and nonintervention in domestic affairs. Brazil and Paraguay shared concerns about the communist threat, particularly after the 1964 coup, which brought to power in Brazil a national security doctrine regime. Military and security cooperation rapidly became the cornerstone of Brazil-Paraguay relations. Stroessner maintained relations with Argentina, but Brazil's massive economic expansion and Argentina's political and economic crises of the 1960s made the choice clear: Brazil offered a stable partnership with tremendous economic and political benefits (Abente 1988: 89).

In the period between 1954 and the late 1960s, Brazil provided approximately U.S.$120 million in addition to signing accords that offered trade concessions and financing to build roads, bridges, and port facilities.[12] More important, duty-free port facilities were granted to Paraguay in Paranagua and Concepción, and after years of negotiation and study, construction was begun on the $12 billion Itaipu hydroelectric dam (the largest in the world), which became a great source of wealth to the Paraguayan economy. Finally, changes in trade patterns were also significant. Paraguay's exports to Brazil increased from less than 1 percent in 1965 to 25 percent by 1981. Imports experience a similar trend (Rodriguez Silvero 1987; Franco 1988). Therefore, as Alfredo Da Mota Menezes (1990) describes, Brazil, principally for geopolitical reasons (though there were some economic gains to be made), was more than happy to provide Paraguay with another "economic lung" that would free it from its historical dependency on Argentina. Therefore, Stroessner used Brazilian economic and political support to diminish Argentine dominance and strengthen his domestic position.

Democratization and Foreign Policy, 1989–1998

One of the limitations of a transition from above and within, as was Paraguay's, is that there is little change in the structure and elites from the previous authoritarian regime. The structural legacies of the Stroessner regime coexist with democratization and political and civil rights.[13] The motivation behind the putsch against Stroessner in 1989 was not so much democracy as an attempt to restore a much maligned Colorado Party–military alliance. The transition relied on the support of many of the political, economic, and military interests associated with the previous regime. Democratization provided the means to an end for an authoritarian elite seeking to manipulate and "control the pace and scope of the transition" in order to retain a "high degree of political and economic power" (Nickson 1989; Galeano 1989). Therefore, change in this "protected democracy" is occurring in the context of structural continuity and immobility. If there were ever a case in which the old dictum "the more things change, the more they stay the same" was appropriate, it would be Paraguay.

Foreign policy change has not been dramatic, but rather a shift in emphases. The transition and the new international context of the post–Cold War period have altered the regional and global context of Paraguay's international relations. However, the decisionmaking process has not adapted itself to the new context, largely because of the institutional and administrative deficiencies of the new democratic regime. As a result, Paraguay lacks a cohesive, well-defined, and articulated foreign policy. Two Paraguayan scholars of international relations describe the country's foreign policy as "presidential," because of the dominance of the executive, and "dragged," with respect to how Paraguay was pulled into regional political organizations and economic integration arrangements by its neighbors (Argentina, Brazil, and Uruguay) (Masi and Simon 1993; Masi 1991a). The absence of a professional diplomatic service coupled with the level of bureaucratic politicization institutionalized by Paraguayan sectarianism allowed foreign policy to be manipulated or hijacked by ambitious politicians. The incompetence and passivity of the foreign ministry are the principal reason why foreign policy was delegated to the Palace of Lopez and regional capitals.

From the time General Andres Rodriguez staged his successful coup on February 3, 1989, and was elected president three months later, the most notable feature of his government's foreign policy was the active and personal diplomacy of the president, characterized by the frequency and intensity of his international contacts. The Ministry of Foreign Affairs, under the leadership of Luis Maria Argaña (1989–1990), a longtime Colorado Party boss with no experience in international relations, was plagued by the legacy and weight of the previous regime's bureaucratic perversions. Argaña showed little interest in foreign policy matters and spent most of his time engaged in domestic politics, using the ministry as a staging point for his political ambitions.[14] The ministry was incapable of redefining a modern and coherent national foreign policy, mostly because the ministry itself lacked a modern and professional structure and personnel sufficiently independent of partisan politics.

The foreign ministry continued to operate under the same ideological, anticommunist paradigm of the previous regime until 1991, and only changed course not because of a process of modernization but by simply being "dragged" or "regionally pulled" along by changes in the international system (i.e., the collapse of communism in the Soviet Union and regional political and economic cooperation). Argaña's replacement, Alexis Frutos Vaesken, made an effort at reforming and modernizing the foreign ministry, but it was largely superficial and insufficient to turn the ministry from a passive observer to an active participant in the nation's international relations.[15]

As a result of these limitations, the responsibility of reintegrating Paraguay into the international system, particularly the Rio Group and the regional economic integration process, fell to Paraguay's neighbors (Argentina, Brazil, and Uruguay), which pushed President Rodriguez to take the lead in accelerating Asunción's participation in light of the deficiencies of the foreign ministry (Masi 1991a: 12). For example, Uruguayan president Julio Sanguinetti convinced Rodriguez to attend the 1989 inauguration of Bolivian president Jaime Paz Zamora in order to end a long-standing bitter relationship and begin the process of regional infrastructure integration. Moreover, upon the insistence of Argentina and Uruguay, Paraguay was invited to join the Rio Group, and in 1990 it was President Sanguinetti who initiated the process by which Paraguay was invited to participate in the regional economic integration scheme that ultimately led to the creation of the Southern Cone Common Market (Mercosur) (Masi 1993). Despite these cases of successful "pull," there were many squandered opportunities because of the absence of a coherent and functioning foreign policy bureaucracy. For example, Paraguay's role in the negotiations leading to the 1990 Mercosur Treaty was minimal at best. The lack of experts in economic integration resulted in Uruguay taking on the role of Paraguay's negotiator (Masi 1990). As can be expected, Uruguay's and Paraguay's interests did not always coincide. Therefore, the failure to respond to new opportunities with regard to neighboring countries revealed the limitations of the Rodriguez policy of presidential diplomacy, the absence of expert advisers on foreign policy formulation, and the weakness of the Ministry of Foreign Affairs when faced with new challenges and opportunities (Simon 1995b).

The Rodriguez administration (1989–1993) pursued three key foreign policy objectives: (1) end Paraguay's international isolation from which it suffered during the latter years of the Stroessner era; (2) reactivate a ravaged economy by joining regional economic integration systems and attracting foreign investments and credits; and (3) perhaps most important, seek international support for the Rodriguez government. President Rodriguez considered such support and the reintegration of Paraguay into the community of democratic nations to be vital to the regime's legitimacy (Simon 1989; Salum Flecha 1989; Labra 1990). He hoped that by demonstrating a commitment to democracy and economic reform, Paraguay would gain access to foreign investments, trade concessions, and credits needed to reactivate the economy and sustain democratization. In other words, Rodriguez considered these to be critical requirements for domestic legitimacy. Interestingly, the external factor, which had played a secondary role in the demise of the Stroessner regime, acquired new potency and relevance to the strength and legitimacy of the Rodriguez government. The weakness of Paraguay's democracy has made external actors particularly influential in mediating conflict and strengthening institutions.

Since the regime's image and legitimacy were so intricately linked to Paraguay's reintegration into an international system—one that insisted on democratic rule for participation—Rodriguez called in international fora for a strong commitment to the strengthening of Paraguayan democracy. For example, he constantly assured the international community that he would not seek reelection or extend his rule beyond 1993. President Rodriguez immediately ratified the Pact of San Jose (American Convention on Human Rights) and signed other agreements that demonstrated his commitment to democracy and human rights. The president dropped the virulent ideological-praetorian content of the previous regime's foreign policy, and replaced Stroessner's pendulum policy with a more balanced approach in its relations with Argentina and Brazil. He worked to mend relations with Argentina. He had four private visits with Argentine president Carlos Menem and signed a series of agreements on trade, communication, customs, and transportation, and moved toward resolving pending problems concerning the Yacyreta hydroelectric plant and the Rio Pilcomayo ecological dispute (Simon 1991). In terms of Brazil, relations maintained their steady course with respect to trade and investments, while diplomatic contacts and negotiations on the Itaipu hydroelectric project and foreign debt were emphasized. In the end, as Paraguayan analyst Fernando Masi (1997: 180) asserts, "the Rodriguez government sought to avoid conflict with neighboring countries for fear that it might hinder its overriding diplomatic objective of securing a new democratic image for the country."

The Rodriguez government also considered improving relations with the United States a key priority of its foreign policy. Again, Asunción understood that U.S. approval of Rodriguez and his government was an essential condition for Paraguay's reinsertion into the international system, which would translate into certain economic benefits needed to reactivate the economy and consolidate democratic rule. The fact that the United States stood as the only superpower in the post–Cold War period and as leader of the free and democratic world had symbolic meaning for Paraguayan elites and a regime that desperately sought to translate international support into domestic legitimacy (Mora 1997: 71). U.S. support not only helped in promoting a new democratic image in the international arena, but it also strengthened Rodriguez's position against the opposition and sectors of the Colorado Party opposed to the transition.

The first Bush administration not only conferred recognition and full support for the Rodriguez government, but it also restored General System of Preferences (GSP) trade concessions and military assistance and cooperation agreements. Between 1989 and 1992 there were five visits by U.S. political and diplomatic officials, including Vice President Dan Quayle. During the same period, five visits by high military officials, mostly from U.S. Southern Command, visited Asunción to restore and enhance military and antinarcotics cooperation and to observe several joint operation exercises. Rodriguez effectively translated the presence and expression of support from U.S. officials into domestic legitimacy by holding up the U.S. stamp of approval as a necessary requirement for legitimacy (*abc color* 1991).

Foreign Policy and Political Crises: Muddling Through

Since 1989, but particularly during the administration of President Juan Carlos Wasmosy (1993–1998), Paraguay's democracy has been under tremendous pressure from authoritarian enclaves within the Colorado Party and the armed forces. It has also been under stress brought on by socioeconomic deterioration, labor protests, corruption, and weak and ineffective institutions. These combined forces have eroded the regime's credibility (Nickson 1997). Paraguay is an example of what Larry Diamond and others have (1997) aptly described as an "incomplete democracy" or "low-intensity democracy": shallow, illiberal, and poorly institutionalized. Political crises coupled with economic recession and a weak president did not allow for much discussion or change in foreign policy. The government and society, particularly political parties, were too engrossed in domestic political matters (i.e., containing threats from the armed forces) to engage in an open and effective debate on foreign policy. The bureaucratic-administrative structures remained highly politicized and corrupt, incapable of meeting the political, economic, and international challenges of Paraguay. The foreign ministry of the Wasmosy administration continued to operate under the same rules of the previous administration, limiting its ability and role in foreign policy decisionmaking.

The fragility of Paraguay's democracy and the political impotence of President Wasmosy, who was beholden to the civil-military interests that had brought him to power, increased the degree to which Paraguay relinquished responsibility for not only its international relations, but also the stability of the transition, to regional neighbors and other external actors, such as the OAS, Mercosur, and the United States. The predominant role played by these external actors in safeguarding democracy from an internal threat in April 1996 confirms the extent to which the systemic impacts and shapes the domestic.[16] In other words, a weak president (owing his presidency to an alliance of civilian and military nationalists opposed to an active foreign policy agenda for Paraguay) grappling with insurmountable domestic challenges, specifically the indefatigable threat from General Lino Oviedo, further crippled the development of a coherent national foreign policy. Thus the need to focus inward diverted attention and interest away from framing a foreign policy that a complex and challenging international system required.

The foreign ministry continued to suffer from the same institutional deficiencies and politicization of the previous regime. Three foreign ministers (Diogenes Martinez, Luis Maria Ramirez Boettner, and Ruben Melgarejo Lanzoni) served in the Wasmosy administration, none of them with any expertise or interest in modernizing and pushing the ministry into the center of Paraguayan foreign policy decisionmaking. Ramirez Boettner was an experienced diplomat, but perhaps more than any of his predecessors (and successors) reacted negatively to suggestions that the ministry needed restructuring.[17]

However, in the first six months of the administration, Foreign Minister Martinez assembled a group of journalists, scholars, and other experts of international relations to present a plan that would help the ministry design a foreign policy for the Wasmosy administration (*Ultima Hora* 1993; *abc color* 1993).[18] Several programmatic and strategic plans were presented but were immediately shelved and ignored once Martinez resigned and the government focused its attention on domestic political crises.[19] Finally, there was no attempt by either the Rodriguez or the Wasmosy administration to include other key government agencies or the legislature in the process of foreign policy decisionmaking.[20] In this environment, society at large was nearly ignored, despite the regime's pronounced democratic ideals.

Rather than being pulled by regional neighbors, as was the case with the previous administration, the foreign policy of the Wasmosy administration suffered from drift and nearly total neglect. Initially, Wasmosy tried to personalize Paraguay's international relations by taking numerous trips, attempting to establish a direct and personal relationship with other presidents. However, as a result of Paraguay's incomplete and precarious democracy, the country's international image began to suffer despite these international contacts (Simon 1995a: 10). In the meantime, a number of important foreign policy matters remained unresolved, such as the Rio Pilcomayo dispute with Argentina, relations with the United States (drug trafficking and intellectual property), Itaipu renegotiations, Mercosur, and global concern over the validity of Paraguayan democracy.

Foreign policy inaction worsened as Paraguay sank deeper into political crises after President Wasmosy left office in August 1998. The embattled administrations of Presidents Raul Cubas (1998–1999) and Luis Gonzalez Macchi (1999–present) continued to lack the strength, legitimacy, and focus to address critical foreign policy issues, such as challenges emanating from disputes within Mercosur. Between January 1998 and August 2001, Paraguay had three presidents and eight foreign ministers. Moreover, during this period there were several impeachment proceedings held against each president, the assassination of Vice President Luis Maria Argaña, two failed coup attempts, over a dozen labor and peasant strikes and protests (including road blocks), and a quickly deteriorating socioeconomic crisis. The lack of leadership in the executive and the relative disinterest of the legislature and society (deeply preoccupied with the deteriorating domestic situation) in regional and global matters of importance to Paraguay's national interest contributed to what can be characterized as a nation without a foreign policy.

Conclusion

This study of foreign policy during Stroessner's patrimonial or neosultanistic regime and that of the two democratic transition governments demonstrates the enduring potency of two explanatory variables of Paraguayan foreign policy. The individual or idiosyncratic level of analysis of foreign policy is particularly significant because of the weight of Paraguay's personalist and authoritarian heritage on politics and foreign policy decisionmaking. The monopolization of power in the hands of the executive is a function of Paraguay's patrimonial culture, geopolitics, and record of despotic rule. Stroessner was the culmination of this tradition, except that he created a political system that enhanced the degree to which power was vested in the executive. Foreign policy personalization by *el actor único* allowed Stroessner to design a foreign policy the objective of which was to help strengthen and consolidate his regime. In other words, it was Stroessner's foreign policy, not Paraguay's.

The role of the president remained critical in the foreign policy of the democratic transition, particularly under Andres Rodriguez. The absence of a functional and professional Ministry of Foreign Affairs forced the president to assume full responsibility for the country's international relations at a critical time when the regime needed international support to strengthen democratic rule. When the executive neglected or was ineffective in pursuing a "presidential" foreign policy, as was the case with the politically weak Juan Carlos Wasmosy, Paraguayan foreign policy drifted and Paraguay's international image suffered as a result.

The other important explanatory variable of Paraguayan foreign policy is systemic. Because of Paraguay's weak political and economic power base and its landlocked position between two regional powers, its foreign policy is vulnerable to external actors and strategic realities. Paraguayan foreign policy under both the *Stronato* and democratic regimes is conditioned by regional and international contexts. Examples include the Cold War, U.S. policy, Argentina-Brazil rivalry, and trends toward democracy and globalization. In fact, domestic stability, in large part, hinged on the ability of the authoritarian and democratic regimes to use foreign policy for purposes of obtaining much needed political and economic support and legitimacy. The systemic weighed heavily on foreign policy in both political systems. Once again, as in the case of President Wasmosy, when the executive is weak, the system fills the void and indirectly manipulates foreign policy. This was the case with Paraguay's entrance into Mercosur, in which Uruguay seemed to be the key advocate of Paraguay's membership while leaders in Asunción passively watched and consented. For the most part, domestic actors and the military remained left out of foreign policy formation. Small states like Paraguay, with a long tradition of authoritarianism, economic dependency, and a vulnerable geopolitical position, are bound to have a "presidential and dragged" foreign policy regardless of regime type.

Notes

1. Paraguayan authoritarian heritage is examined in Hicks 1971; Kaufman 1984; Rodriguez Alcala 1987; and Sondrol 1990.

2. On the historical and cultural roots of the Stroessner dictatorship, see Lewis 1980.

3. Description of a sultanistic regime is offered in Linz 1975: 268. For the application of sultanism to the Stroessner case, see Riquelme 1994.

4. Some of the best studies of the Stroessner regime include Lewis 1980; Delich 1981; Abente 1989; Miranda 1990; Arditi 1992; and Lambert 1996, 1997.

5. Research on Paraguayan foreign policy during the Stroessner era includes Hoyer 1975; Estigarribia and Simon 1987; Mora 1988, 1993; Simon 1990c; and Yopo 1991.

6. For a discussion of Stroessner's foreign policy objectives, see Yopo 1985, 1991: 31–32; Mora 1988, 1993: 89–90; and Simon 1993: 47–67.

7. For an analysis of the formal and informal powers of Stroessner, see Lewis 1980: 105–123. The legal basis of Stroessner's control of foreign policy was stipulated in the constitution of 1967 in Article 180, Section 6, which grants the executive branch complete authority over Paraguay's international relations.

8. The two major universities in Paraguay, Universidad Nacional and Universidad Católica, other than offering a few courses on international law and Paraguayan diplomatic history, did not have academic programs in international relations or foreign policy.

9. Also, Executive Decree 24.450 of 1972 amends the 1970 law, creating the Academy of Diplomacy and Consular Affairs.

10. For studies on U.S.-Paraguay relations, see Mora 1995, 1997, 1998.

11. The expansion of trade and investments is discussed in Rodriguez Silvero 1986; and Borda and Masi 1994.

12. The total amount of aid is provided in Da Mota Menezes 1990.

13. The literature on Paraguay's transition is relatively extensive. See Rivarola 1990a, 1990b; Sondrol 1992a; Abente 1993; Simon 1994; and Lambert and Nickson 1997.

14. For a critique of Argaña's poor performance as foreign minister, see a series of six articles authored by Jose Luis Simon in *abc color,* July 1989.

15. On November 6, 1990, Resolution 70 of the Ministry of Foreign Relations reformed the outdated organizational structure of the ministry. Also in 1990, curricular reforms were instituted in the Academy of Diplomacy and Consular Affairs of the ministry. However, direction of the academy remained in the hands of loyal Colorado Party members, such as Luis Martinez Miltos and Juan Bautista Rivarola Paoli, who had little or no experience in international relations and related curricular matters.

16. For an analysis of the role of external factors in Paraguay's democratization, see Valenzuela 1999; and Mora 2000.

17. For an analysis of Paraguayan foreign policy during the Wasmosy administration as explained by the foreign minister, see Ramirez Boettner 1995.

18. The specialists assembled by Foreign Minister Martinez included Jeronimo Irala Burgos, Carlos Plate, Ramon Silva Alonso, Jose Luis Simon, Ramon Casco Carreras, Fernando Masi, Hugo Marinoni Rodriguez, Juan Andres Cardozo, and Mauricio Schwartzmann.

19. One detailed study presented to the foreign ministry included Masi and Simon 1993.

20. Martin Sannemann (1995), president of the Commission on Foreign Relations of the Chamber of Deputies and member of the opposition, noted with some consternation the absence of the legislature and society in formulating a "national" foreign policy.

3

The English-Speaking Caribbean States: A Triad of Foreign Policies

Jacqueline Anne Braveboy-Wagner

The islands of the English-speaking Caribbean are among the smallest independent nations in the world. These island nations—Antigua and Barbuda, the Bahamas, Barbados, Dominica, Grenada, St. Kitts/Nevis, St. Lucia, St. Vincent and the Grenadines, and Trinidad and Tobago—range in territorial size from 13,939 square kilometers (the Bahamas) to 269 square kilometers (St. Kitts/Nevis), and from 2.6 million inhabitants (Jamaica) to 40,700 (St. Kitts/Nevis). Two other members of the English-speaking Caribbean family, Guyana and Belize, are mainland territories. Although they are relatively large in territorial size, with Guyana having a territorial size of almost 215,000 square kilometers and Belize 23,000 square kilometers, their population sizes are smaller than those of the larger Caribbean islands: 782,400 people live in Guyana and 238,500 in Belize.[1] By any definition, these states are small.

It is the emergence of these countries to independence in the 1960s that helped stimulate the debate in the international community about "small states," and refined it to include the now abandoned concept of the "mini" or "micro" state. The Caribbean territories, with populations of under or close to 1 million in the 1960s, spurred a debate about the "viability" of small states, not only as a matter of political and economic capacity, but also as a matter of diplomacy: Could such small nations be expected to carry out the international responsibilities expected of sovereign states? As time went on, the debate shifted from the discourse on principles (sovereignty, equality, responsibility) to a practical emphasis on policy measures to help these states overcome their inherent vulnerabilities.

Interestingly, although all these small countries self-identify as "small" in a global context, four of them—Jamaica, Trinidad and Tobago,

Guyana, and Barbados—are considered to be "big" in the regional context, and from that perspective are generally seen by the smaller countries as having much more capacity to exert global influence than they actually do. Related to this is the fact that the decisionmakers of all these small states sometimes adopt attitudes and policies that suggest that they see themselves as more influential than does the rest of the world. Typifying this attitude was the determination of Grenada's decisionmakers during the revolutionary period of 1979 to 1983 to play, with the help of like-minded allies, a highly effective role on the world stage—well beyond the expectations of a state of that size.

In the following pages, I discuss relevant elements of the small state debate, reviewing some aspects of the relevant literature. I then highlight the main themes and strategies of the foreign policy of the English-speaking Caribbean states since their independence, and second, seek to explain their behavior.

Changes in Foreign Policy, 1960s–2000

Because of the very fact of their smallness, it is convenient to analyze the foreign policies of the twelve independent English-speaking Caribbean countries as a unit. Each of these countries is still jealous of its sovereignty, notwithstanding what we shall see is their greater reliance on regional strategies today. There are nuances in the behavior of the individual states that highlight their differences. We distinguish between the more developed countries (MDCs) (Jamaica, Trinidad and Tobago, Guyana, Barbados, and the Bahamas) and the less developed countries (LDCs) (comprising the Eastern Caribbean and Belize).

While recognizing that the differences of these states are important from regional or local perspectives, the fact is that the rest of the world tends to see these nations as a group, and that given their common history and culture, a discussion of their foreign policy can be parsimoniously, if cautiously, undertaken within this aggregated approach. Economically, the countries suffer from the dependence, openness, and vulnerabilities associated with small size. Socially and culturally, the British legacy can be seen in the institutions and values that permeate these societies, despite some dilution in favor of North American values over time. Politically, they all maintain the Westminster system of government in a modified form that reflects the authoritarianism inherent in the making of policy and politics in the region, even today, when the older postindependence leaders have been replaced by younger, more pragmatic ones (Braveboy-Wagner 1992).

Hierarchy of Foreign Policy Goals

These Caribbean states have sought to use foreign policy to achieve three goals: territorial and political security, economic and social development, and global and regional prestige. A general Malthusian assumption with respect to the hierarchy of these goals or interests for the region is that development comes first, except during crises when a country's territorial integrity is under threat from within or without. "Prestige" refers to activities undertaken to increase or preserve global or regional status or to define and assert important principles, and normally ranks last of the three sets of interests because it bears the least tangible rewards.

Although the typical foreign policy statement of goals in the English-speaking Caribbean lists principles—respect for human rights, democracy, the rule of law, noninterference, promotion of international peace and security, friendly relations with other countries—as basic tenets of foreign policy, the arrangement of objectives by the Barbados government in 2000 is more reflective of what these small states emphasize today. The Barbados Ministry of Foreign Affairs and Foreign Trade counts among its major objectives not only the promotion of trading relationships with third states and economic groups and the protection of Barbados's interests within the framework of international, commercial, and economic policymaking, but also its attempt to procure concessionary financing for Barbados's development effort. Other goals of the Ministry of Foreign Affairs and Foreign Trade are the attraction of investment capital for industrial development in prescribed sectors of the economy and the promotion of Barbados as an offshore financial sector. Moreover, it supports the promotion and expansion of tourism, the strengthening of the regional integration movement, and the concept of Caribbean unity. Strengthening ties with traditional allies and fastening new ties with friendly countries based on the principles of peaceful coexistence and the sovereign equality of states present another objective, besides collaborating with like-minded countries to advance the concepts of morality, justice, and respect for human rights in international affairs. The ministry also pursues peaceful relations among states, and through constructive collective action, a new social, political, and economic order. Finally, it protects and promotes interests and welfare of Barbarian nationals abroad.

These objectives can be seen as a descending scale, from economic initiatives to political, and on to consular activities. This is a reflection of the fact that since the end of the Cold War, the English-speaking states have been preoccupied with economic diplomacy with the aim of maximizing opportunities for trade and investment. Though more visible today, this objective is not new. For the English-speaking Caribbean countries, which have had "neither the resources nor the desire to exercise military power" (speech by George C. R. Moe, minister of external affairs, 1975: 24), the most consistent strand of foreign policy since independence has been a focus not on military security, but on development.

Economic Strategies

Even with the global changes of the 1990s, the basic strategies of Caribbean states, filtered through foreign or economic bureaucracies, have not so much changed as intensified. Overall, the basic foci have been preservation of traditional linkages and the preferential arrangements that characterize those relationships (i.e., with Britain/Europe, the United States, and Canada), diversification of trading partners (primarily in the direction of Latin America and Asia), and promotion of regionalism.

Four ideological stages correspond to changes in foreign economic strategy. In the early postindependence period (1962–1970), in view of their continued dependence on Britain, increasing dependence on the United States, and pro-West political orientation, the English-speaking states opted for the open economy model of development. By the 1970s, the second period, they had become more nationalist in keeping with the new assertiveness of the rest of the third world, as well as the increased flexibility of the Western powers, especially the United States in the wake of the Vietnam War. Under some pressure from within, the English-speaking Caribbean countries began to participate more effectively in third-world economic forums where the New International Economic Order (NIEO) was taking shape. They espoused the third-world strategies of diversification and cartelization, with Jamaica and Guyana participating actively in the new International Bauxite Association (IBA) and Trinidad and Tobago supporting the Organization of Petroleum Exporting Countries (OPEC), even if the latter's application to join OPEC was rejected. They supported the strategy of "delinking" from the international economic system, and south-south collaboration, including regional integration. It was during this time that these Caribbean states moved from having a basic free trade area (CARIFTA) to a common market in 1974. The close integration of foreign economic and foreign political policy was exemplified by Jamaican Michael Manley's politicization of the issue of International Monetary Fund (IMF) conditionalities. Manley's election loss on an anti-IMF platform paved the way for the return of the U.S.-promoted open economic model, not only in Jamaica but in the rest of the region as well.

Toward the end of this second period, the Eastern Caribbean islands became independent. Though St. Lucia and St. Vincent flirted briefly with nationalist economic strategies, these countries emerged to independence at a time when the United States was beginning to return to a "hegemonic" approach to Cold War issues. The Eastern Caribbean countries, preoccupied with economic survival, depended heavily on trade preferences extended by the European Community (which Britain had joined). Some, Antigua and Barbuda for example, were already oriented toward the United States. By then, the integration movement had been weakened not only by political arguments over the unconstitutional coup in Grenada in 1979, but also by economic disagreements engendered by the adverse effect of oil price increases on all the members save Trinidad and Tobago. Some members had moved to seek more external trade and assistance rather than focus on the limited regional market.

In the third period, the 1980s, the movement to restructure Caribbean economies consolidated. Like much of the third world, these states experienced a "lost decade," mired in debt and preoccupied with the social fallout from IMF-imposed or voluntary structural adjustment measures. Though retaining a third-world bargaining outlook, the English-speaking Caribbean states turned for help to bilateral economic initiatives, including preferences extended by the United States, Canada, and Europe, and to cooperation with multilateral agencies. Though attempts were made to reinvigorate the integration movement, not much progress was made in the 1980s.

In the fourth period, the 1990s, and continuing into the new century, there has been a considerable focus on a regionalist strategy as a way to achieve economic goals. Regionalism is seen as a way to step up the pace of market expansion and increase bargaining strength in crucial "free trade" negotiations. With this in mind, a Regional Negotiating Machinery (RNM) was created in 1997 to oversee the process of negotiating trade arrangements with key external countries and integration movements.

The 1990s saw the loss of leverage for the small Caribbean countries, which to that point had managed to attract a good deal of developed-country financial assistance by virtue of their status not only as former colonies, but also as democratic allies of the United States. Alternatively, at certain times, leftist Jamaica, Guyana, and Grenada had also been able to attract more diverse, albeit quantitatively less, international assistance from socialist, social democratic, and nationalist allies. With the end of the Cold War, financial assistance diverted to the reconstruction and democratization of Eastern Europe, and to the increasing number of fractured communities in war-torn areas. Moreover, the emphasis on economic liberalization forced Caribbean countries to realize that the preferential systems on which much of their revenue was predicated would soon end. The specific triad of preferences that had been granted to the Caribbean over the years comprised the following: the European Community/Union (EU) preferences under the Lomé Accords, first negotiated by the African, Caribbean, and Pacific (ACP) countries in 1975 and renewed for four successive periods; the Caribbean Basin Initiative (CBI), established by the Reagan administration in 1982–1983; and the Caribbean-Canada (CARIBCAN) preferences, first negotiated in 1986. Under these programs, which went beyond the Generalized System of Preferences (GSP) extended to developing countries in general, most Caribbean products entered the markets of Europe and North America duty-free, though important products such as garment and leather goods, footwear, sugar, and petroleum products remained subject to various tariffs. With the advent of a united and widening Europe and the establishment of the World Trade Organization (WTO), it was time to amend the key protocols governing trade with the EU. On the U.S. side, the broadening of the North American Free Trade Area (NAFTA) to include Mexico in 1994 realized fears that investment and trade would be lured away from Caribbean economies.

The region's basic strategy has been to marshal forces in a determined fight to retain preferences as long as possible, accompanied, with respect to NAFTA, by a decision to seek collective admission to NAFTA and in the meantime to seek "NAFTA parity" (i.e., equal status with Mexico). This strategy has been carried out through sustained collective lobbying in Brussels and in Washington, even when the outlook looked far from promising. For indeed the NAFTA parity issue, though eventually successful, dragged on for most of the 1990s, with prolabor U.S. congressmen as reluctant to grant these limited preferences as they were to grant the president the capability to fast-track the admission of more countries to NAFTA. On the European side, the fight by the Caribbean Community (CARICOM) was not so much over the preferences themselves (in that Europe proved willing to extend certain key preferences for a grace period), but over the fate of the important banana preferential regime in the face of U.S. challenges. Although these challenges were initially stoked by U.S. multinational companies in Central America,[2] as time went on the issue became incorporated into far broader U.S.-European concerns over agricultural subsidies and other invisible barriers to free trade. In these circumstances, the solutions rested with the developed countries and not the small state complainants. CARICOM's lobbying efforts have therefore been directed primarily to appealing to European nationalism to secure Europe's continued support in the face of sanctions and other threats to Europe emanating from the United States.

Enhanced regionalism has been reflected not only in the deepening and widening of CARICOM itself to secure a "fallback" expanded market, but also in greater determination to bury political and economic differences and espouse collective approaches to negotiation. An earlier piecemeal approach by CARICOM to joining NAFTA was transformed in 1994 into a more comprehensive hemispheric strategy when the United States agreed to work with the nations of Latin America toward a goal of hemispheric free trade by 2005. Clearly the United States was interested in broadening its own market to better confront a united Europe and an economically strong Asia. In these hemispheric talks, the prime concern of CARICOM (not yet secured) has been to ensure that small states are granted preferential treatment, without which a country as small as Dominica would have to compete on near-equal terms with one as huge as Brazil.

The move toward hemispheric unity has been complemented by strategies to enhance intra- and interregional trade. In fact, given the expansion of regional trade, some countries are in no hurry to integrate with the United States (this is, for example, the position of members of the Southern Cone Common Market [Mercosur]). For CARICOM nations, the new global environment has served to push forward the deepening and widening of the core integration movement. As a result, beginning in the 1990s, there have been gradual moves toward a single economic market reflected in the planned adoption of a common external tariff. Monetary unity is being debated, but because of the great variation in currency strengths throughout the region (except for the Eastern Caribbean), monetary union appears unlikely. Complementing these market and currency considerations have been decisions by CARICOM members to allow free movement of skilled labor and easier travel within the region. CARICOM has also deepened functional cooperation, and has become more proactive in helping to resolve regional political problems, ranging from postconflict reconstruction in Haiti to ethnopolitical problems in Guyana.

At the same time, CARICOM has sought to widen the integration movement, not only to expand the market but also to present a stronger bargaining front in free trade negotiations with North America. First Suriname was accepted as a member (1994), then Haiti in 1995. Cuba had applied for membership in 1993. Despite CARICOM's support for Cuba dating to 1972 (though with some distancing in the late 1970s and early 1980s), it was not surprising that Cuba was rejected for membership. Both economically and politically, Cuba could have a destabilizing influence on CARICOM. Instead, CARICOM created a commission to explore ways to cooperate economically with Cuba. Similarly, Venezuela, which had applied for full membership in 1991, was initially rejected but later (1993) allowed to participate in CARICOM via a one-way free trade arrangement that was later copied by Colombia (1994). At the same time, CARICOM reached out to Central America and to the Dominican Republic, including them in the new Association of Caribbean States (ACS), established in 1993. The ACS also includes Mexico, Venezuela, and Colombia, and associated nonindependent Caribbean territories. The ACS was heralded as having the potential to increase the integrated market to a size of more than 200 million. However, like the Asia Pacific Economic Cooperation (APEC) body, albeit weaker, the ACS has remained an informal arena for cooperation rather than an organically integrated unit. Since 1994, CARICOM has also reached out to its South American counterparts, completing integration agreements with Mercosur and with the Andean community, and continuing to negotiate with the Central American Integration Association (SICA).

In short, this period in CARICOM foreign relations can usefully be viewed as regionalist and institutionalist. Not that the forces of nationalism and individualism have been dormant. For example, Trinidad and Tobago as well as Jamaica have sought individual entry into NAFTA (as well as the collective CARICOM entry); there have been continuous arguments among the MDCs about trade violations; and the fact that in the mini oil crisis of 2000 the oil-dependent CARICOM states signed a preferential pact with Venezuela that explicitly excluded Guyana (see below) highlighted the continuing tendency to place national interests over the collective. However, the externally engineered drive by CARICOM states to present a united front is a major departure from the past and may have the effect of cementing the internal cracks that have long kept these countries from working together in any consistent manner.

Social Development Strategies

A subset of economic development interests focuses on what might previously have been considered truly domestic issues, but are now international: issues of social "security."[3] For the Caribbean, the most pressing have been health issues, in particular the urgency of dealing with the AIDS epidemic, narcotics trafficking, and environmental issues. With respect to the first, the Caribbean has the highest rate of adult HIV/AIDS infection among all world regions (2.11 percent compared to 1.67 percent for sub-Saharan Africa, the region with the most infected persons) (United Nations 2000). Caribbean states have pursued a strategy of active cooperation with UN and regional health agencies. In the area of narcotics, the Caribbean's geographic vulnerability to trafficking has been well documented (Griffith 1997). The adverse effects of narcotics trafficking (and production) include increased levels of drug abuse and crime; corruption of the judicial, security, and governmental systems; and money laundering, often through the many offshore operations that exist in the smaller countries of the region. The governments of the region have cooperated, in particular, with the United States, the United Nations, and regional agencies. However, on this issue of great importance to the United States, the potential for conflict with the U.S. interests has been consistently high, primarily due to the use of threats of Congress-mandated decertification (denial of aid) and other penalties against noncooperative countries. Among the most visible controversies was the contentious negotiation in 1995 of shiprider agreements to allow U.S. personnel to arrest suspected traffickers in Caribbean territorial waters. Arguments by Jamaica, Barbados, and Guyana about potential violations of sovereignty eventually led to revisions of the original agreement.

The English-speaking Caribbean islands have also focused on unique environmental problems, including global warming as it affects rising sea levels, ozone depletion and its health consequences (potentially affecting tourism), tropical biodiversity issues, the alarming erosion of coral reefs and the natural habitat, and disaster reduction measures. One of the successes of CARICOM states in dealing with this issue has been their proactive role in founding the Alliance for Small Island Developing States (AOSIS) in 1990. AOSIS, which has Pacific, Asian, and African members as well as members from the broader Caribbean, has lobbied for more global attention to island states' special concerns. Another consideration that has promoted a focus on sustainable development has been the need to satisfy aid donors, which now generally add environmental conditions to their aid arrangements, and which also grant low-cost environment-related loans that small Caribbean nations are eager to request.

Traditional Security Concerns and Strategies

Only two countries in the region, Guyana and Belize, have had to endure traditional threats to their territorial integrity: Guyana with Venezuela on the west and Suriname on the east; Belize with Guatemala. For these countries, the strengthening of external ties has been not only an economic imperative but also a way to counter threats to their territorial sovereignty.

A natural strategy for small countries is to try to counter the effects of size by allying and cooperating either with as many countries as possible or with one powerful ally. Belize has used both strategies, relying on British guarantees for its protection, and also reaching out for support to the UN and CARICOM. Independent Guyana, on the other hand, eschewed military alliances and relied on its many nonaligned and socialist allies as well as its neighbors within CARICOM. Both countries were excluded from the regional Organization of American States (OAS) because of their disputes with Latin American members, but CARICOM states helped to support their causes within that organization, and by force of numbers as well as persistence engineered changes in the OAS charter that allowed Belize and Guyana to join in 1990. The OAS has since mediated (somewhat successfully) in the Belize-Guatemala dispute.

In addition to these threats to territorial integrity, the period of the middle 1970s to the early 1980s is often viewed as a highly militarized one for the Caribbean region (Young and Phillips 1986). During this period, the conservative English-speaking Caribbean countries perceived threats of subversion emanating from Grenada and Cuba, whereas left-leaning Jamaica, Grenada, and Guyana were subject to destabilization efforts by the United States. Moreover, social and political agitation in Trinidad and Tobago (1970), and in Jamaica under Michael Manley, among others, brought threats to the region's political stability, culminating in Grenada's descent into disorder in 1983. This internal instability was often associated with development issues—either societal groups protesting about the particular development path taken by a country (Trinidad and Tobago) or governments adopting development strategies that were politically polarizing (Jamaica, Grenada). Although the region returned to relative domestic calm after the Grenada crisis, an attempted coup by Black Islamic elements in Trinidad and Tobago in 1990 served as a reminder that social instability is not guaranteed in these formally democratic small nations.

Prestige Interests and Strategies

Prestige is a catchall term referring to "status" activities intended to increase a state's visibility and influence in the international system. There are two types of activities that can be subsumed in this category: "participatory" diplomatic activities, such as international conferences, organizational participation, and diplomatic visits; and "hosting" activities, wherein the country serves as an arena for major conferences and events, including such nonpolitical activities as sports and entertainment when officially sanctioned and supported. For a small state to divert resources to hosting events, it must expect to gain some tangible benefits in the short or long run (e.g., increased revenues from tourism in the case of the Caribbean). On the other hand, the first activity is usually undertaken primarily to gain some intangible influence in international affairs.

The importance of participatory activities to CARICOM states has varied depending on the size of the country, its ideology, leadership preferences, and the nature of the international system. In general, the smaller Eastern Caribbean countries have been less engaged in hosting activities, and less interested in what St. Lucia's John Compton once called "posturing" on the international stage (Braveboy-Wagner 1989: 205). Their attention tends to be focused more on the subregion (CARICOM and the Organization of Eastern Caribbean States [OECS]), unless, like revolutionary Grenada, ideological considerations have broadened foreign policy goals and fostered greater international involvement. While all the smaller states have been anxious to sustain a presence at the United Nations, some—for example Dominica and St. Kitts/Nevis—have found it particularly difficult to sustain the costs of adequate representation in that body. In the late 1980s the Commonwealth stepped in to lend financial support for some of the Eastern Caribbean states to maintain their permanent missions to the United Nations. Alternatively, with respect to the OAS (served by the embassies to Washington), the OECS countries have joined together to share facilities.[4] Still, with small staffs of three to four persons at the United Nations and in Washington, Eastern Caribbean states are at a disadvantage in their attempts to participate in global affairs. Most participate only on issues of direct concern to them, although Antigua and Barbuda are known for having been active in the 1980s on the issue of the legal disposition of Antarctica, and Grenada continued, even after the end of the revolutionary regime, to be more active than its smaller neighbors.

The larger English-speaking Caribbean states suffer from fewer resource limitations, in terms of both finances and skills, and have generally been more active in global forums, especially the United Nations, than their size might predict. At the United Nations, from the early postindependence period, they consistently supported the principle of decolonization (although, on some specific cases involving certain Pacific islands, East Timor, and U.S. Virgin islands, among others, they were sometimes divided), and they were active in support of UN actions on behalf of the Palestinians and against the apartheid regime in South Africa. They cast their votes for noninterference, nonuse of force, and respect for international law—important issues for small states unable to resist aggression.

Support for human rights, however, has been qualified. The English-speaking Caribbean states have stood in favor of general human rights declarations and their delegations have served on the UN's human rights committees. Nevertheless, these states have been divided on specific cases, especially Central American situations during the 1970s and early 1980s, and Chile during the years of Augusto Pinochet (see Braveboy-Wagner 1989: 134–139). Moreover, support for human rights principles has not necessarily translated into action at home in that these states continued to work with Guyana's authoritarian regime even when it was widely condemned for human rights violations, involved themselves in nearby Haiti only after global attention focused on the crisis in the 1990s, and hesitated with respect to action to preserve political rights in Grenada between 1979 and 1983. In recent years, they have condemned human rights violations in Cuba but at the same time roundly condemned the U.S. embargo of Cuba and sought to work with the country economically. So the effect of this condemnation is minor. In addition, since 1998, Caribbean states have done some damage to their global reputation as human rights advocates by their support of the death penalty, which is generally perceived by the populace as a criminal deterrent. Adverse rulings by the UK's Privy Council, which remains the final court of appeals for these countries, with respect to the unconstitutionality of long delays in carrying out the death penalty, have pushed them to support the creation of a Caribbean Court of Appeals (known also as the Court of Justice). Further, to shorten the delays caused by prisoners' appeals to international bodies, Jamaica as well as Trinidad and Tobago have decided to opt out of the American Convention on Human Rights and the UN International Covenant on Civil and Political Rights.

Caribbean states' representation on certain UN bodies and their election to high offices provide an assessment of their influence. Guyana has served twice as a nonpermanent member of the Security Council, Trinidad and Tobago once, and Jamaica twice. In 1993, Guyana's representative became the first (and only, up to 2002) CARICOM person to serve as president of the General Assembly. By the late 1990s, Trinidad and Tobago (seven times); Antigua, Bahamas, St. Lucia, and St. Vincent (once each); and Belize (twice) had all held the vice presidency of the General Assembly. CARICOM states have been particularly active in the Economic and Social Council, with Jamaica and Trinidad and Tobago serving seventeen and fourteen years respectively, the Bahamas nine, and St. Lucia six. Finally, Guyana, Jamaica, Trinidad and Tobago, and Barbados have served many times as officers of the General Assembly's committees.

Despite this reasonably high level of participation in the UN's main bodies, there is skepticism at both official and societal levels in the region about the benefits of participation in global conferences. Illustrative of this was the debate about Jamaica's successful bid to sit on the

Security Council in 2000, in view of the internal economic decline and social turmoil that some felt needed the government's full attention. Indeed, in the 1990s and in 2000, there appeared to be more interest among Caribbean states in extended regionalism than in global diplomacy, leading some nongovernmental groups to complain about the region's absent or low level of representation at key global conferences and their preparatory committees.

Explaining CARICOM Foreign Policy

I have identified certain behavior patterns common to these twelve states: the emphasis on economic diplomacy, the reliance on North America and Europe even as attempts are made to diversify in the direction of Latin America in particular, the search for friends in both security and socioeconomic areas, and the attempt by some to exert some global (in addition to regional) influence. I have noted that their strategies have at various times focused on bilateral relations, the third world (nonaligned), multilateral cooperation, coalition behavior, and regionalism. I now turn to the question of what motivates and explains the behavior of these small countries in the external arena.

The System

The decisionmakers of the small CARICOM states have had to be cognizant throughout their independent history of their location in the international hierarchy (low, based on size), their geopolitical location close to the United States, and the changes in structure as well as norms of the international system. The system both influences and constrains their behavior. System structure influences the basic alliance or coalition-type behavior that defines the actions of Caribbean small states. Coalition behavior increases their bargaining power, and close relationships with North America and Europe are determined by the vertical interaction encouraged historically by an imperialist system structure (Galtung 1971). Moreover, constraints have stemmed from geopolitical location close to the United States, particularly during the Cold War, and geopolitical factors continue to influence economic, political, and immigration issues with the United States. Geopolitics also has influenced the subregion's move to deepen its relationship with Latin America, despite earlier perceived cultural barriers to such integration. As to the influence of international regimes, conformity to the global dominance of norms of economic liberalization is reflected today in the way

Caribbean states have felt compelled to divest and restructure their economies so as to be able to compete economically. In this regard, the influence of the system is reflected in the ways in which leaders themselves describe system interaction. Thus, for example, according to one Caribbean leader's description of the changes of the 1990s: "emerging from the developed countries was the point of view that we all needed to make adjustments to the (economic) order as it existed . . . *Immediately* . . . developing countries had to re-think the course of action that they were pursuing by closing their borders, because *if the changes were not made, sooner or later you would find yourself isolated*" (Manning 1997: 225; emphasis added). The explanation here contains a highly voluntaristic element: that the leadership could choose *not* to make changes. However, the result would be detrimental—global isolation. In sum, the nature of and events in the international system are influences on all states, especially in such an interdependent system as today's, but they are major influences on small states' choices and behavior.

Although the international system is a heavy constraint on choice for small states, on some issues the decisionmaking elite can choose to make this environment the primary consideration, try to ignore the environment, or seek to change or overcome its impact in some way. For small states, the international system determines the majority of the actual issues on the foreign policy agenda: as an example, concern for environmentalism was largely the product of activities by groups in developed countries, diffused to the south; economic liberalism norms were similarly diffused. These issues require attention because they usually involve major tangible gains or losses. These are the "big" issues on which system influence is key. But in some instances, system considerations can be ignored. Illustrative are the cases of Caribbean withdrawal from human rights conventions and the decision to establish relations with Cuba. In other instances, Caribbean small states have sought to try to change the system (thereby overcoming some constraints), primarily through coalition behavior. We should also distinguish between the global system and the various regional or subordinate systems with which these countries interact. Sometimes the small state may deliberately make a decision that is rational for the region but goes against the grain in terms of the larger global context. The collective decision on Cuba in 1972 again falls into this category, as do integrationist and protectionist policies in the 1970s, which went against the global free trade regime, or the region's acceptance of ideological pluralism in the early 1980s, despite the heightened polarization between the United States and the Soviet Union. As we will see, in the final analysis, how these states deal with system constraints depends on how the issues are perceived and filtered through the leadership.

The State

To understand the nuances of state behavior and why the individual Caribbean states differ in this regard (despite the general commonalities outlined earlier), one must look at the state and substate levels. Here I examine four state-level factors—attributes, values, public opinion, and institutions.

"Small" is a national attribute, one that affects policy by considerations of size and wealth. Certainly the earlier substantive discussion substantiates the fact that the Caribbean small states do not have the resources to get involved in every aspect of global affairs and generally confine their participation to key global issues and to regional affairs. Also, whether seen through Bruce Moon's compliance or consensus perspective (1985), Caribbean "dependent" states have generally been anxious to maintain traditional external ties. Even during the turmoil of the 1970s, they exhibited more interest in reformist economic strategies than in revolutionary stances, Grenada notwithstanding. This does not mean that these states have always been acquiescent or reactive; on the contrary, many have been highly vocal and proactive with respect to key international principles and events. Certainly, within the region, relative size (Jamaica) and wealth (Trinidad and Tobago) are significant: they translate into greater *regional* influence, and the assumption of strong global or hemispheric roles *on behalf of* the region.

In the area of societal values, policymaking is influenced by the English-speaking Caribbean countries' embedded democratic value system, despite its authoritarian modifications. Traditions of representative democracy (though not necessarily always "good governance"), freedom of association and religious expression, and a free press are particularly strong, even though there have been attempts by various regimes to curb some of these freedoms. As multiethnic societies, these countries are generally highly tolerant of diversity; and as small open countries, freedom of travel and emigration (both inter-island and to northern countries) has been important for their social value and for practical economic reasons. The region's support for human rights, democracy, and self-determination, and its fight to preserve immigration outlets stem in large measure from these societal values and expectations. Economically, capitalist values are widespread. Ownership of property has long been both an upper-class and a "petite bourgeoisie" goal, and the entrepreneurial values held by the relatively small "comprador" class have spread through broader sectors of the society over time. Not only are these values inherent in the leadership as well as the broader society, but also in themselves they translate into policies that generally support capitalist economic approaches. Beyond these norms, nationalist, anticolonial, and other public attitudes have been embedded through historical and political legacies.

Public opinion has generally been muted on foreign policy issues, not unlike the case in most countries of the world, where such policy has traditionally been seen as the domain of the elite (Galtung 1969). But increasingly, popular concern has been vocalized on the broader social, if not the political, foreign policy issues: for example, what to do about refugees fleeing from repression in Haiti or Cuba to certain Caribbean countries, drug issues, AIDS, environmental decay stemming from unregulated tourist or development activities, disaster reduction issues, forced return migration, violence against women, and other issues on the international policy agenda. As elsewhere, the media, which is proactive throughout the region, and nongovernmental organizations are the main channels for debate and information on these issues. Global sensitivity to democracy has brought civil society partners, labor and business in particular, into consultative decisionmaking at both national and regional levels. Especially in foreign economic policy, the state has retreated to assume the role of facilitator (Benn 1997). Thus, in essence, economic progress rests with business groups and multinational investors. Business groups are not only influencing the governments more strongly but also are conducting their own "foreign policy" by making international/regional economic and financial exchanges that are barely policed by the bureaucrats. This is a major change from the postindependence open economy period, when, although investment and trade were unregulated, they still were monitored by the state.

The major government institutions in the English-speaking Caribbean—civil service, judiciary, police services, and so on—are relatively strong and time-tested, though in many cases they have been somewhat weakened by corruption and drug-related violence. As in most developing countries, the state has been the largest employer. However, bureaucrats are normally implementers rather than decisionmakers, and in the Caribbean they are often left out of the policymaking process, except insofar as they provide necessary information to the decisionmakers. They do often resist, delay, and oppose the implementation of programs for a variety of reasons, including the fact that they are heavily unionized and more politicized than is the case in developed or larger countries. But leadership preferences are not *shaped* by the bureaucrats unless a particular bureaucrat finds favor with the elite, and the issue of delaying implementation is more problematic in domestic policy than in foreign policy. In the latter, the bureaucrats tend to be conservative and politically vulnerable in terms of selection for choice assignments abroad and promotion to ambassadorial and subambassadorial levels. In these countries, bureaucrats are also upstaged by the economic and financial ministries, which are more closely integrated into the planning process and are heavily involved in negotiations with the international financial institutions. Thus bureaucratic politics is not a prime influence on the foreign policy decisionmaking process, though a complete view of foreign policy would have to include analysis of the implementation process as well. It is noteworthy that successes in small state foreign policy depend very much on the skill and training of the small core of high-level diplomats, and that the Caribbean is often praised for the quality of its diplomats.

The Individual

The key to understanding Caribbean foreign policy lies at this level, or rather lies in understanding the interplay between this level and the other two. In essence, the determining factor is *elite choice*. In an interdependent world, anything approaching self-reliance is an elusive ideal for any state. Yet there must be something unique about the Caribbean small states that has caused them to be so vulnerable to system influences even in the 1960s, when technically these states could have closed themselves off to the world after independence as did some third-world countries. In fact, Guyana early on chose a somewhat isolationist and self-reliant strategy, even eschewing the influence of television broadcasting. The point is not whether such a strategy would have hindered economic growth but rather that it was not so much history, culture, or size that kept these countries as open to the system as they have been as it was the elites' choice of development strategy.[5] Almost every Caribbean government has chosen to integrate into the global and regional economic environment, on the assumption that this would bring economic development. In the 1970s, when nationalist policies were put in place in most countries that were then independent, the selective delinking from the international economic system did not substantially change the region's exposure to the outside. Thus Michael Manley's democratic socialist Jamaica, "cooperative socialist" Guyana, and revolutionary Grenada all chose to call on IMF help just as readily as did conservative Dominica or moderate Trinidad and Tobago. Of course in the 1990s all governments, even Guyana, moved to liberalize their economies. Although much is made of the systemic pressures to do so, the attributes and nature of the society and leadership preferences seem to be just as important determinants of this behavior as the international system.

Why governments have chosen this path of "openness" is a matter of the government elites' choices influenced by two main factors: leadership assessment of societal norms and values; and personal ideology, beliefs, and motivations. These two factors are somewhat related in that leadership values are shaped to a large extent by socialization. A third factor, the nature of the institutional-leadership relationship, contributes to the key role played by the leadership in the first place.

The stress on the elite or the leadership—meaning the leader and his coterie of advisers who, in the Caribbean context, are not necessarily cabinet members—stems from the fact that these countries have had a history of personalist governance, so that policy has been defined largely from the top down. From the 1960s into the 1980s, these countries were governed by dominant leaders—Eric Williams in Trinidad and Tobago, Forbes Burnham in Guyana, Lester Bird in Antigua and Barbuda, Eric Gairy in Grenada, and John Compton in St. Lucia, to name a few. Not only was decisionmaking highly personalistic, but also many leaders opted to assume the foreign affairs ministries themselves or to place only highly trusted aides in that portfolio. Despite the change to younger, pragmatic leaders in the 1990s (Braveboy-Wagner 1992), the nature of the decisionmaking system has not changed that much. First, the Westminster system of government gives the leader of the majority party in parliament control over the policy agenda, so there is little incentive to bipartisanship. When this system is coupled with the tendency toward authoritarianism inherent in these societies, decisionmaking becomes highly centralized. Moreover, since the legacy of personalism remains strong in the party system through which the governors get elected, it carries over into cabinet decisionmaking. The effect on foreign policy making is to stifle "bottom-up" initiatives and even dissent in the cabinet in favor of sometimes heavy-handed top-down decisionmaking.[6]

Thus it is the leadership elite, not the party functionaries or the bureaucrats, who are the key to understanding foreign policy making in these small states. As noted, elite preferences are influenced by both personal factors and societal values: sometimes these work together, sometimes they are at odds. Democratic and capitalist norms, for example, are generally shared by leaders and the people at large. But in certain specific instances, leaders influence popular values. For example, Trinidad and Tobago's policy, mentioned earlier, of keeping a distance from the United States after independence can be traced to the experiences and attitudes of the charismatic leader Eric Williams, anti-U.S. nationalist attitudes that succeeded in permeating the society. Likewise, certain nationalist and antiregional attitudes spread to the Jamaican masses after independence. During the 1970s, some leaders tried to foster socialist values: Jamaica's social policies and related foreign policy strategies during the 1970s were attributable to the personal ideological beliefs of Michael Manley, shared by his advisers and certain intellectuals, but these leaders were somewhat successful in promoting these beliefs among a certain mass segment of society. In contrast, Grenada's Maurice Bishop and a circle of advisers who had formed socialist ideas during their university days in England found it difficult to implement them in the strong bourgeois environment of Grenadian society. Yet again, Cheddi and Janet Jagan's adherence to Marxism and social justice dating to their youthful days in the United States never quite took hold in Guyana. Clearly, the illusive concept of "charisma" also has much to do with whether leaders succeed in legitimizing their ideas and attendant policy choices.

Apart from the issue of whether or not there is societal concurrence in certain value systems, the leadership elite are generally influenced by their backgrounds and experiences. The personal experiences that contribute to policy are many and varied, but in small-sized societies such as these, key influences stand out. Personal factors not only account for development of ideas and attitudes but also affect perception. How other societal and system elements are perceived depends on these experiential factors, including too the leadership's learning curve, especially in situations where the leader returns to power after a hiatus in opposition. In one obvious example, Michael Manley returned to power espousing more conservative domestic and foreign policies, having learned from the societal divisions and external antagonisms that his earlier socialistic policies engendered. Cheddi Jagan returned to power in the 1990s (after being in opposition since the 1960s) and, despite retaining his Marxist beliefs, "learned" and adapted to international changes and demands.

System, State, and Individual

How do the influences at these three levels work in concert to explain foreign policy in these small countries? Caribbean foreign policy results not from these states' place in the international hierarchy (though low position influences coalition formation), and not from bureaucratic machinations, but from the leadership elite's choices, which are in turn influenced by personal and societal norms, as well as, in certain instances, public opinion. Leadership plays a key role because of the small size of these countries, and because of the institutional arrangements (specifically, the particular manifestation of the Westminster system, and the subsidiary role played by bureaucracies) that contribute to focusing policy decisions, especially the more "removed" foreign policy decisions, in the hands of a few people. The elites evaluate the domestic and external circumstances (including important system constraints) through the prism of these small countries' vulnerabilities and capacities, which are two sides of the same coin. In terms of vulnerabilities, small size, openness, and dependence are important influencing attributes. There are some particular vulnerabilities already noted related to these qualities—among them, diseconomies of scale, heavy dependence on external trade and aid, and vulnerability to natural disasters and to various external threats. Vulnerabilities also include some more dynamic considerations, for example adverse changes in the international system, changes in the domestic economy, changes in national political and social integration (ethnic problems, crime, drugs), and political problems such as the level of stress on institutions (for example, through refugee/immigration influxes or drug cartel operations, and changing levels of popular support for the regime).

The other side of the coin, country capacity, determines whether particular policies that the leadership elite perceive as needed to deal with prevailing vulnerabilities can actually be made operational. Capacity depends on factors such as differing levels of industrialization, wealth, and human and technological resources. Trinidad and Tobago, for example, has the most viable economy, and therefore the elite can and have opted for a broad and diversified trade strategy. On the other hand, the smaller Eastern Caribbean countries, with undiversified economies, are forced to focus on retaining trade preferences in North America and Europe. Of course, as already seen, capacities in the diplomatic sphere are directly related to these factors. In plain terms, Caribbean foreign policy depends on leadership choices made within the constraints of domestic capabilities *and* small-state economic and political vulnerabilities. Judicious juggling of these two sets of factors is always necessary.

Conclusion

Although the twelve independent English-speaking Caribbean states that used to be termed "ministates" are not major players on the world stage, they have exerted influence in a number of ways over the years: by allying with one superpower or the other during the Cold War, by sheer voting power in international organizations (especially in the OAS), by coalition behavior (for example, the ACP alliance with the EU or AOSIS on environmental matters), and through other strategies elaborated above. Although most of these states have very limited resources, capacity has been strengthened through use of these strategies, especially regionalism, even though sometimes the pull of nationalism and differing vulnerabilities and interests have made regional action difficult. The prime motivation of English-speaking Caribbean states in foreign policy is economic—meeting their domestic economic and related social needs. In the 1990s and into the twentieth century, these countries have been faced with dramatic challenges as a result of their loss of leverage as Cold War allies of the United States; the global drive for economic liberalization, which has brought home the prospect of loss of crucial trade preferences; and the vulnerability of their societies to "uncivil" transnational forces. Regionalist strategies offer some hope for resisting marginalization, and the Caribbean history of adaptation to global events suggests a capacity for resilience. This analysis suggests, however, that if creative foreign policy strategies are to be devised, the Caribbean must look to its leadership for the ideas and initiative and to its skilled diplomats for the implementation of these strategies. Whether the region can look beyond the tunnel of the "banana issue" and other problems and move toward achievement of positive goals remains to be seen.

Notes

This chapter is abstracted from Braveboy-Wagner 2001.

1. All figures are from Caribbean Development Bank 2000: 13.

2. The fact that Carl Lindner, the chairman of Chiquita Corporation, has been a major donor to both Republican and Democratic political parties was also a factor in stirring sustained U.S. intervention over the banana issue.

3. Since the 1980s there has been acceptance in the third world of the redefinition of security to include not only traditional military concerns but also economic and social issues. Both the literature and the policy discourse reflect this redefinition.

4. In terms of bilateral diplomacy, the OECS maintains shared missions in London, Ottawa, and Brussels.

5. The term *development strategy* as used here refers to the mix of economic, social, and political choices and cannot be referred to by simple categories such as "democratic," "socialist," and "moderate."

6. There are other adverse effects—for example, personalization of the process of ambassadorial appointments, and bypassing of the foreign ministry in decisionmaking. For a discussion, see Braveboy-Wagner 1989.

4

Panama: A "Hegemonized" Foreign Policy

Peter M. Sanchez

Panamanian foreign policy cannot be analyzed fully without a thorough understanding of U.S.-Panama relations. Panama gained its independence from Colombia in 1903 only when Washington decided that its goal of building a canal through the isthmus would be achieved more easily by dealing with a small, weak Panama than by dealing with the more powerful and nationalistic Colombia. Although Panamanians had already developed a sense of national identity, in 1903 U.S. power and influence were decisive in quickly and bloodlessly creating the Republic of Panama. A resulting accord, the 1903 Hay-Bunau-Varilla Treaty, granted Washington the right to build and defend the canal, as well as near-sovereignty rights over a ten-mile-wide swath of the isthmus. As a result, throughout the twentieth century Panama's independence was conditioned by a sizable U.S. civilian and military presence and by repeated U.S. intervention in the country's affairs.

The relationship that developed between the Republic of Panama and the United States has been fascinating but also enigmatic and contradictory. The history of this relationship, spanning over one century, is replete with events and relationships that have filled the pages of novels and books, documenting Panama's often tragic struggle for independence and the U.S. quest for hegemony in Latin America. What U.S. policymakers labeled a "special relationship" was fraught with conflict, tragedy, and frustration, to a large extent owing to the asymmetry of the U.S.-Panama partnership. Although ties have been close and at times quite amicable, all too often intense differences have arisen to sour the U.S.-Panama partnership. Any analysis of Panama's foreign policy must therefore take into account this difficult, unbalanced relationship.

This chapter examines Panama's foreign policy after the 1989 U.S. invasion of the isthmus, which ousted General Manuel Noriega from power. The analysis will focus on U.S.-Panama negotiations over the perpetuation of a U.S. military presence on the isthmus past 1999. That year was paramount because the 1977 Panama Canal treaties, negotiated by President Jimmy Carter and Panamanian military strongman General Omar Torrijos, stipulated that only Panamanian defense forces would be stationed on the isthmus after December 31, 1999, thus requiring the end of the U.S. military presence. The two 1977 treaties, one concerning the neutrality and defense of the canal and the other concerning the operation of the canal, promised to end Panama's neocolonial status, by eliminating the Canal Zone in 1979, ending the U.S. military presence in 1999, and turning over the operation of the waterway to Panama in 1999.

The focus on the negotiations over a continued U.S. military presence is particularly useful since Panama's government insisted that it be limited to very specific antidrug functions, a condition that Washington eventually rejected. In the end, all U.S. troops left Panama as required by the 1977 treaties, a bittersweet moment for many Panamanians and Americans, who had become accustomed to the extensive U.S. presence. The conclusion of the negotiations, at first brush, suggests that a small state was able to achieve an important foreign policy objective despite resistance by a large and powerful state. After careful analysis, however, I suggest that Panama's foreign policy is still highly influenced by the power asymmetry that exists between the two nations. Panama's foreign policy success in these negotiations can be attributed principally to watershed changes in the international system rather than to Panama's ability to exert influence in the international arena. The world may seem to be moving toward globalization and interdependence, but state power and systemic forces still exert significant pressure on diplomatic affairs, particularly in the interaction between a small and a large nation-state.

Panamanian Sovereignty vs. U.S. Neocolonialism: The Troubled "Special Relationship"

A thorough examination of U.S.-Panama negotiations over a continued U.S. military presence on the isthmus requires an understanding of the historical precedents that conditioned those negotiations. In this section I underscore that the U.S.-Panama relationship from 1903 to 1989 was influenced greatly by Panama's weakness vis-à-vis the United States and by a fundamental clash of interests.

Panama's vulnerability vis-à-vis the United States stemmed principally from its smallness and weakness as a nation-state. As late as 1999 the nation's population was estimated only at about 2.74 million and its gross domestic product (GDP) only at about U.S.$18 billion. Panama is roughly the size of South Carolina, or just over 30,000 square miles (Goodwin 2000: 45). U.S. hegemony in the Western Hemisphere and U.S. interests and actions in Panama tended to underscore the smallness and weakness of the isthmus. The United States occupied the position of a near-colonial power since the mid-1800s, severely limiting Panama's sovereignty and independence (LaFeber 1989).

At the same time that the isthmus was under U.S. tutelage, Panama and Washington became increasingly committed to very different foreign policy goals. On the one hand, the United States carefully protected its interests in Panama, mainly the safe and efficient operation of the Panama Canal and the use of Panama as a strategic platform for its Latin American geostrategic policy. On the other hand, Panama desired to achieve true sovereignty and some degree of economic independence. These competing interests inevitably led to conflict between the two countries.

Panama's importance to Washington increased over the years as the United States expanded its economic and military reach. By the 1930s the U.S. military presence on the isthmus had grown significantly. Two factors led to this militarization. First, the growing crisis in Europe compelled Washington to place greater importance on the canal as a means of communication. Nazi Germany became increasingly interested in Latin America, and Panama served as a linchpin in this strategic battleground. Concurrently, nationalist social forces in Panama were growing stronger, with ever-increasing lunges toward anti-Americanism, compelling Washington to increase its military presence to defend the canal against social turmoil. In 1946, for example, the United States wanted to extend the lease on defense sites that it had acquired during World War II, but Panama's government rejected the plan. Nevertheless, the following year, Washington was able to negotiate a treaty to keep fourteen military facilities. While the Panamanian oligarchy seemed somewhat agreeable to the request, nationalist groups organized against maintaining even this more limited U.S. military presence. As Panama's congress debated the issue, thousands of demonstrators took to the streets and forced the legislators to unanimously reject the agreement (Conniff 1992; LeFeber 1989). Panamanian nationalists had won the day. In Washington's eyes, therefore, the United States had to defend the canal not only from a potential external attack but from internal "threats" as well, further intensifying Panamanian anticolonialism.

The 1960s were a repeat of the 1930s. Soon after the Cuban Revolution in 1959, Washington, as it had done during the World War II period, assembled a sizable network of military installations in Panama designed to protect vital U.S. strategic interests and to safeguard the efficient operation of the canal. The defense sites in Panama were directed by the U.S. Southern Command (SOUTHCOM), led by the Commander in Chief SOUTHCOM (CINCSO) and headquartered at Quarry Heights, on the Pacific approach to the canal and just outside of Panama City. During the Cold War, these facilities were crucial for achieving U.S. interests, at least in the eyes of high-level policymakers (Gurdian Guerra 1998; U.S. Southern Command 1997; Leis 1985).

Increasing numbers of Panamanians reacted violently to this augmented military presence. In 1964, over twenty-one Panamanians died as a result of several days of anti-U.S. rioting over the right to fly Panama's flag in the Canal Zone. U.S. troops, deployed to defend the Canal Zone, fired into the crowds and were blamed for the Panamanian casualties.[1] The 1964 riots represented a watershed event in U.S.-Panama relations. Until then, Panama's oligarchy had simply wanted Washington to accept some principally economic and symbolic changes to the hated 1903 treaty. However, the riots brought Panama's oligarchy and nationalists together into an alliance demanding that Washington abrogate rather than amend the 1903 treaty. Washington finally paid attention and President Lyndon Johnson pledged to establish a new relationship with Panama.

In 1968 the Panamanian National Guard overthrew a democratically elected government and by the next year General Omar Torrijos had established himself as "maximum leader." Torrijos headed a military regime that was repressive and antidemocratic, but at the same time carried out needed social and economic reforms (Ropp 1982). The military regime brought order and stability to Panama, greatly satisfying U.S. interests. The new order allowed Washington to drop its efforts at renegotiating the hated 1903 treaty and prevented leftist and anti-U.S. sectors from assuming power in the isthmus.

By the mid-1970s, General Torrijos became insistent that Washington should again take up the diplomatic quest for reshaping the U.S.-Panama relationship. In 1977, Washington and Panama finally restructured their troubled relationship by agreeing to two treaties that almost immediately gave Panama sovereignty over the infamous U.S. Canal Zone and would give Panama control of the canal itself on December 31, 1999. The accords also stated that after this date "only the Republic of Panama shall . . . maintain military forces, defense sites and military installations within its national territory." The canal treaties seemed to signal the victory of a small nation over a superpower, a David and Goliath denouement in global diplomacy.

Previous conflicts over the U.S. military presence on the isthmus set the stage for the canal treaties and Panama's insistence that U.S. troops leave after December 31, 1999. Although the Carter administration agreed to the withdrawal of U.S. troops on that date, other U.S. power brokers wanted to ensure that the door remained open to a continued U.S. military presence after 1999. The U.S. Senate eventually inserted a proviso into the Neutrality Treaty (one of the two treaties) that states:

> Nothing in the treaty shall preclude the Republic of Panama and the United States of America from making . . . agreements or arrangements for the stationing of any United States military forces or the maintenance of defense sites . . . in the Republic of Panama . . . that the Republic of Panama and the United States of America may deem necessary or appropriate. (LaFeber 1989: 244–245)

This U.S. change to the treaties ultimately led to confusion and controversy, since both sides saw the amendment very differently. U.S. officials, but principally those most wedded to maintaining U.S. forces in Panama, interpreted this provision as a green light for the perpetuation of a U.S. military presence on the isthmus past 1999. Critics in Panama, however, argued that the change was made after Panama's National Assembly ratified, and a national plebiscite accepted, the two treaties. From the isthmian perspective, then, this proviso had little legitimacy, owing to its late insertion into the treaty process. The result was that prior to the start of the U.S.-Panama negotiations over a continued U.S. military presence, some voices in the United States were saying that Panama had already agreed to a continued U.S. presence, while some in Panama argued that the treaties required that U.S. troops exit the isthmus not later than December 31, 1999.

In 1983, two years after Torrijos's death, General Manuel Antonio Noriega took control of Panama's military, renaming them the Panamanian Defense Forces (PDF), and established himself as de facto ruler. At first Noriega seemed to be a U.S. lackey, allowing Washington to do as it wished in Central America by using Panama as a strategic platform for U.S. military and intelligence operations (Kempe 1990). However, all too quickly Washington's general turned "nationalistic" and into a liability for several reasons. Washington came under scrutiny when Noriega's involvement in the drug trade became public, since U.S. decisionmakers had maintained a very intimate relationship with this tyrant and drug trafficker for decades (Koster and Sánchez 1990). Of additional concern to Washington was Noriega's close relationship with the Castro regime, the Salvadoran leftist guerrillas, and the Colombian drug cartels.

High-level U.S. officials had overlooked these major faults owing to Noriega's covert contribution to Washington's containment policy in Central America. However, once the U.S. Congress forbade the Reagan administration to assist the Nicaraguan Contras in 1986, Noriega's blemishes became major liabilities, leading to an important shift in Washington's perception of the Panamanian general. Very quickly Noriega became anathema and Reagan administration leaks to the U.S. Congress and to the U.S. press (Hersh 1986) were just one tool in the diplomatic struggle to discredit the general. Washington took calculated, systematic steps to force the general from power. These steps included diplomacy, threats, military maneuvers, inciting military *golpes,* clandestine operations, and economic sanctions (Kempe 1990; Koster and Sánchez 1990; and Scranton 1991). Noriega resisted Washington's efforts at removing him from power for three years, eventually compelling President George Bush to authorize an invasion in 1989, which resulted in taking Noriega to the United States to stand trial for drug trafficking. Although Torrijos and Noriega had seemed to defy Washington and do as they pleased, in the end Panama's sovereignty was shown to be insignificant when compared to U.S. military power and interests.

The Diplomatic Struggle over U.S. Military Bases After 1999

The context for the perpetuation of a continued U.S. military presence in Panama appeared optimal after the 1989 U.S. invasion, despite the continued existence of strong nationalist/anticolonial sectors in Panama. The Neutrality Treaty, while calling for the departure of U.S. troops, committed Panama to take on primary responsibility for canal defense after 1999. Panama's postinvasion government, however, with much prodding from Washington, had dissolved the country's armed forces soon after the U.S. invasion. Also, opinion polls showed that many Panamanians seemed willing to accept a continued U.S. military presence, believing that U.S. soldiers brought economic and political stability.[2] But Panama's new president, Guillermo Endara, was a member of the Arnulfista Party, which tended to favor the departure of U.S. troops. Even though Endara took office thanks to the U.S. invasion, he decided not to negotiate with Washington on the issue of U.S. military bases. Realizing that Endara had scant public support, Washington decided to wait to negotiate with the next elected government, announcing publicly that negotiations would be held only if Panama asked for U.S. troops to remain.[3]

The 1994 election in Panama threw a curve ball at the United States. Rather than rejecting the nationalism of the past, the plurality of

Panamanians voted for the Democratic Revolutionary Party (Partido Revolucionario Democrático [PRD]), the political organization that General Omar Torrijos had founded and that had supported General Noriega until the 1989 U.S. invasion. Ernesto Perez Balladares became Panama's new president, now being billed as a banker rather than as a backer of the PDF. While the PRD did not receive a majority of the vote, nationalist parties soundly won the popular vote. The political parties that received the lion's share of the vote tally were the PRD (33 percent), the Arnulfistas (29 percent), and Papa Egoro (18 percent), a new but also nationalist party that called for the removal of all U.S. troops (Scranton 1995). Even though the majority of Panamanians appeared to want U.S. troops to stay, the political lineup in the national legislature was now potentially at odds with Washington's hopes of keeping a U.S. military presence on Panamanian soil. Additionally, nationalist groups, deeply committed to ending the U.S. neocolonial presence, were ready to mobilize to prevent any agreement from taking place. Washington was now facing an uphill battle.

The Multilateral Antidrug Center Talks

The negotiations for a possible perpetuation of U.S. troops in Panama tentatively began in November 1995 and lasted until September 1998, although some have argued that Washington made some efforts to keep troops in Panama as late as the beginning of 1999.[4] At first, the United States and Panama discussed the possibility of allowing the U.S. government to keep military bases past 1999. Eventually, however, the talks focused on the establishment of a Multinational Antidrug Center (Centro Multinacional Antidrogas [CMA]). The CMA talks began in earnest in July 1997 and concluded in failure around mid-1998.

The initial efforts toward an agreement of some kind were quickly dashed. At first, the Perez administration appeared to be amenable to reaching an accord that would allow U.S. bases to remain on the isthmus. He appointed Gabriel Lewis Galindo, a man who was positively inclined toward the United States, as his foreign minister. But almost as soon as exploratory talks began, in February 1995 they came to a halt because the United States stated that it would not pay a lease on any future bases in Panama. President Perez countered by stating, "No payment. No bases." At the end of 1996, however, Perez proposed the creation of a CMA that would have civilian leadership and a small, mostly U.S. military component. This proposal represented a political compromise. It allowed Washington to hold firm on not paying for bases, while the Panamanian government could say that it had stood firm on the issue of U.S. bases after 1999. On a visit to Washington, President Perez discussed the CMA issue with President William Clinton, giving the proposal the necessary impetus to start negotiations anew.

An important part of this diplomatic struggle centered on the economic value of the U.S. bases. On the one hand, the Department of Defense argued that Panama stood to lose about $370 million if U.S. forces left the isthmus. A study by two Panamanian economists, however, put the loss at around $180 million (*Latin America Weekly Report,* April 11, 1996: 165). For many years, very few Panamanians had focused on the potential benefits of the vast areas and numerous properties that would be reverted to Panama under the provisions of the canal treaties. As time passed and as Panama became more democratic, an increasing number of Panamanians began to think about the financial benefits that could potentially accrue to the nation if these properties were used for economic rather than military purposes. Nicolas Barletta, a friend of the United States, former president, and director of the Authority of the Interoceanic Region (ARI), argued that Panama could stand to gain about $1.5 billion from the use of the reverted properties (*Latin America Weekly Report,* June 15, 1995: 263). Architect Ricardo Bermudez also pointed out that Panama's urban development had been severely hampered by the linear growth forced upon the city by the plethora of U.S. defense sites contiguous to the canal. He argued that the civilian use of the bases would allow the city to grow in a more rational, concentric pattern (Bermudez 1998). It is clear that Washington had tended to overestimate the financial value of the military bases in Panama, principally because it ignored the potential financial rewards of using those territories and facilities for commercial purposes. Panama, for example, as a maritime crossroads, had never been able to build a port for cruise ships, owing to the monopoly held by U.S. military bases on land adjacent to the Caribbean and Pacific approaches to the canal. Panama had also never been able to provide much needed services to transiting ships, a potential commercial bonanza. Clearly, the closure of U.S. bases would allow Panama to more fully take advantage of its strategic geographic location. In fact, from the time of independence, Panama's leaders had quarreled with Washington over economic opportunities and benefits that the former believed the isthmus should be able to derive from the canal (Major 1993). There was of course an important unknown that benefited Washington greatly: What would happen to Panama politically and economically once the U.S. bases were gone? This troubling unknown convinced many Panamanians that they should support bilateral negotiations with the United States on the establishment of a CMA.

The selection of negotiating officials also generated conflict. When the bargaining over the creation of the CMA first began, the U.S. government's chief negotiator was Ambassador John Negroponte, a veteran U.S. diplomat intimately involved in the Reagan administration's Central American containment policy and who had acquired the nickname "Mr. Death-Squad." Negroponte was not liked by the Panamanian negotiators, who were forced to choose a new negotiating team in June 1996, owing to Lewis Galindo's death. Ricardo Alberto Arias became the new foreign minister. The new chief negotiator on the issue of bases was Jorge Ritter, a well-known Torrijista who had supported Noriega's regime up to the last moment as foreign minister and then as ambassador to the United Nations. Washington classified him as "nationalistic" and as "anti-American." Second in command in the negotiations was Adolfo Ahumada, another Torrijista, who had played a role in the canal treaty negotiations in 1977 and who had been classified as a "radical" and a "Marxist" by U.S. negotiators during those years (Jorden 1984: 270–271). Negroponte appealed to conservative power brokers in Washington who wanted to ensure that the United States did not "give in" to Panama, as they believed had happened with the 1977 canal treaties. Ritter appealed to the powerful Torrijista element within the ruling PRD, with one party official saying, "We knew if Ritter was negotiating the deal, we wouldn't have to worry that the Americans would trick us somehow" (*Miami Herald,* September 30, 1997). The playing field had certainly changed for Washington, since these new "nationalist" Panamanian negotiators had serious reservations about Negroponte and about a continued U.S. military presence on the isthmus. By September 1997, Negroponte left his position as chief U.S. negotiator, citing retirement as the reason for departure. Just prior to his "retirement," *Miami Herald* reporter Glenn Garvin wrote: "The talks between Negroponte and Ritter grew so tense that the two men decided to recess for four days before meeting again in Washington" (August 18, 1997). Although both sides minimized the importance of Negroponte's departure, it was clear that if there was to be any chance for reaching a CMA agreement, the Cold War warrior had to exit the scene. The United States replaced Negroponte with Thomas E. McNamara, assistant secretary of state for political and military affairs, a respected career diplomat without an incriminating past.

From a personal perspective Jorge Ritter and Panama had won. Ritter had been successful at removing Negroponte from the negotiating table. He quickly paid a price, however. Less than two weeks after Negroponte's retirement, *El Nuevo Herald,* Miami's Spanish-language newspaper, published a story charging that Ritter, while ambassador to

Colombia, had become involved in illegal financial activities with at least one known drug trafficker. Later that month, the *Miami Herald* reported that Ritter might have also been involved in money laundering (September 30, 1997). Officials in Panama, if they had forgotten the Noriega affair, were bluntly reminded that U.S. intelligence agencies had volumes of information on Panamanian officials that Washington could use at any time to place them in a precarious position. Nevertheless, despite the U.S. pressure, the Perez administration kept Ritter on as chief negotiator and the talks resumed at a faster pace.

From September to December 1997, half a dozen rounds of negotiations took place. Both sides had argued that talks needed to be finalized by December, since both nations had lengthy constitutional and fiscal processes that needed to be accomplished prior to the time that U.S. troops were scheduled to depart Panama. In addition, in 1998 a national election would take place in the United States and Panama would hold a referendum on a constitutional amendment allowing for a second, consecutive presidential term. Negotiators on both sides were eager to take as much domestic politics as possible out of the CMA talks. Finally, on December 23, 1977, the two negotiating teams triumphantly announced that they had reached an agreement, adding that the signing of a final accord would take place one week later owing to rudimentary legal details and the need for some minor language translations.

Collapse of the Negotiations: No CMA!

The optimism that existed at the end of December quickly turned into frustration and finger pointing on January 12, 1998, when the Perez government announced that it could not sign the agreement as written. This quick about-face infuriated U.S. officials. A new and catastrophic round of discussions replaced what was considered to be a fait accompli. Several key elements of the accord were no longer acceptable to the Panamanian side. Instead of signing the accord, the Perez administration demanded that important changes be made to the preliminary agreement reached at the end of December. The situation was complicated further when vice foreign ministers from Brazil, Colombia, and Mexico, in Panama at the time and considering their countries' membership in the antidrug center, demanded that the CMA concern itself with both the production and *consumption* of illegal drugs, a clear allusion to the U.S. responsibility in the illegal narcotics traffic. Panama then suggested that more nations be brought into the CMA discussions prior to reaching a final agreement. In that same week, a broad grassroots coalition emerged in Panama for the purpose of defeating the CMA in a national referendum. The group, calling itself MONADESCO

(National Movement in Defense of Sovereignty) comprised fifty labor, human rights, and academic organizations. McNamara left the isthmus without a signed agreement, infuriated, and with very difficult diplomatic and political hurdles ahead of him. If the agreement became multilateral, would the U.S. Senate have to ratify the accord as a treaty? If the United States continued to negotiate after this dramatic change in Panama's position, would Washington be allowing Panama to set the agenda? If an agreement were ever reached, would violence erupt in Panama? The controversy climaxed on January 27, 1998, when the Mexican newspaper *Excelsior* published the text of the accord reached in late December, along with an article revealing that high-level Mexican officials were very critical of the agreement (Becerra Acosta 1998). Although Panamanian officials had leaked some bits and pieces, until then the Panamanian public knew very little about the CMA negotiations, criticized by many as "secretive" and "nondemocratic." The Perez administration had revealed only that the CMA would be a civilian, multinational antidrug center, with a small military component. President Perez repeatedly refuted charges made by critics that the center would constitute "hidden U.S. bases." Once *Excelsior* made the accord public, though, it became clear that the CMA was much more than had been advertised and that under the agreement the U.S. military would retain many of the same rights and privileges it had enjoyed during the entire century.

To many Panamanians, the CMA was indeed a ruse for the perpetuation of the U.S. military presence and of U.S. neocolonialism. First, the accord did not stipulate how many U.S. troops, or troops from any other country, would be stationed at the center. Second, Panama put several key facilities at the service of the CMA and basically under the control of the U.S. military, including Howard Air Force Base, Fort Kobbe, Rodman Naval Base, Galeta Island, among others.[5] Third, the agreement included existing U.S. military bombing ranges, meaning that Panama would have to maintain these ranges, a costly prospect, and that the U.S. government would be able to depart Panama without cleaning them up, as stipulated by the 1977 canal treaties. Fourth, and most important, the agreement would allow the United States to carry out "other missions," in addition to the counternarcotics operations for which the CMA was supposedly designed. The clarification of what would constitute these "other" missions became a key point of contention.

The Perez administration quickly decided to pull out of the agreement reached in late December 1997. While the above concerns were important in reaching that decision, Panama's internal politics also played a role in President Perez's hasty withdrawal from the agreement. Almost immediately after the two sides had reached an accord, President

Perez turned the agreement over to top PRD officials and to other "prominent" Panamanians. The president was shocked to find that these individuals were highly critical of what the Panamanian negotiators had conceded to Washington. PRD leaders also conveyed to President Perez that the PRD would probably not back such an accord. In fact, the PRD had for years clearly stated its opposition to a continued U.S. military presence. Since Perez needed his party's support to change Panama's constitution to allow for his reelection, he decided to take a more nationalistic stance on the CMA agreement. His decision was to demand that Washington omit the "other missions" clause from the agreement and that the CMA operate initially for three rather than twelve years, as the United States had desired. These were two changes that Washington would not accept.

The talks deteriorated very quickly and never recovered momentum. By April 1998, President Perez was stating publicly that he had made a mistake in the CMA negotiations and that the draft CMA accord that had been reached had turned into a "*mamotreto,*" essentially an unwieldy ream of papers. He added that the United States had insisted on having jurisdiction over its military personnel and insisted on performing "other missions," and that Panama could not accept those two privileges (*El Panama America,* April 2, 1998). The U.S. secretary of defense, William Cohen, then announced a plan to accelerate the closure of U.S. military bases in Panama, perhaps to send a signal that the U.S. military would leave Panama unless the two sides quickly reached a compromise. In mid-April 1998, McNamara issued a statement saying that a CMA agreement could guarantee the continuation of the "special relationship" between the United States and Panama, but that the United States would have to begin to implement alternative plans very soon. "Once these alternate plans are implemented the opportunity for an antinarcotics center in Panama will be lost," he warned (USIS 1998). But President Perez, the PRD, some prominent Panamanians, and numerous nationalist groups had already decided to reject the CMA. In September 1998, after several more months of diplomatic waltzing, negotiators acknowledged that the talks had reached their end. All U.S. troops would have to depart from isthmian soil by noon on December 31, 1999, as required by the 1977 Panama Canal treaties. Those who had demanded that Panama regain complete sovereignty rejoiced.

Explaining Panamanian Behavior

The conclusion that analysts might reach, and have reached, concerning U.S.-Panama relations is that Panama was able to get what it wanted from the United States (Falcoff 1998). Panama was able first to convince the United States to renegotiate the hated 1903 Hay-Bunau-Varilla Treaty in 1977 despite U.S. hesitance; and then to ensure that Washington did not perpetuate its military presence in Panama past 1999, despite U.S. efforts to maintain that presence. These appear to be very notable accomplishments for a small nation-state, especially considering that Panama's success has apparently come at the expense of a superpower's interests. I will now employ the three levels of analysis commonly used in the study of international relations in order to gain a better understanding of the motivations and forces behind these dramatic changes in the U.S.-Panama relationship and to determine whether the conventional explanation is accurate.

The International System: Did David Slay Goliath?

When looking at U.S.-Panama relations at the international system level, I identify two important changes in the system that weighed heavily on these relations: the end of colonialism in the twentieth century and the end of the Cold War circa 1991. The U.S.-Panama relationship, beginning with the building of the Panama Canal Railroad by a U.S. company in the mid-1800s, has been one of neocolonialism (LaFeber 1989; Marques 1989). The United States did not control Panama directly as Spain had done prior to 1821. However, the United States did control part of Panama's territory, the ten-mile-wide Canal Zone, from 1903 until 1979, when the canal treaties were officially implemented. Additionally, as highlighted above, the United States stationed ever-increasing numbers of U.S. troops in the country from 1903 until 1999. LaFeber has characterized this relationship as "informal colonialism" (1989: 46). Regardless of how U.S. scholars and policymakers characterized the relationship, many Panamanians viewed the "special relationship" as exploitative and imperialistic, necessitating major changes in favor of Panama's sovereignty and security.

As early as the 1930s, widespread and intense anti-U.S. sentiments arose in Panama. These sentiments were consistent with the ideas found in national liberation movements that emerged in colonies of imperial powers all over the world. Despite the fact that the United States saw itself as a promoter of liberty and self-determination, Panamanian nationalists saw Washington's policies as colonialist in form and substance. The anticolonial wave that spread the globe after the end of World War II manifested itself in Panama as well: first in the rejection of a treaty that would have allowed the U.S. military to keep additional bases in Panama, then as anti-U.S. riots in 1964, and then as the Carter-Torrijos treaties of 1977.[6] Even the leaders of Panama's independence in 1903, who have often been characterized as U.S. lackeys, were disconcerted by Washington's assertiveness in acquiring a Canal Zone and rights of sovereignty in Panama. By the middle of the century, more and more oligarchs looked at the United States with skepticism, even though they tended to benefit economically from the "special relationship." Eventually, however, nationalism, combined with anticolonialist ideas, unified most Panamanians in calling for complete sovereignty for the isthmus.

The failure of the CMA negotiations represented simply the last Panamanian effort to regain the sovereignty it had lost in 1903. While decolonization principles mostly affected Panama, they must have influenced U.S. decisionmakers as well. Although the U.S. government desired to establish a CMA in Panama, as the most cost-effective way to fight the drug war and maintain its military contacts in Latin America, pressing Panama for a continued U.S. military presence on the isthmus could have created a violent eruption of nationalism that might have been very costly for Washington's regional interests.[7] Perhaps most extraordinary is that the United States held on for so long to its colonial remnants in Panama despite the existence of anticolonial sentiments in the country for so many decades.

U.S. strategic concerns during the Cold War help us to understand Washington's long-term colonial interests in Panama. Thus the end of the Cold War represents another paramount systemic change affecting the CMA negotiations. Beginning in 1954, when U.S. policymakers became convinced that Soviet interests were making headway in Guatemala, Washington viewed Panama as a strategic linchpin in its global containment policy. The isthmus represented a key economic asset, as well as a platform for U.S. strategic policy in the region. As late as 1989, Washington viewed Panama as vital to U.S. strategic interests, invading the country to ensure that the Noriega regime did not control the canal and did not threaten U.S. military defense sites. Conservatives in Washington wished to keep bases in Panama even after 1999. However, with the end of U.S.-Soviet rivalry, most key U.S. policymakers no longer viewed Panama as vital to U.S. strategic plans. At the end of the millennium, Panama had lost much of its economic and military importance to the United States, allowing Washington to finally take a softer position vis-à-vis Panama.

Undoubtedly, some sectors in Washington still desired permanent U.S. military bases. For example, conservatives in Congress, particularly Senator Jesse Helms, continued to view Panama as vital to U.S. strategic interests and fought hard to press the Clinton administration for a new agreement. Some segments within the Department of Defense, principally those officers and organizations that viewed low-intensity conflict and the antinarcotics mission as vital to military strategy, lobbied to keep U.S. bases in Panama as well. The intelligence community also pushed for a U.S. military presence in Panama owing to the various espionage facilities already in operation on the isthmus, such as Galeta Island. U.S. agencies involved in the fight against the illicit narcotics trade were perhaps most interested in keeping a U.S. military presence on the isthmus, since the United States already operated in Panama the largest counternarcotics operation in Latin America. The CMA would have represented a post-1999 replacement for that effort. Despite these calls for a continued U.S. presence, there simply was no important overarching imperative, like the containment of communism, for Washington to keep defense sites on Panamanian soil. On the contrary, by the end of the millennium, several factors militated against keeping U.S. soldiers in Panama. A continued U.S. military presence would be costly and might have incurred sizable political costs, like fomenting anti-U.S. sentiment in Panama and ill will among Latin American nations. The best solution was simply to accept Panama's rejection of the CMA and abide by the provisions of the 1977 Carter-Torrijos treaties, requiring the removal of all U.S. troops from the isthmus.

A long-range historical examination of U.S.-Panama relations enables the analyst to see the systemic factors that impacted heavily on the relatively brief CMA negotiations. The fact that Washington withdrew all of its military forces from Panama does not mean that David slew Goliath. Two factors convinced Washington not to use a heavy hand in the negotiations. First, Panama no longer served as a key U.S. strategic platform in a superpower struggle. Second, keeping U.S. troops in Panama would run counter to one of the major developments in world politics in the twentieth century—the process of decolonization. U.S. military bases in Panama were no longer critical for U.S. interests. A heavy-handed effort on Washington's part to keep those bases would tarnish the image of the United States as the leader of the democratic world and potentially create a volatile situation on the isthmus. During the entire century, anticolonial forces in Panama had called for the departure of U.S. troops from the isthmus. Only when the Cold War ended and Panama seemed less important strategically were these forces able to convince the "eagle" to release its "talons" (Smith 2000).

The State: Woes of a Democratic but Weak Panama

Unlike the negotiations in 1977, which led to the watershed Panama Canal treaties, the CMA talks took place in a relatively democratic political environment. In 1977, President Carter had dealt with a populist, military strongman, General Omar Torrijos, who had a firm control on the nation. In 1997, on the other hand, President Clinton dealt with an elected leader subject to popular opinion and the political interests of various sectors.

At first, the Perez administration appeared ready to fashion an agreement with the United States to establish a CMA in Panama. A multinational, civilian-led antidrug center seemed to be a good compromise for Panama. With such an arrangement Perez could perhaps satisfy the nationalists, who demanded the end of U.S. military bases, while at the same time satisfying the majority of Panamanians, who apparently wanted the "gringos" to stay. A CMA accord would also keep Washington at bay, since U.S. troops would be able to stay on the isthmus and Panama could show that it was cooperating with the U.S. antinarcotics effort.

Panama's president, however, was unwilling to sacrifice his political ambitions and his political party's legacy for the establishment of a CMA. Perez's reelection ambitions jeopardized the CMA once PRD leaders made it clear that they would not support him for reelection if he negotiated a deal with Washington that allowed U.S. soldiers to stay in Panama with a carte blanche, rent-free, and with near-diplomatic immunity. Nationalists, particularly student organizations and educators, made it clear to President Perez that they would vigorously assault any effort that allowed U.S. troops to stay in Panama after 1999. It was clear that, although many Panamanians desired U.S. troops to stay, a vocal and sizable segment of the population was willing to go to the streets to stop any CMA agreement.[8] Neither Panama nor Washington wanted anti-U.S. violence to break out on the isthmus, as it had in the past. Finally, President Perez was also influenced by economic elites, who saw the reverted properties as a potential economic bonanza for themselves and for the country. These domestic forces and interests were sufficiently powerful to convince Panama's president to sideline the CMA agreement, risking U.S. ire and retribution.[9]

The democratic character of the Panamanian government greatly affected Panama's foreign policy during the CMA negotiations. When General Torrijos was in power, he was able to push through a treaty despite extensive opposition simply because he was "maximum leader." Perez did not have that luxury. Press freedom allowed for a great deal of coverage to those who opposed the continued U.S. military presence. During 1997 and 1998, there were many public discussions and lectures in Panama on the U.S. military presence by political analysts as well as by technical experts. As a result, during the period of the CMA negotiations, the Panamanian public received a great deal of information about the U.S. military presence and its negative economic and political effects. In the past, Panamanians had simply been told that U.S. soldiers fueled the Panamanian economy. Now Panamanians also heard the other side of the story, that the U.S. military presence had negative ramifications for the country's economy and that the reverted properties, if wisely employed, could potentially bring even more economic benefits to Panama. President Perez was also constrained by grassroots organizations and political parties that favored a U.S. withdrawal. Interest-group pressure was strong and thus President Perez decided to favor strong domestic interests rather than Uncle Sam.

Would Panama's democratic government have been able to resist a U.S. government demand for bases if Washington still perceived the isthmus as strategically and economically vital? This is an impossible question to answer. The historical record, however, provides clues. During the Cold War, Washington was certainly more than willing to criticize and even subvert democratic governments, if those regimes stood in the way of U.S. strategic interests, as it did in Guatemala in 1954, Brazil in 1964, and Chile in 1973 (Smith 2000), and as it did when Panama's Arnulfo Arias was elected president in 1940 and in 1968 (see LaFeber 1989; Conniff 1992). Therefore, simply the existence of a democratic government in Panama might not have guaranteed success with Washington. In the final analysis, the end of the Cold War, along with anticolonial sentiments, were the conditions that made it possible for a democratic Panama to succeed in its negotiations with Washington on the issue of a continued U.S. military presence on the isthmus.

Perhaps the most important factor at the state level, particularly for a small state, is the power of the state itself. While it was able to prevent U.S. soldiers from remaining on the isthmus, Panama's success resulted principally because there was no longer a Washington consensus that the canal and adjacent U.S. military bases were vital for U.S. strategic interests. Even so, Panama had a reasonably difficult time dealing with U.S. officials during the CMA talks for two reasons: first, because of the asymmetrical U.S.-Panama relationship, and second, because of Panama's almost nonexistent diplomatic corps. Jorge Ritter, who had been described as an extreme nationalist by U.S. agencies and who had vehemently supported the Noriega regime, was principally responsible for the agreement that resulted at the end of December 1997 granting "excessive responsibilities" to the U.S. government (Becerra Acosta 1998). Such generosity, from someone like Ritter, at worst may have resulted from intelligence the U.S. government had acquired concerning his alleged illegal activities, and at best may have resulted from Panama's inexperience with diplomacy. The Panama team rightly assumed, for example, that the United States, through communications surveillance, was aware of its negotiating positions. In fact, some months after the failure of the negotiations, it became public knowledge that the U.S. government had been spying on the Perez administration (Marquis and Garvin 1999). Panama, as a small, weak state, could not even dream of the instruments of state power available to the U.S. government during the negotiations, and as a result could not have been expected to perform very well during the CMA talks. Nevertheless, since there was no solid Washington consensus on the need to maintain U.S. bases on the isthmus, the Panamanians were able to say no to the U.S. government without an adverse reaction from Washington.

Despite its democratic regime, Panama will remain at a disadvantage in its relations with powerful nations such as the United States. The weak Panamanian state, in addition to having a very small and sometimes inexperienced diplomatic corps, is always subject to economic, technological, political, and military disadvantage. For example, Washington always has instruments of power at its disposal, such as economic aid, that it can employ against its enemies and uncooperative friends. Panama has no such instruments of power and thus must either comply with Washington or accept the costs of not cooperating.

The Individual: Diplomacy on the Fringe

Individuals can affect the character of diplomacy in many ways. However, individuals cannot rapidly change either the international system or the extant domestic forces during a particular diplomatic effort. For example, General Omar Torrijos was clearly able to get the United States to renegotiate the hated 1903 Hay-Bunau-Varilla Treaty in 1977. But Torrijos was able to do so only because nationalist forces in Panama had reached such a boiling point by the 1960s that U.S. foreign policy experts had become convinced that Panama could erupt in social revolution if the U.S.-Panama relationship was not restructured.[10] Additionally, the United States at the end of the 1970s was involved in the process of détente, designed to minimize U.S.-Soviet rivalry and conflict. Thus, while Omar Torrijos and Jimmy Carter certainly made a new treaty possible, the systemic and domestic forces that would promote a change in the nation's relations were already present at that earlier date.

During the CMA negotiations individuals affected much of the character of the talks, but not necessarily the outcome. Unfortunately the particular mix of diplomats was less than conducive to effective diplomacy. At the start of the talks, Panama's chief negotiator, Gabriel Lewis Galindo, was quite amenable to a continued U.S. military presence. By the time the talks were seriously under way, however, he had died and the chief negotiators were John Negroponte for the United States and Jorge Ritter for Panama. Negroponte reminded Panamanians of the "special relationship," during which Panama was Washington's neo-colony and subservient to U.S. interests. Ritter, on the other hand, irritated the U.S. side, owing to his support for the Noriega regime and his "nationalism." Washington agreed to push Negroponte aside and put McNamara in charge of the talks, potentially increasing the chances of success.[11] Washington at that point wanted Panama to reciprocate by easing Ritter out of the picture, but President Perez kept Ritter as his chief negotiator. The U.S. ambassador in Panama, William Hughes, did not play a positive role in the talks. Washington had chosen Hughes principally because of his experience in dealing with the illegal narcotics problem, showing that U.S. diplomacy focused on the outcome rather than the process. But Hughes, a former member of Congress, was neither a diplomat nor an effective U.S. representative in Panama. The Panamanians often complained about his inability to speak Spanish and lack of desire to learn the language, and of his frequent trips away from the isthmus. During a time of important negotiations, an absent and almost disinterested ambassador greatly detracted from good and effective diplomacy.

If Lewis Galindo had lived through the process, if McNamara had been appointed as chief U.S. negotiator at the outset, and if an experienced and more engaged ambassador had been present, would the CMA talks have succeeded? Certainly some sort of counternarcotics center, with a U.S. military presence, may have resulted from such a diplomatic "dream team." However, the factors that led to the failure of establishing a CMA—the end of the Cold War and decolonization—would still have exerted a great deal of influence on the diplomatic process. If an agreement allowing for U.S. bases in Panama had been reached, the talks might have been deemed a success, but the U.S.-Panama relationship would perhaps have entered another period of uncertainty and potential conflict.

Conclusions and Implications: Sharks and Sardines

Small states, regardless of how they are defined, are at a clear disadvantage in the international system, especially when dealing with a superpower in a hegemonic context, as is the case with Panama and the United States. Panama did not succeed in the talks over continued U.S. military presence on the isthmus because of skilled diplomacy, its ability to exert influence, or other nonsystemic factors. Panama's success can be attributed principally to the end of the Cold War and the gradual process of decolonization that flourished at the end of World War II. The end of the U.S.-Soviet rivalry meant that U.S. decisionmakers no longer felt threatened by Soviet/Cuban influence in the Western Hemisphere. Although some Cold War hard-liners still wandered the halls of Congress, most U.S. policymakers focused on institutional missions and on fiscal bottom lines when thinking about the possibility of keeping U.S. troops in Panama. Also, the end of socialism meant that Washington focused more on a global economy in which its direct control of the canal was less critical. At the same time, keeping a U.S. pseudocolonial presence in Panama would have been out of step with the "new world order." In July 1997 the United Kingdom had finally returned Hong Kong to China. How would the world react to Washington's insistence on keeping U.S. troops and territory in Panama past 1999? More practically, as some in the State Department argued, the continuation of a U.S. military presence in Panama could have resulted in the perpetuation of a rocky relationship between Washington and Panama, a dangerous outcome considering the turmoil in nearby Colombia. It seemed much more prudent to simply end the U.S. physical presence on the isthmus. As one longtime observer of Panamanian affairs noted: "The US government should have quickly abided by the Canal Treaties and removed all US troops well before 1999; then it would have been Panama's decision whether they wanted us back or not" (Koster 1998). The international context was ripe at the end of the twentieth century for ending the U.S. military presence in Panama, and thus the Perez administration was able to say no, and Washington was willing to accept that decision.

This somewhat deterministic conclusion does not exclude the importance of other factors, however. The system sets the parameters of what is possible or most likely. Characteristics of the state and individuals determine the most likely, specific outcome of policy within those parameters. For example, diplomacy in a democratic Panama was markedly different from diplomacy under an autocratic Panama. President Perez had to respond to domestic forces that General Torrijos could control or ignore. Also, negotiations would certainly proceed differently under someone like Gabriel Lewis Galindo than under Jorge Ritter. My argument, however, is that systemic power distribution and particular forces and ideas in the international system have a sizable effect on international interactions, particularly in the interactions between weak and strong states. Consequently, even in an era of globalization, small states are hostage to the interests of powerful states and to strong international forces. Sovereignty for small states is more a matter of principle than of practice, and leaders of these states must take this reality into consideration in their diplomatic ventures.

Notes

I acquired much of the information used in the development of this chapter from a variety of sources while in Panama on a lecturing/research Senior Scholar Fulbright grant during July 1997 to July 1998, a key period for analyzing the CMA negotiations. The newspapers *El Panama America* and *La Prensa* provided most of the chronology and Panamanian perspective. Personal interviews provided a great deal of inside information from both the U.S. and the Panamanian perspective. While I interviewed over 100 people formally and informally, only a few key interviews are listed in the bibliography.

1. There are conflicting accounts of what happened during these social disturbances that spread beyond Panama City. Some Panamanians blame all of the deaths on U.S. troops and Canal Zone police, while some U.S. accounts have argued that U.S. military personnel did not fire into the crowds. Nevertheless, the violence that ensued on January 9, 1964, represented to a large extent pent-up hostilities toward the United States on the part of many Panamanians, who were tired of U.S. colonial attitudes. For one recent account by a Panamanian, see Mendez 1999.

2. Various surveys, often funded by the U.S. Information Service, have shown that about 70 percent of Panamanians favored the permanence of U.S. troops in Panama. When asked for a reason to support such a presence, respondents usually cited economic benefits. However, when respondents were initially asked if U.S. troops should stay in Panama if the U.S. government did not pay for the bases, only about 50 percent of Panamanians supported a continued military presence. See, for example, *Latin America Weekly Report,* June 1, 1995: 240.

3. For many years, Washington had employed two basic strategies without success to get Panama to accept U.S. troops past 1999. One was to try to convince Panama that time was running out, that a deal had to be struck or the Department of Defense would have to start the withdrawal of troops. The United States tried to use this strategy as early as 1983. Second, Washington attempted to convince Panama that it was not that interested in keeping troops on the isthmus, and thus Panama would have to ask the U.S. government for the permanence of U.S. soldiers. These U.S. strategies rested on the assumption that Panama desperately needed the U.S. military presence.

4. The U.S. government has not given up on its quest to use Panama as a strategic platform. Most recently Washington has proposed a "visiting forces" agreement that would allow U.S. troops certain rights and protections when visiting or traveling through Panama. While the U.S. government has similar agreements with about seventy countries, such a deal would open the door for a U.S. military presence or function in Panama.

5. Galeta Island was important to the U.S. intelligence community since it was a valuable communications and intelligence-gathering facility.

6. Here I am highlighting only a few major events. Panama's history is replete with incidents that demonstrate anticolonial attitudes aimed at the United States, beginning with the well-known "Watermelon War" of the mid-1800s.

7. In several informal discussions with U.S. and Panamanian officials, it appeared that the State Department was most attuned to the potentially negative repercussions that could manifest themselves if the U.S. government pushed Panama hard for the perpetuation of U.S. military bases on the isthmus.

8. In fact, in August 1997 the Perez government sent riot police after students who were demonstrating outside the U.S. embassy in Panama City against the continuation of U.S. bases. One student lost a finger in the encounter, making the front page in all of the local newspapers.

9. After he left office, Perez became involved in a conflict with the U.S. government over visas that his administration allegedly sold to Chinese citizens wishing to go to the United States. Washington eventually denied the former president a visa, barring him from visiting the United States. If Perez had reached an agreement with Washington over the establishment of a CMA, it is doubtful that the evidence on the Chinese visas would have seen the light, especially since such evidence originated from U.S. intelligence sources.

10. In 1978, Torrijos had put in place Operation Smells Burning, a plan of the national guard to sabotage the canal if the U.S. Senate did not ratify the canal treaties. During the canal treaty debates, U.S. foreign policy experts knew that U.S.-Panama relations would become highly volatile if the treaties were not ratified (LaFeber 1989: x).

11. At the time, Washington stated that Negroponte was being removed as chief negotiator only because he was "retiring" from the State Department. In 2001, ending the diplomat's brief "retirement," President Bush named Negroponte U.S. ambassador to the United Nations.

5

Luxembourg: Where Small Works (and Wealthy Doesn't Hurt)

Jeanne A. K. Hey

The small size of the Grand Duchy of Luxembourg belies its influence and success in international matters, especially in the European theater.[1] Any discussion of Luxembourg's foreign policy necessarily begins with a note on the country's size. Less than 1,000 square miles in area, Luxembourg is smaller than the U.S. state of Rhode Island (Apple 2002). Its resident and citizen population is about 450,000, more than a quarter of whom carry foreign passports. One can circumnavigate the entire country by car in an afternoon. Luxembourg's tiny physical size no doubt explains why many in the United States appear to think it is a city in Germany, rather than an independent nation-state. Europeans, however, make no such mistake, as they are fully aware of Luxembourg's longstanding diplomatic influence on the continent.

Luxembourg has a precarious geopolitical position. It borders Germany, France, and Belgium and has over the years been treated as a spoil of war by a variety of European powers. Indeed, its independence is a historical accident that could easily have been (and was) denied at a variety of points throughout centuries of European interstate conflicts. In the twentieth century, Luxembourg suffered terribly during both world wars and was in fact liberated from German control *twice* during World War II. Luxembourg is nestled in that part of the Ardennes that was retaken by the Germans from the Allies during the Battle of the Bulge. Not surprisingly, Luxembourg became a founding member of European economic and political integration, aimed primarily at minimizing Franco-German hostilities.

Despite these disadvantages, Luxembourg has been remarkably successful in foreign policy. Foreign policy "success" here is defined as a state's ability to achieve the goals it sets in the international arena. Luxembourgers are more fortunate than most national constituencies in that they have a strong sense of national interest, which helps their leaders to articulate and achieve clear foreign policy goals. That they do so with very limited national resources, especially military resources, makes the achievement all the more notable.

This chapter reviews some of the major themes and events in Luxembourg's foreign policy during the 1990s. It then analyzes this empirical content from the perspective of different levels of analysis. It reveals that while many factors help to explain Luxembourg's foreign policy behavior, the country's wealth is crucial in determining the successes of its foreign policy makers.

Luxembourg's Foreign Policy in the 1990s

Luxembourg's foreign policy makers share a remarkably strong consensus about the country's major foreign policy goals. First is to ensure peace between France and Germany. Luxembourg's geography and history reveal its vulnerability to hostilities between the two major continental powers in Europe. Alphonse Berns, a career diplomat who is now the secretary-general of the Ministry of Foreign Affairs, explained that "we wouldn't survive . . . another round of military tourism in our territory" (Berns 2000). This bedrock of Luxembourg's foreign policy presents a paradox. Avoiding Franco-German conflict is at once of paramount importance and unnecessary, as no one really believes that such a conflict would erupt. As one former foreign minister explains, "people know that a war between Germany and France is unthinkable, but at the same time it's the bottom line of our foreign policy" (Flesch 2000).

The second prime directive of Luxembourg's foreign policy is to maintain and enhance the nation's prosperity. Luxembourg is cited as the world's wealthiest country. With a per capita gross domestic product (GDP) of U.S.$37,346, Luxembourg is by far the wealthiest country in the Organization for Economic Cooperation and Development (OECD), according to that organization's own sources. Even by a measure of purchasing power parity (PPP), which takes into account its high prices, Luxembourg remains by far the wealthiest, with a PPP of U.S.$33,119 (OECD 1999: 38). Luxembourgers are very aware of their good financial fortune, and of the fact that it enhances their regional and global voice. As such, they are keenly focused on maintaining and enhancing their wealth.

These goals, to keep peace between France and Germany and to protect the nation's fortune, are neither surprising nor unusual. Indeed, realist theory has for centuries told us that states will seek national security and prosperity. But unique to the Grand Duchy are the clarity and consensus of its foreign policy makers in prioritizing and pursuing these objectives over all others. In a country where partisan rancor can be quite intense, party leaders fully agree on these goals and in general fail to dispute a government's foreign policies. Interviews with Luxembourgers within and outside the government, including cabinet officials, members of parliament, union leaders, teachers, and journalists revealed absolutely no dispute about the general direction and purpose of Luxembourg's foreign policy. As a former secretary of state for foreign affairs remarked, Luxembourgers of all stripes agree that there is "no alternative to the basic policy" (Goebbels 2000).

Foreign policy analysts remind us that there is a difference between foreign "policy" and foreign policy "behavior" (Hermann and Peacock 1987). The issue here, therefore, is not so much what Luxembourg's general policy thrust is, but how it is manifest in observable actions. The principal answer is that much of Luxembourg's foreign policy behavior aims to increase European political and economic integration in a way that enhances intra-European cooperation and gives Luxembourg greater access to markets. In other words, Luxembourg is a most enthusiastic member of the European Union (EU).

Luxembourg and the European Union

It is difficult to overstate the degree to which the European Union is integrated into Luxembourgish life. This is true not only because Luxembourg City is a seat of EU institutions and the workplace of thousands of EU employees, but also because Luxembourg depends so heavily on the EU for its foreign policy goals. "Life outside the EU would be completely unthinkable for Luxembourg," remarked one local journalist, because the country "lives and dies by free trade" and because the EU enhances Luxembourg's "diplomatic voice" (Gray 2000). Specifically, the European Union ameliorates many of the adverse consequences of Luxembourg's small state status. The EU's equality-of-states doctrine provides small states with the same rights as large ones. Its *acquis communautaire,* or body of community law, protects treaties and decisions from being overturned and is overseen by the European Court of Justice. In effect, the *acquis communautaire* ensures that the rights of small states, once acquired, will not be forfeited (Baillie 1996: 2–3, 1998: 196). Luxembourg, as founding member of European integration, thus ensured rights and benefits for itself half a century ago that it might have difficulty acquiring today. What are Luxembourg's specific goals within the EU? The first is to maintain and enhance Luxembourgish power within the institution. This means maintaining a high diplomatic presence, especially within the Council of Ministers and the European Council, where Luxembourg's representation is the same as that of all other member states (Manners 2000). Wary of appearing too presumptuous, Luxembourg has a low-profile diplomatic style. Luxembourgers choose their issues carefully in the EU and help others seek their goals (Flesch 2000). As a tiny state, but one with clout, Luxembourg can be at once influential and nonthreatening. As Sasha Baillie, a scholar and now an officer in Luxembourg's Ministry of Foreign Affairs, explains, "a small state's behaviour in negotiations is determined by its aim of endearing itself to the other parties" (1998: 196).

A second goal is to keep EU employees in Luxembourg. Luxembourg is home to the European Court of Justice, the Court of Auditors, the European Investment Bank, the European Parliament Secretariat, the Official Publications office, Eurostat, the European Translation Centre, and some offices of the European Commission (Baillie 1996). The 7,500 EU jobs, many of them high-paying, provide the national economy with a crucial influx of funds and help account for the very high cost of housing in Luxembourg City (Apple 2002). Maintaining those posts is crucial not only to Luxembourgish prosperity but also to Luxembourg City's reputation as a cosmopolitan center of European life. No longer the "small, sleepy Grand Duchy," as it was described when chosen as the site of the European Coal and Steel Community in 1952, Luxembourg today hosts many of the EU's most important negotiating sessions and is a common destination for European prime ministers (Dinan 1994: 29). So when the European Commission proposed restructuring EU institutions in 1999, Luxembourg had reason to fear the loss of jobs to Brussels or Strasbourg. Luxembourg's foreign minister, Jacques Poos, intervened and gained assurance from the commission that the EU would honor a previous commitment to keep at least 2,000 European Parliament officials in Luxembourg City. Luxembourgish pressure in Brussels also contributed to securing a statement by the office of EU Commissioner Neil Kinnock to the effect that only "very limited movements between the different places of work" would occur in any restructuring and that proposed changes did not require any movement of staff from Luxembourg to Brussels. Luxembourg's representative in the new commission is Vivian Reding, a seasoned diplomat and politician and one who has made a priority of securing and expanding EU jobs in Luxembourg (*Luxembourg News* 1999).

A third goal of Luxembourg's foreign policy in the European Union is to see that Luxembourg's power in the institution is not diluted by the coming expansion. Luxembourg currently holds six seats in the European

Parliament, a number that is disproportionate to Luxembourg's relative population within the EU while also representing the smallest delegation. The parliament has passed a bill, as of this writing not yet ratified by the commission, ensuring that no delegation would have fewer than four seats. There will also be a limit on the total number of seats allowed in the parliament, independent of how many new members join. Luxembourg and other small states will need to employ skillful diplomacy to generate a system that guarantees them four seats while larger states need to share a fixed number of remaining seats. Expansion similarly threatens Luxembourgish influence in the Council of Ministers, where Luxembourg currently enjoys both an equal vote and a veto. Currently, the council is considering a "relative majority" rule that would eliminate Luxembourg's veto and seriously threaten Luxembourg's influence on the council (*Luxembourg News* 2000a; Haag 2000).

Given the threat that EU expansion poses to Luxembourg's longstanding influence within the European Union, one would expect Luxembourg to oppose future expansion, or at least to advocate a slow pace. In fact, Prime Minister Jean Claude Juncker has fervently and with broad support promoted EU enlargement. His position is rooted in his understanding of Luxembourg's investment and trading interests in a "large Europe." Juncker has also been mindful of the prospects for peace brought about by the inclusion of former communist states in the EU, especially in the aftermath of the North Atlantic Treaty Organization's war against Yugoslavia in 1999. Recalling the EU's peacemaking foundations, Juncker stated that "the founding fathers of Europe had just one concern: to ban the demons of war from the European continent. The zone of peace and stability we know today in the Western part of Europe has to be extended to Central and Eastern Europe—that is the EU's challenge at the start of the 21st Century" (*Luxembourg News* 2000a: 4). Juncker and his compatriots believe that Luxembourg's future, as well as Europe's, lies in integration, even if that means including former communist states that present economic and political challenges to an organization that has for most of its history been a club of the most wealthy and politically stable European states. Behind that high-minded principle, of course, remains the fact that Luxembourg's profit-making potential in the east also increases if former Warsaw Pact members join the EU.

Aside from these broad goals within the European Union, Luxembourg of course pursues specific objectives on a whole host of issues too numerous to mention here. It should be noted that Luxembourg's relationship with the EU is not always easy. This was perhaps most clear in 1999 when former Luxembourgish prime minister Jacques Santer resigned as

European Commission president after an independent investigation found that he was blind to corruption committed by some commissioners working under him. As Santer's affiliation at the time was with the EU, and not with Luxembourg, the drama did not taint Luxembourg's foreign policy reputation so much as it did Santer's and the commission's. Luxembourg also squabbles with its EU partners over issues ranging from specific items such as French nuclear policy and Luxembourg's tax code to broad issues like the European Monetary Union. Nevertheless, Luxembourg is clearly a member of the highest standing within the organization and one whose influence and prestige far exceed what the country's small size might indicate. As a founding member of European integration and a tireless operator in EU advancement, Luxembourg merits the benefits it enjoys (Baillie 1998). EU founder Robert Schuman is known to most of the world as a former French prime minister, but Luxembourgers know that his mother was a national and that he was born and schooled in Luxembourg. Hence they claim him as their own (*Luxembourg News* 2000c: 8).

The Grand Duchy's good behavior and economic and political stability enhance its standing within the EU. While other members are scolded or even punished for their noncooperative behavior (France), their aspirations to a special status within an organization of equals (the United Kingdom), their inability to get their economic house in order (Greece), or the frightening nature of their domestic governing coalitions (Austria), Luxembourg remains out of the news precisely because it so rarely presents the EU with any real problems. A 1999 report released by the Council of Ministers praised Luxembourg "with satisfaction that the situation of public finances improved further in the last two years and the budgetary targets set in the initial stability program of Luxembourg have been exceeded" (*Luxembourg News* 2000c: 8). This is typical. Without fail, Luxembourg not only follows EU guidelines but exceeds them, while other countries fail to meet the criteria for joining European Monetary Union or even the EU itself.

Luxembourg and Economic Prosperity

Luxembourg boasts the highest per capita income in the world (U.S.$48,000) and would like to keep it that way. Luxembourg's pursuit of economic prosperity centers on policies that seek to expand free trade within Europe and elsewhere, to promote Luxembourg's business interests abroad, and to maintain a banking code that ensures Luxembourg's status as a highly profitable financial center. Luxembourg is home not only to the headquarters or branch offices of nearly 200 world banks, but also to global corporate giants such as Goodyear and Radio Television Luxembourg (Apple 2002). Luxembourg promotes free trade first by its activities within the EU and its advocacy of EU expansion. It is of course also a member of all the major international economic organizations and pursues free trade in these as well. Luxembourg's mantra, born in its total reliance on trade, is the freer the trade, the better.

While working to create a global system in which free trade flourishes, Luxembourg is not shy about promoting its own business interests. Grand Duke Henri, who assumed that title in September 2000, was an active global traveler on behalf of Luxembourg's business interests during his years as crown prince (Roberts 2000). The state has long enjoyed an excellent relationship with ARBED, the private steel company that brought enormous wealth to Luxembourg in the wake of World War II's devastating impact on the tiny country. As ore deposits declined, ARBED shifted its activities to steel recycling in Luxembourg and to steel production in foreign lands. When local production waned in the 1970s, threatening thousands of jobs, Luxembourg participated in the famed "tripartite agreement," in which labor unions, ARBED, and the government restructured the industry's labor agreement in a way that left no ARBED employee without a job or a solid retirement income.

Banking replaced steel as the center of Luxembourg's economic engine in the early 1980s. By mid-decade, Luxembourg ranked as the third largest banking center in Europe, behind London and Paris (Black et al. 2000: 534). A primary economic priority now is to ensure a legal code that maintains the flow of funds from foreign depositors into banks based in Luxembourg. Charles Doerner (1983) explains that Luxembourg's attraction to foreign depositors was not initially that Luxembourg was a "tax haven" per se, but that Luxembourg, unlike other European states, did not require banks to post a minimum reserve. This gave advantages to banks doing business through a Luxembourgish subsidiary. By 1981, however, Luxembourg's policymakers realized the importance of banking secrecy in attracting foreign investors. In that year, they codified secrecy into law, making it a criminal offense to make public a depositor's identity (Sackx 2000: 54). Since then, Luxembourg's position is that depositors themselves, rather than Luxembourg-based banks, have the responsibility to inform home countries' tax agencies about earnings (Gray 2000).

European Union neighbors, as well as other countries including the United States, have expressed frustration about the lost tax revenues resulting from Luxembourg's secrecy laws. As one Luxembourgish academic put it, "we thrive on the frauds of Germany, France and Belgium" (Haag 2000). Luxembourg has deflected criticism and maintained its banking system by adhering scrupulously to the law and by cooperating with international investigations into fraud. Banking lawyer Andre Lutgen explains that "banking secrecy has been lifted in Luxembourg at least 400 times." He added that the Grand Duchy also enacted a law on insider trading in 1999 and had one of the first money-laundering laws enforced worldwide (in 1989) (quoted in Sackx 2000: 54). At the same time that Luxembourg cooperates with foreign countries in cases of banking fraud, it assures local bankers that it will do all it can to maintain the current system. For example, treasury and budget minister Luc Frieden recently assured the Luxembourg Bankers' Association that Luxembourg would maintain banking secrecy despite external pressure to relax it (Sackx 2000: 54).

Minister Frieden's promise may be difficult to keep, at least in the long run. In 2000 the European Union's large members pushed hard for reforms that would make tax cheating difficult. They asked for either a common withholding tax to apply across all member states or an "exchange of information," by which national banks would supply information on foreign depositors to home countries. In June 2000, EU members agreed to a deal, to be implemented in 2010, that would "water down" confidentiality rules and allow the exchange of information. The Grand Duchy had preferred a common withholding provision, but agreed to the exchange of information under pressure from the United Kingdom and others. The deal allows Luxembourg a long transition period and is "so hedged with caveats and conditions that it . . . is far from a done deal" (*Luxembourg News* 2000d: 4). In other words, the arrangement gave Luxembourg a cooperative image while at the same time ensuring that no major changes in the banking laws would occur anytime soon. "Luxembourg is keen not to be seen as obstructing things," noted one journalist (Gray 2000). But it also seeks to ensure that it will not be made to give up privileges that others would continue to enjoy. Luxembourg has succeeded in maintaining an image of a fair player, even though Europeans all think of it as a tax haven. This good reputation received a recent and important boost. In a crucial OECD report on tax havens released in spring 2000, Luxembourg was not listed as a primary offender.

The Grand Duchy's very careful adherence to the law and its willingness to cooperate with international criminal investigations keep it in good standing with most of its EU neighbors on the tax issue. The fact that many of the banks operating in Luxembourg (and therefore contributing to hiding foreigners' taxable income) are themselves German, Belgian, and French undermines the strength of those countries' criticisms against Luxembourg. Luxembourgers know that some change in tax policy is in the making and that the EU will eventually demand a common withholding or sharing of information on depositors. But that day is still far off and Luxembourg will by then have fully prepared for the transition.

Explaining Luxembourg's Foreign Policy

In the language of Marshall Singer (1972: 402), Luxembourg compensates for its absence of "coercive instruments" of foreign policy (i.e., military power and threats) with "attractive instruments," such as a strong market, an educated population, excellent diplomatic skills, and a commitment to European integration. Luxembourg's making the most of what it has, and making unimportant what it lacks, is a theme running through the following analysis of the Grand Duchy's foreign policy behavior. This strategy accounts for Luxembourg's surprising stature within Europe and the world, despite its Lilliputian size.

A question that arises when categorizing different inputs into Luxembourg's foreign policy behavior is where to place the country's smallness. Physical size has typically been considered a "national attribute," and would therefore be part of the state level of analysis. Based on that perspective, one would expect Luxembourg to exhibit a host of behaviors such as those listed in Chapter 1 of this volume. But Luxembourg's smallness is also a system-level feature, given that it situates the country in a low position on the world power scale, and especially noting its location between regional superpowers France and Germany. In other words, Luxembourg's peculiar geography creates special problems (and opportunities) within a regional and global context. As a top Luxembourgish diplomat noted, "the smaller the country, the larger the outside world" (Berns 2000). With this in mind, smallness here is treated at both the system and state levels. Its influence in determining major foreign policy guidelines and its behavior within the European Union are discussed under the system level of analysis. The degree to which smallness affects how Luxembourg develops and implements foreign policy is discussed under the state level of analysis.

The System

Luxembourg's small status explains much of its basic foreign policy tenets. First, smallness explains in part Luxembourg's preoccupation with easing tensions between France and Germany. Luxembourgish diplomat Guy De Muyser (1999) explained the European Union as Luxembourg's "life insurance" against Franco-German antagonism. Larger European countries certainly also see the EU as a key component of their antiwar program, but for Luxembourg the EU is "life" insurance indeed, as Luxembourgers know that their statehood itself is put in jeopardy by any war pitting Germany against France. That Luxembourg has essentially no military force, also a product of its smallness, exacerbates the country's vulnerability to European warfare. Rather than try to construct a meaningful military force that would draw on limited resources (as the Swiss have), Luxembourg has placed its bets on a strong European Union as a guarantor against another European war.

Second, smallness accounts for Luxembourg's reliance on the European Union, as the institution provides Luxembourg with a voice stronger than it would have in a nonintegrated Europe. This is true both inside and outside the European theater. Colette Flesch (2000), a career politician and diplomat, explains that Luxembourg would have essentially no standing in the World Trade Organization and other global organizations if it tried to negotiate alone. Because the EU negotiates on behalf of its members, Luxembourg's interests are well served. Small-state status helps to explain certain positions Luxembourg takes within the European Union as well, such as securing a minimum number of parliamentary seats in an expanded parliament and keeping voting rules that favor small states in the commission. Luxembourg has also sought special exemptions to EU rules based on its small size. These include exemptions to agricultural rules in the 1950s and 1960s and to immigration rules in the 1980s. In both cases, Luxembourg successfully argued that it could not bear the hardship of new rules as easily as could larger states (Berns 2000).

Third, smallness explains Luxembourg's success as a negotiator inside the European Union. Luxembourg's European partners recognize its diplomats' skill within the EU. Baillie (1998) argues convincingly that the country's tiny size creates a perception of weakness that translates into a strategic opportunity. Because Luxembourg is not seen as a threat and clearly has no hegemonic interests within Europe, other states are more likely to grant requests and be open to Luxembourgish initiatives. In other words, sympathy to a Luxembourgish request incurs no concerns that one is succumbing to threats or power plays. There is therefore less political gamesmanship surrounding issues in which Luxembourg is involved than those involving France, Germany, or the United Kingdom.

The State

In this section, I discuss how smallness influences policymaking at home, as opposed to how smallness influences the way Luxembourg acts and is perceived beyond its borders. Does the Grand Duchy's small size help to explain how its foreign policy goals are developed and implemented? De Muyser (1999) observed that "we have almost no foreign policy interests except the stability of our borders, many good relationships with our neighbors and economic prosperity." Two things can be said about his observation. First, it accurately points out that small size means that Luxembourg cannot afford to extend itself beyond these most basic foreign policy objectives. Size, it would seem, has an absolute effect on foreign policy scope. Note, however, the goals that De Muyser lists: stability of borders, good relationships with neighbors, and economic success. These are exactly the foreign policy priorities that a political realist would attribute to any state, be it a superpower or a tiny duchy (Morgenthau and Thompson 1985). To the extent that this is true, Luxembourg is no different from others, only more limited in its means. It should also be pointed out here that Luxembourg has a generous foreign aid program and is therefore not so limited as it first appears (Berns 2000).

Certainly small size limits what Luxembourg can do in the foreign policy realm. It has perhaps a more important effect on the atmosphere within which policy is created. Small size creates consensus about foreign policy goals. Luxembourgers share a sense of vulnerability and national identity. This leads to widespread agreement on international matters. Partisan bickering in Luxembourg's parliament is largely absent on matters of foreign policy. Politicians know that any divisiveness would weaken Luxembourg's already small voice in the international arena. Because they also largely agree on foreign policy matters, political actors are willing to remain supportive in regional and global matters. As Flesch (2000) explains, the Grand Duchy's size accounts for the civility that the parliament exhibits on foreign policy matters. So long as a government does not seek policies that exceed the agreed-upon principles, it is unlikely to receive domestic opposition.

Smallness also affects foreign policy strategies. Luxembourg often allies with other European states, especially Belgium and the Netherlands. The Benelux Union, established in 1948, is famous not only for its advancement of its members' interests, but also as a model of European integration (Black et al. 2000: 535). A well-known adage among Luxembourgish diplomats is, "If you have a good idea, whisper it to your Dutch neighbor," in the recognition of the historical influence of the Netherlands in Europe (Berns 2000). This is not to say that Luxembourg never acts alone, but that it can only exert individual influence on a few matters. It certainly cannot bully anyone. Luxembourg finds that its voice is better heard when united with others. This has been particularly true at the biannual summits of the European Union and during negotiations for the common currency (Christophory 1999).

A second state-level characteristic that influences foreign policy making in Luxembourg is the country's wealth. The more one looks at the Grand Duchy, the more one realizes that its status as a rich country is as much or more important than its status as a small country. Colette Flesch (2000) spoke directly to this issue when remarking on a conference of small states she attended with diplomats from the Caribbean and Andorra. "I had nothing in common with those people," she remarked, because of development discrepancies and because Luxembourg is an EU member. Luxembourg's wealth compensates for its small size in the European theater. It suffers none of the lack of respect that Greece or Portugal sometimes do because they are the least developed in the EU. Wealth also helps to explain the foreign policy consensus described above. "When you're basically the richest country in the world, the model works," said Simon Gray (2000), editor of *Luxembourg Business*. Gray went on to explain that Luxembourgers are happy with their wealthy situation and know that they owe it to a series of governments' adherence to a policy that promotes Luxembourgish business abroad and a pro-European stance in the region. Though they may disagree on a host of domestic issues, none argues with this most basic success.

Prosperity also contributes to a host of specific policies, ranging from maintaining Luxembourg as a financial center, banking secrecy, and free trade. Wealth, combined with domestic consensus on foreign policy issues, permits Luxembourg to take the high road on controversial issues. The country's economic success gives it a buffer to soften any negative effects stemming from EU expansion and the immigration that will most likely follow. Luxembourg is progressive on these issues compared to most of its neighbors. Luxembourg argues that it is better to welcome laborers from the east and south to good working conditions than to deal with an illegal immigrant work force that would surely come if the EU does not expand (Flesch 2000).

Luxembourg's wealth accounts for the influence of the private business sector on policy. All individuals interviewed for this chapter agreed that business groups were the strongest private influence on government behavior, more than the church, popular groups, or unions. "Foreign policy makers and business groups are in such close contact that the Prime Minister wouldn't think of choosing a policy that goes against business interests" (Haag 2000). For many years the most prominent business interest was the steel company ARBED. Today it is banking. Luxembourg sends business delegations around the world (Roberts 2000). When asked how the business community effects its influence on government decisions, Gray (2000) responded, "It doesn't have to," going on to explain that in a small country in which personal contacts are crucial, the business community can communicate at parties and receptions, knowing that it "is pushing at an open door. There is no need for lobbyists or lawyers."

Even Luxembourg's vocal trade unions understand that their interests are tied to the success of private business. So their efforts are aimed at achieving good contracts, rather than criticizing the government for being too cozy with private industry (Gray 2000). Indeed, labor enjoys a good relationship with the government and rarely interrupts foreign policy. Because Luxembourgish laborers enjoy some of Europe's highest wages and most generous benefits, they avoid the high-stakes tactics that their peers in neighboring countries often employ. "A strike is 'going nuclear' in industrial relations here," said Gray (2000), pointing out how easy Luxembourg's governments have it compared with the French and Germans.

James Rosenau (1990) argued that public opinion would be a crucial state-level determinant of foreign policy in democracies. Luxembourg is a thriving democracy, albeit one that remains very loyal to the grand duke and his family. Indeed, even though Luxembourg's royal family is among the world's wealthiest, Luxembourgers engage in virtually none of the talk one finds in Britain about abolishing a parasitic monarchy. The grand duke is a constant presence in public life, but strictly defers to the elected officials in policy matters. Despite a strong democratic structure, the influence of public opinion in Luxembourg is notably weak. This owes largely to the foreign policy consensus described above, which exists not only within the halls of parliament, but also in the urban centers and countryside. Constituents largely leave their leaders alone on international matters. One observer noted, for example, that "even public opinion and the trade unions are aware that we are totally dependent on the tax revenues from the business community," and therefore do not criticize the country's working in the banking industry's interests (Haag 2000). Luxembourg has no university that could act as a center for either agitation or even grand-scale debate on foreign policy issues.[2] The intellectual community is rather small and cordial. Additionally, Luxembourg faces few foreign policy crises or major controversial questions (such as military spending). Furthermore, Luxembourgers know that because their country is small, its international activities will have only marginal effect on global outcomes.[3] Duncan Roberts (2000) adds a cultural explanation, noting that Luxembourgers are "reserved people" who prefer to keep their opinions to themselves. They are also internationalists. Not only do they live at the crossroads of Europe, but they are also multilingual and schooled in other cultures. "No [Luxembourgish] parliamentarian would be proud of not having a passport," commented Berns (2000), contrasting legislators in his country with some in the United States who boast that they have nothing to learn from foreign study or travel. These factors combine to weaken pressure from domestic constituents on foreign policy makers. It would be wrong to say that Luxembourg's foreign policy makers ignore public opinion. It is simply that public opinion rarely acts as an obstacle to the actions policymakers want to take.

Although some analysts have treated the bureaucracy as its own level of analysis, such an approach is better suited to large countries with bureaucracies that take on a life of their own and act independently of elected leaders. This problem is less likely to arise in a small state like Luxembourg, where the bureaucracy itself is small and connected to the government. Indeed, the bureaucratic and government communities in Luxembourg are a tightly knit group of people who typically have known each other for years.

One can imagine both drawbacks and benefits to a small bureaucracy. Of the former, the most obvious is that a small state will have fewer people dedicated to running foreign policy than in large or medium-sized states. Even though Luxembourg must maintain diplomatic relationships with all countries in the world, it can only dedicate a fraction of the manpower used for the same purpose in Germany, Russia, or the United States. This means that Luxembourgish diplomats suffer a very heavy workload, a fact that becomes apparent during a visit to the foreign ministry, which is clearly not a haven for underworked bureaucrats taking advantage of the taxpayers' funds.[4] Benefits of a small bureaucracy include a conduciveness to developing relationships with relative ease (Baillie 1998: 196). Institutional barriers do not divide government employees to the degree that they do in larger bureaucracies, minimizing duplication and failures of communication. Luxembourg also enjoys two particular benefits. First, it can depend on the European Union to carry out much of the diplomacy it would otherwise have to do itself. Second, bureaucratic leaders spend their careers in a variety of different government offices. Government ministers frequently command numerous issue portfolios at the same time, and sometimes move from one ministry to another when not serving in parliament. Furthermore, these same politicians often serve in Brussels or Strasbourg, adding an EU element to their experience (Flesch 2000). That said, the foreign affairs ministry also relies on long-serving diplomats who bring continuity to policymaking. Jacques Poos was foreign affairs minister for fifteen years until the Christian-Socialist coalition broke down after the 1999 national elections. That his was the face at international meetings year after year lent Luxembourg the influence that comes with experience. Added to this continuity is the fact that the foreign affairs ministry is staffed almost entirely with career servants. Only the foreign affairs minister and his or her top deputy change with the government. The top staffer at the ministry, the secretary-general, is a career diplomat (Berns 2000).

Some might argue that this lack of turnover would lead to a lack of creativity or innovation in policy. Berns (2000) says that in decades of experience at the foreign affairs ministry, the embassy in Washington, and other posts, he has witnessed the diplomatic corps's commitment to maintaining flexibility, whether it be to a new problem or to a new government. He also points out that to have real turnover with each new administration would mean a tripling of the current available manpower, given that there are three main political parties. "We just can't do that," Berns says, adding that excellent training, a tradition of nonpartisanship among diplomats, and a high degree of professionalism make up for the small numbers in the diplomatic corps.

The bureaucracy also enjoys a relatively compliant parliament. Aiming to present a united front to the world, lawmakers rarely present obstacles to foreign policy makers. This is true for coalition partners, whose party typically is awarded the post of foreign minister. But it is also true for the opposition, who generally save their most vociferous complaints for domestic issues. Robert Goebbels (2000) explains that foreign affairs is usually criticized in a "symbolic way," rather than on issues about which political opponents feel strongly. Luxembourgish politicians in the EU also remain united on crucial issues. In the European Parliament, members sit (and usually vote) not with fellow nationals but with members of their party from other states. Colette Flesch (2000), a current member of the European Parliament, explains that her votes in Strasbourg are "80 percent party, 20 percent Luxembourg," meaning that most of her votes are in accordance with her political ideology and not devoted to the interests of her homeland. But this is because the vast majority of votes have little or no impact on Luxembourg. She and her compatriots of all political stripes vote as a unit when the issue at hand is crucial to Luxembourg. She cites the current debate over the reshuffling of seats in the European Parliament as a crucial example on which all Luxembourgish members are united.

Luxembourg's foreign policy bureaucracy is fortunate: it enjoys a reputation free of any hint of corruption or incompetence, it works in a fluid and adaptable manner, it benefits from the offices of the European Union, and it meets only minimal barriers from domestic political actors. Citizens of the Grand Duchy are careful to present a united front on international issues, greatly enhancing the platform upon which foreign policy is presented to Europe and the world.

The Individual

There is no question that particular individuals have influenced Luxembourg's international behavior and reputation. Jacques Santer and Robert Schuman are just two with notable careers in European politics. The Grand Duchy's smallness can increase the visibility of individual ministers and the prime minister. Given that the country's entire population is comparable to that of a midsize European city, the prime minister can easily visit any part of the nation. Luxembourgers appear to feel less distance between themselves and their leader than U.S. citizens do. To that degree, the Luxembourgish prime minister is under careful scrutiny, but he can also communicate with relative ease. This section's focus is on Luxembourg's prime minister since 1995, Jean Claude Juncker. He became prime minister after his mentor, Santer, left office to assume command of the European Commission. Until 1999, Juncker led the Christian-Socialist coalition, which came to power in 1984. Although he hoped to continue that alliance, the 1999 electorate preferred the business-oriented Democratic Party over the Socialists. The prime minister, however, remained more popular than ever and now presides over a Christian-Democratic coalition that brought longtime Luxembourg City mayor Lydie Polfer into the Ministry of Foreign Affairs.

Critics and supporters alike point to Juncker as a crucial component of Luxembourg's regional and global success in the 1990s. He is universally respected, both within and outside the Grand Duchy. What accounts for his success? First, he is not ideological, or at least is not perceived to be. He hails from the most right-wing of the mainstream parties, the Christian Socialists, yet he is of the left within that party. He is sympathetic to labor and other populist economic causes, but remains conservative on social issues. Juncker appears to have more critics within his own party, who want him to move to the right, than from opposition parties.

Second, he is an internationalist who seems most content working on a European scale. His diplomatic skills are formidable, yet he is a former finance minister who speaks the technical language of global finance. He is an expert on economic matters, which are at the heart of most of the EU's business. Furthermore, his language and cultural faculties make him a key negotiator within the EU, especially between Germany and France. Juncker is fully fluent and equally comfortable in Luxembourgish, French, German, and English. Unlike his counterparts in France and Germany, who almost always speak publicly in their native language, Juncker follows the model of the Dutch and Scandinavians. He speaks whatever language his companions find most comfortable. He translated for Jacques Chirac at the crucial EU meetings in Dublin where much of the detailed work on the European Monetary Union was worked out. His technical and language expertise made him a crucial go-between in those delicate negotiations, even if he received little public commendation for it (Christophory 1999; Berns 2000). As a Luxembourger, he is also uniquely suited to seeing difficult issues through the eyes of the French and the Germans.

A third factor accounting for Juncker's success is his keen interest in foreign policy matters. Indeed, critics have complained that he is too focused on Europe, to the expense of domestic matters (Roberts 2000). Although Foreign Minister Poos enjoyed a long and influential career, Juncker is undeniably the diplomatic face of Luxembourg. Whereas Poos was not charismatic, Juncker is remarkably so and outshines many of his government's ministers. Although the current foreign minister, Lydie Polfer, carries a certain charisma of her own, Juncker's public persona ensures that he will remain at the forefront of Luxembourg's international efforts (De Muyser 1999; Haag 2000). Juncker's charisma helps him not only in regional and global debates, but at home as well. It aids his popularity, his political longevity, and therefore the stability of his government. Opponents and supporters alike agree that Juncker is extraordinarily intelligent and a positive frontman for Luxembourg in the global arena. "Everyone agrees that he is head and shoulders more talented than anybody else," Gray (2000) said in explaining why Juncker has been so successful at the polls for so long, despite his party's waning popularity. Luxembourgers like that Juncker is well respected in the European Union and that former German chancellor Helmut Kohl called him "junior" (both were of Christian parties). Juncker wears his arrogance on his sleeve, castigating politicians and the media alike with an abandon that U.S. politicians could only dream of. Juncker's public approach is not to suffer fools. Luxembourgers seem to appreciate his bravado because it is accompanied by integrity and competence (Roberts 2000).

Luxembourg's small foreign policy bureaucracy permits a prime minister with initiative and expertise to assume a great deal of influence over the foreign policy process. Although some condemn him for focusing too much on the international, Juncker enjoys the benefits of presiding over a country whose livelihood is very dependent on regional and global exchange. This gives a prime minister such as Juncker political room to spend as much time on foreign policy as he likes. If Luxembourg's prime minister were less interested or competent in the international arena (an unlikely prospect), the efficient and competent bureaucracy could certainly manage foreign policy. But that bureaucracy is also small and adaptive enough to work with new leaders.

* * *

Although factors at each level of analysis contribute to explaining Luxembourg's foreign policy, it is possible to rank them. The system level, including Luxembourg's small status and its geopolitical position, constrain the country's foreign policy scope and generate the "prime directive" of Luxembourg's external relations: to prevent an outbreak of war in Western Europe. These factors also account for Luxembourg's devotion to European integration. To the extent that much of Luxembourg's foreign policy is dedicated to these efforts, the system level can be said to offer the strongest explanatory determinants. Yet a state-level factor, Luxembourg's banking industry and the wealth owed to it, explains the Grand Duchy's preoccupation with maintaining its status as a financial center. The country's riches also account for the remarkable national consensus that permeates the decisionmaking process, freeing Luxembourg's foreign policy makers from the domestic political squabbles that so hamper policymaking in most states. The states' well-oiled bureaucracy and small status also contribute to a smooth-running foreign policy machine that behaves in a manner approaching a rational actor, that is, one that defines national interests and pursues them in an apolitical way. The individual level became important during the 1990s as an especially well-trained and charismatic leader assumed the top post in the Luxembourg government. Yet incompetents and purely politically motivated people rarely make it to the high levels of government in Luxembourg. While Juncker is certainly to be credited for his initiatives and diplomacy, it is also true that factors at the state and system levels create an environment in which nearly every Luxembourgish prime minister is able to stand out.

Conclusion

Luxembourg is a country where small works. Smallness rarely hinders Luxembourg's foreign policy; in fact it often enhances it. The Grand Duchy is unique in its ability to define foreign policy goals clearly and to devise successful strategies to pursue those goals. This review of policy and its foundations suggests an important conclusion about Luxembourg's foreign policy success. Because it is wealthy and a long-standing member of the European Union, Luxembourg is able to enjoy the benefits of small state status while avoiding most of its pitfalls. Many of the key components of Luxembourg's foreign policy owe to the fact that the country is so financially successful. The consensus about foreign policy objectives and strategies that exists at the governmental and popular levels is largely a function of the dictum: if it works, don't fix it. In other words, Luxembourgers, regardless of political affiliation, are happy with their successful model and have little incentive for change. At the parliamentary level, this translates into a willingness on the part of members of parliament to refrain from grand-scale critique of the government's foreign policy activities. An extremely well qualified bureaucracy is also a function of wealth and the educational benefits it brings. The bureaucracy enjoys the benefits of Luxembourg's smallness as well, since all foreign service officers have necessarily completed their university studies abroad. Although Luxembourg has limited financial resources to devote to foreign policy in absolute terms, it remains a wealthy country that can and does devote substantial funds to the international activities in which it chooses to participate.

That Luxembourg is a long-standing democracy in the heart of Western Europe similarly contributes to its foreign policy success. It need not worry about internal political turmoil, and its devotion to the European Union calms worries about a continental war. The EU is undoubtedly the most successful political-economic regional organization in the world and helps its members, particularly the small ones, to have an enhanced global voice. In short, Luxembourg does not suffer so many of the problems that plague most of the world's small countries: lack of funds for international programs, a weak foreign policy bureaucracy, border disputes, being overwhelmed by a regional hegemon, and internal political instability that spills over into foreign policy. It is because it is so blessed with economic resources, a favorable history, geography, and educated talent that Luxembourg, even though a nation of less than half a million, can afford to exhibit such confidence on the global stage.

Notes

1. The country is often referred to as "the Grand Duchy," or simply as "Luxembourg." Unlike Europe's other constitutional monarchies, which are either kingdoms or principalities, Luxembourg is a duchy in that its monarch is a grand duke, currently Henri.

2. Luxembourg City does have the Centre Universitaire de Luxembourg, which offers two-year programs and prepares students who complete their degrees in foreign universities.

3. These points were made by a foreign ministry officer who asked to remain anonymous, consistent with the ministry's policy.

4. Indeed, I have interviewed foreign policy bureaucrats in Colombia, Ecuador, and the United States. None have appeared so busy as a desk officer in Luxembourg.

6

Austria: The Burdens of History

Paul Luif

Austria, as we know it today, is the mostly German-speaking remnant of the large Hapsburg monarchy, which broke up after World War I. The new state survived barely twenty years. A civil war between the Catholic conservatives and the Social Democrats led to the Austro-fascist regime by the Catholic conservatives in 1934. In March 1938, just before the Austro-fascists could organize a referendum to prove to the world that the population would opt for Austria's independence, Austrian-born Adolf Hitler ordered German military occupation of the country. The Austro-fascists yielded to the overwhelming power of Nazi Germany without firing a shot.

On November 1, 1943, the United Kingdom, the Soviet Union, and the United States published a declaration in which they stated that "Austria, the first free country to fall victim to Hitlerite aggression, shall be liberated from German domination." They wished to "see reestablished a free and independent Austria." But, they added, Austria "has a responsibility which she cannot evade for participation in the war on the side of Hitlerite Germany."[1]

On April 27, 1945, as Vienna was liberated by Soviet troops, a provisional government declared Austria's independence. The politicians who created this Second Republic drew some lessons from the experiences of the First Republic. After the first general elections of November 1945 the adversaries of the civil war decided to cooperate closely and formed a coalition government. This Grand Coalition of the conservative Österreichische Volkspartei (ÖVP; Austrian People's Party) and the Sozialistische Partei Österreichs (SPÖ; Socialist Party of Austria) dominated Austrian politics for the remainder of the twentieth century.[2] These politicians had to cope with several important foreign policy challenges after 1945, the interwar experiences offering no useful guidance.[3] The first challenge was the gaining of full independence, since Austria, as Germany, was divided into four zones, and its capital, Vienna, into four sectors, each ruled by one of the four victorious Allies.

In the 1940s, both parties tried to keep Austria away from the incipient Cold War and were already thinking about a "neutral" stance for foreign policy to rid the country of the Allied occupation.[4] At the height of the Cold War, between 1950 and 1952, the Austrian government attempted to win the support of the Western powers to push the Soviet Union out of Eastern Austria; these efforts failed. In February 1955 the Soviet government finally hinted that it could imagine its troops leaving Eastern Austria independent from the solution of the German question.

A visit by an Austrian governmental delegation to Moscow in April 1955 led to a compromise between Austria and the Soviet Union, which only hesitantly was accepted by the Western powers. The Soviet government agreed to completely withdraw its troops from Eastern Austria, the precondition being that Austria would not join a military alliance (i.e., the North Atlantic Treaty Organization [NATO]) and would accept the status of "neutrality." The Austrian government won two important concessions in regard to the latter. First, neutrality would be "of the type maintained by Switzerland,"[5] and not something more vague (and possibly Soviet-friendly) like "nonalignment," as practiced at that time by Yugoslavia and India. Second, the neutrality clause was not to be included in the State Treaty, the legal instrument to end the four-power occupation, but would be a unilateral declaration of the Austrian parliament. Thus Austria avoided a direct droit de regard of the four Allies, in particular the Soviet Union, concerning its neutrality policy.

On October 26, 1955, one day after the last foreign soldier had left Austrian soil, a constitutional law establishing Austria's permanent neutrality was passed in parliament:

> 1. For the purpose of the lasting maintenance of her independence externally, and for the purpose of the inviolability of her territory, Austria declares of her own free will her perpetual neutrality. Austria will maintain and defend this with all means at her disposal.
>
> 2. For the securing of this purpose in all future times Austria will not join any military alliances and will not permit the establishment of any foreign military bases on her territory. (Stourzh 1985: 239)

By stressing "free will," Austrian officials wanted to demonstrate that their country was not "neutralized," not pushed by the Allies (especially the Soviet Union) to adopt that status, but that it was their own choice. In fact it was their decision, but the alternative would have been the further stationing of foreign troops in the country.

The years of Allied occupation laid the foundations for a democratic "corporatist" structure of the Austrian political and economic system. This structure consisted on one hand of the Grand Coalition government, which had ruled Austria since 1945. The enemies of the civil war in 1934 now worked closely together to end the occupation, but also divided practically all political positions among themselves. With the consent of both parties, large parts of the Austrian industry were nationalized and "divided" among the ÖVP and SPÖ, each party creating its own fiefdom. On the other hand, corporatism meant a close cooperation of the social partners (trade unions with strong links to the SPÖ, and business usually connected with the ÖVP) and their far-reaching influence on economic and social policies. The government, together with the social partners, shaped the policies of Austro-Keynesianism between the 1950s and 1970s: (1) low unemployment guaranteed by the nationalized industry and the deficit spending of the government (in particular during economic downturns); and (2) a hard-currency policy by connecting the value of the Austrian schilling to the deutschemark. Until the mid-1980s, these policies were successful, and Austria became one of the richest countries in the world.

Austria's "Active Neutrality"

In contrast to the more restricted wording of the constitutional law on neutrality, the Swiss interpretation of "permanent neutrality" was broad at that time and included not only military obligations (prohibiting membership in a military alliance) but also political and economic restrictions (such as excluding membership in a customs union). In 1955, Austrian politicians apparently had no intention of interpreting neutrality in such a broad way. The limited extent of Austria's neutrality was stressed by Chancellor Julius Raab (ÖVP) when he introduced the bill in the Austrian parliament. He called Austria's neutrality a "military neutrality" that would include "no obligations and commitments whatsoever in the economic or cultural field."[6] In contrast to Switzerland, Austria joined the United Nations in December 1955 and then, in April 1956, became a member of the Council of Europe, which comprised only "Western" countries. At the same time, politicians started to talk about Austria joining the European Coal and Steel Community, the nascency of European integration. Austria could have been well on the way to becoming one of the founding members of the European Economic Community (EEC).

But in October–November 1956, only a year after the Allies had left Austria, the Soviet Union intervened militarily with tanks and troops on the Austrian border, some forty miles from Vienna, to crush the Hungarian uprising. The Austrian government strongly criticized the Soviet action. This verbal support of the Hungarian freedom fighters led to an abrupt deterioration of Austria's relations with the Soviet Union. The quarrel with the Soviets made the Austrian government more careful in its external relations, especially in its integration policy. In view of the Soviet opposition to such a move, any plans to join the EEC slowly disappeared from the political agenda.

But there were also domestic reasons for such a development. Representatives of the SPÖ's left wing became critical of closer relations with the Common Market. In June 1959 even the chairman of the SPÖ, Bruno Pittermann, denounced the EEC as a "bourgeois bloc" and excluded EEC membership. This came as a surprise since the SPÖ had been regarded after 1945 as the most pro-Western party and early on reluctantly supported neutrality. The SPÖ opted now for membership in the European Free Trade Association (EFTA). This loose organization created a free trade area (excluding agricultural goods), its members preserving their own import tariffs and other trade restrictions toward third countries. Not only the Socialists saw advantages in EFTA membership. In the eyes of Chancellor Raab, joining the EFTA benefited the ÖVP's supporters among small businesses and the farmers.[7] In contrast, the EEC was assumed by the ÖVP-SPÖ government to pay little attention to Austria's special situation and not grant any exceptions for the weaker Austrian competitors. Toward the outside world, these arguments were usually replaced by references to neutrality—which made the aversion to close integration sound more plausible (Luif 1988: 100–102).

Most of the specialists in international law had started to maintain—as the Swiss model postulated—that a neutral country could not join the EEC, even if it were to be admitted with a neutrality clause. The economic dependence on the other EEC members would be so strong that the promise of a neutral member to freeze relations or leave the organization during a war involving other EEC members (necessary to preserve its neutrality status) would not be credible (Zemanek 1959). There are indications that in the early days after the Allied departure in 1955 the government, in particular SPÖ officials, did not take neutrality as a "permanent" status. Again, Austrian scholars of international law introduced a legal interpretation that made the status more "durable." They assumed a special relationship between Austria and the community of states. As we have seen, the neutrality declaration was purposely a unilateral Austrian act. This act—the Federal Constitutional Law of October 26, 1955—was announced to the states with which Austria had diplomatic relations at that time. The explicit or implicit recognition of this notification had created "quasi-treaty" relations between Austria and these states. All states would have to heed Austria's status; a unilateral renunciation of the status (by other states as well as Austria) would not be possible. In practice, this requirement could bind Austria's adherence to neutrality to the opinion of the important states in the world, especially the Soviet Union (Verdross 1978).

The parliamentary elections of 1966 changed the political landscape. The ÖVP gained an absolute majority in seats and formed a single-party government, and was to reach an agreement on a tight association (resembling full membership) with the EEC. The background to these attempts was the strengthening of the "reformers" in the ÖVP who demanded close relations with Western Europe and consequently stressed the narrow definition of neutrality as being only a "military neutrality." The "reformers" and many economists emphasized the importance of Austrian participation in the more dynamic market of the EEC, but there existed a hidden agenda as well. Close association with the EEC would help to liberalize Austria's society and economy. A permanent exclusion of Austria from the EEC would bring the country closer to the East and to a socialist planned economy.

These attempts failed in mid-1967. After the invasion of Czechoslovakia by Warsaw Pact troops in August 1968, the notion of a specific, limited "military neutrality" was finally rejected by Kurt Waldheim, the foreign minister of the ÖVP government. The obligations of a neutral country would go beyond the obligations of not joining military alliances and not permitting the establishment of foreign military bases. The neutral country "has even during peacetime to conduct a foreign policy that will keep it from getting involved in future armed conflicts and in political struggles which could lead to such conflicts." At the same time, Waldheim stressed the importance of an "active participation in international cooperation" for a neutral country.[8]

These words were early signs of a profound change in Austrian external relations. Bruno Kreisky, chancellor of an SPÖ one-party government from 1970 to 1983, went much further, with a foreign policy focusing less on Western Europe and highlighting Austria's "global" aspects (Luif 1982). Together with the other European neutral and nonaligned states, Austria made important contributions to the realization of the Final Act of the Conference on Security and Cooperation in Europe (CSCE). In the United Nations, Kurt Waldheim was elected Secretary-General in 1971 and confirmed in 1976. Austrian representatives served as chairmen of important UN commissions. Analysis of the voting in the UN General Assembly showed that Austria together with Sweden developed its own independent position (Kramer 1996: 164).

Bruno Kreisky tried to ease tensions in various regions of the globe, like Central America and Afghanistan (Bielka, Jankowitsch, and Thalberg 1983; Höll 1994). The most prominent endeavors were his attempts to solve the conflict between Israel and the Palestinians. He stressed the legitimate aspirations of the Palestinian people and demanded that the Palestine Liberation Organization (PLO) and its political leader, Yasser Arafat, be recognized as the most important partners in the peace talks. In March 1982, Kreisky welcomed Muammar Qaddafi, the Libyan leader, to Vienna.

Looking back, this "active" foreign policy was helped by several factors. First, and perhaps most important, was détente; reduced tensions between East and West in the 1970s gave Austria room for maneuver. Second, Kreisky's foreign policy was helped by the solution of two problems that hampered Austrian external relations in the 1960s: the end of the conflict with Italy on South Tyrol in 1969 and the free trade agreements with the European Community (EC), signed in 1972. And third, in Austria the great popularity of Kreisky and his governing with absolute majorities from 1971 to 1983 gave him significant leeway in external matters.

"Realist" Foreign Policy and EU Membership[9]

In the late 1970s and the early 1980s, in particular after the Soviet invasion of Afghanistan, tensions rose again between East and West. In this new, "second" Cold War, the United States and its somewhat reluctant allies renewed and reinforced the controls for high-technology exports (especially computers) to the East. These exports were suspected to help in modernizing the weapons, in particular the nuclear arsenal, of the communist bloc, which were threatening the West (see, e.g., Melvern, Anning, and Hebditch 1984). The neutral countries, particularly Austria, came under strong pressure by U.S. officials to introduce and strengthen such controls.

As a first reaction, Bruno Kreisky and the Austrian government rejected the demands by the Western allies (Luif 1995: 144). Austria would not participate in a politically motivated embargo. But its industry required secure access to Western, especially U.S., high technology. This was particularly true for the nationalized industry, which at that time wanted to modernize in an effort to improve its competitiveness. The United States threatened to reduce or even stop the exports of high technology to countries not complying with the Coordinating Committee for Multilateral Strategic Export Controls (COCOM), the control regime established by the Western powers during the "first" Cold War and revived in the early days of the Reagan administration. After some hesitation, Austria signed a U.S.-Austrian Customs Mutual Assistance Agreement in 1986. A year later it made the COCOM lists part of the Foreign Trade Act (Roodbeen 1992: 313).

Other countries, particularly Sweden, felt the same pressure.[10] The credibility of the neutral countries' external relations was at stake. Most of their politicians had maintained in the discussions about European integration that membership in the European Community was prohibited, since neutral countries needed to have the final control on trade relations with other countries. Now, they clearly had to heed rules established by the West against trade in high technology with the East. The neutral countries' arguments in defense of their legal requirements were to no avail, as the renewed tensions between East and West had reduced their leeway. Active foreign policy gave way to a more cautious behavior.

About the same time, another challenge appeared on the horizon—the integration of the EC had become more dynamic. Jacques Delors was appointed president of the European Commission in January 1985, the commission published the White Paper on Completing the Internal Market in June 1985, and the EC countries signed the Single European Act, the first substantial change of the EC treaties, in February 1986. At the same time, Austrian industry, in particular its nationalized industry, got into trouble. The financial hardships of November 1985 heralded a deep crisis of the Austrian corporatist model, and another crisis had international implications. In June 1986, Kurt Waldheim was elected president of Austria (a position with little influence on day-to-day politics). Already during the election campaign, he had been criticized for his reluctance to disclose his participation in the German armed forces during World War II, the Wehrmacht. Waldheim's election was an indication for journalists in Austria and abroad that the country had not really coped with its Nazi past.

The general elections of November 1986 brought a significant change in government, after the end of the SPÖ rule in 1983 and a short spell of a "small coalition" government of the SPÖ with the small Freiheitliche Partei Österreichs (FPÖ; Freedom Party of Austria), a party with a right-wing liberal as well as a pan-German tradition. A new version of the Grand Coalition, this time under the leadership of the Socialists, was installed. In its statement of policy of January 1987, the new government declared that intensifying Austria's relations with the EC was a "central objective" of its foreign policy (*Erklärung der Bundesregierung* 1987: 32–33). In May 1987 the Federation of Austrian Industrialists, the association of the bigger Austrian companies and important business organizations, formally demanded EC membership. It would be the only way to fully participate in the emerging internal market of the EC (*Europa: Unsere Zukunft* 1987). A study by two specialists in international law, commissioned by the Federation of Austrian Industrialists, claimed at the same time that membership in the EC would be compatible with Austria's neutrality (Hummer and Schweitzer 1987). In December 1987, in a surprising volte-face, the Federal Chamber of Commerce (which has represented the small and medium-sized enterprises) also opted for Austria to join the EC. Subsequently, in January 1988 the ÖVP, the party with close links to the business groups and the junior partner of the Grand Coalition government, decided to request full membership in the EC. Only in April 1989 did the SPÖ finally accept the idea of applying for EC membership, but with several conditions. In particular it stressed the necessity to preserve Austria's permanent neutrality. For that reason and also because of the continuing opposition from the Soviet Union (the fall of the Berlin Wall would occur only months later), Austria applied for EC membership on July 17, 1989, with an extensive neutrality "clause" with clear references to the tradition of "active neutrality."

Austria's application for EC membership was at first strongly criticized by its partners in the EFTA. But step by step, most other EFTA countries (including all neutral countries) copied Austria's move and sent letters to Brussels as well. The economic integration of the EC members had reached such a quality that staying outside could, at least in the long run, cause extensive harm to the economies of the outsiders.

But when Austria, together with Finland and Sweden, joined the European Union (EU, as the EC has been called since 1943) on January 1, 1995, no exception for its or the other new members' neutrality was made. On the contrary, they had to sign a joint declaration (added to the Final Act of the Accession Treaty) in which they promised that they would be "ready and able to participate fully and actively" in the Common Foreign and Security Policy (CFSP) of the EU and that their "legal framework" would be "compatible" with the rules and traditions of the CFSP.

Behind this acceptance of the CFSP lay several steps in "reinterpreting" permanent neutrality. The first was brought about by the events after the Iraqi invasion of Kuwait in August 1990. The UN Security Council's decision to take action against Iraq (first economic sanctions, then authorizing military measures) made it necessary to bring Austria's constitutional position into line with the country's membership in the UN. The penal code's article punishing actions that could endanger Austria's neutrality had to be quickly modified so that it no longer applied in circumstances where the Security Council had authorized military action under Chapter VII of the UN Charter. The Austrian regulations for approving the import, export, and transit of war matériel were similarly modified.

Austrian policy now started from the premise that the actions in question were steps taken by the United Nations against an aggressor under the international system of collective security. They did not constitute a war within the meaning of the term in international law, and for that reason did not call for the application of neutrality law (*Austrian Foreign Policy Yearbook 1990* [1991]: 64–65).

As a second step, just before starting the membership negotiations with the EU on the CFSP chapter, the government officially defined neutrality in a narrow way, thus finally and officially abandoning the "active neutrality" concept. In a declaration on neutrality, added to the minutes of its meeting of November 9, 1993, the cabinet declared that "the Federal Government proceeds from the assumption that Austria is not obliged to participate militarily in wars, not obliged to accede to military alliances and to establish military bases of foreign states on its territory" (*Die Presse* 1993). One could now argue that a circle was closed. This definition of permanent neutrality went back to the narrow wording of the constitutional law from October 1955. The extensive interpretation of the status, as formulated by the specialists of international law and accepted by practically all decisionmakers since the late 1960s, was discarded.

Third, a bill was passed in parliament, supported by the Grand Coalition parties as well as the two smaller parties, the Greens and Liberal Forum, that introduced a new article into the federal constitution (Article 23f). This new article simply stated that Austria would "participate" in the CFSP, but added that this included participation in "economic" embargoes. The Maastricht Treaty, which entered force during the accession negotiations on November 1, 1993, stated in its Title V that the CFSP covered "all areas of foreign and security policy" and this included "all questions related to the security of the Union, including the eventual framing of a common defense policy, which might in time lead to a common defense." The rules concerning the "common defense policy" and the "common defense" had not yet been implemented when the three new members joined the EU on January 1, 1995. But it was already clear at that time that the CFSP would probably not be confined to "economic" security matters.

Austria and the EU's Security and Defense Policy

It was not without irony that precisely during Austria's first EU presidency (second half of 1998; see Luif 1999) the debate on a European defense identity gained momentum. The events in the former Yugoslavia clearly showed that the EU could not handle the crises by utilizing only verbal behavior—the CFSP did up to the mid-1990s basically produce only common statements. The Maastricht Treaty and the Amsterdam Treaty (in force as of 1999) attempted to change this. But it remained to be seen how these legal texts would be implemented.

Just before the informal meeting of the heads of state and government of the EU member states in Pörtschach, Austria (in the province of Carinthia), on October 24–25, 1998, British prime minister Tony Blair made it plain that he was ready to drop Britain's long-standing objections to the EU having a defense capability. If necessary, Britain would do so without the United States, but it would always be under NATO's authority (Webster 1998). In spite of negative comments by the SPÖ, the coalition partner, Austrian defense minister Werner Fasslabend (ÖVP) organized the first-ever meeting of EU defense ministers in Vienna on November 3–4, 1998. A month later, in Saint-Malo, the heads of state and government of France and the United Kingdom agreed that the EU "needs to be in a position to play its full role on the international stage." To this end, the EU "must have the capacity for autonomous action, backed up by credible military forces, the means to decide to use them and a readiness to do so, in order to respond to international crises" (*Franco-British Summit* 1998).

In 1999, two meetings of the heads of state or government of all EU members, the Cologne European Council and the Helsinki European Council, implemented these ideas. The goal the EU member states set for themselves was to establish by 2003 the ability to deploy rapidly and then sustain forces capable of the full range of Petersberg tasks as set out in the Amsterdam Treaty, including the most demanding, in operations involving a troop level of up to 50,000–60,000 persons. These forces should be militarily self-sustaining with the necessary command, control, and intelligence capabilities; logistics; other combat support services; and additionally, as appropriate, air and naval elements. It is clear that the EU decisionmakers embraced here the lessons of the Kosovo conflict. The seventy-eight-day air war (March to June 1999), which culminated with the occupation of Kosovo by NATO-led peacekeepers, clearly showed that the Europeans were unable to act alone and were heavily dependent on U.S. forces.

Austria, in particular the SPÖ as the senior coalition party, only reluctantly agreed to the new activities of the EU in the security and defense area. The Kosovo crisis clearly indicated the difficulties and inconsistencies Austria incurred with its neutrality policy. NATO started bombing Serbian forces in Kosovo and Serbia proper without a mandate by the Security Council under Chapter VII of the UN Charter. Therefore, the Austrian government did not allow transit flights of NATO planes across Austrian territory, forcing NATO aircraft to make rather significant detours around Austria (and Switzerland as well); Austria thus was not a neutral country, but in fact hampered NATO's military actions. At the same time in the EU context, however, the Austrian government supported the statement of the EU's informal summit in Brussels in April 1999: "The Heads of State and Government reiterate their determination not to tolerate the killings and deportations in Kosovo and believe that the use of severest measures, including *military action,* has been both *necessary* and *warranted*" (cited in Ceuppens 1971: point 2 of the chairman's 1999 summary, emphasis added).

The Kosovo crisis not only exposed the contradictory behavior of Austrian officials, but also clearly showed the importance of NATO's Article 5 (the military assistance clause). Hungary, Austria's neighbor, had been for less than two weeks a member of NATO when the bombing in Yugoslavia started. In contrast to Austria and in spite of its difficult situation concerning the Hungarian minority in Yugoslavia, it opened its airspace for NATO military aircraft.

The contradictory behavior of the Austrian government on security and defense was also caused by the disagreement of the coalition parties on the future of neutrality. The SPÖ insisted on its preservation, whereas the ÖVP, since the mid-1990s, has been ready to discard neutrality and has wanted Austria to join the Western European Union (WEU) and NATO. The bigger opposition party, the FPÖ, headed since 1986 by the outspoken and aggressive Jörg Haider, had discarded neutrality already in the early 1990s. The smaller opposition party, the Greens, has been very much in favor of neutrality and even demanded a return to the "active neutrality" of Bruno Kreisky. Since amending or abolishing the constitutional law on neutrality needs a two-thirds majority in parliament (Nationalrat), a consensus among the three bigger parties is needed, the SPÖ thus holding a veto power as long as it (possibly together with the Greens) has more than one-third of seats in parliament.

Among the general public, neutrality has been popular, being the symbol of Austria's success story after 1945. If one asks the Austrians in opinion polls about Austria joining NATO or maintaining neutrality, usually 60 to 70 percent opt for neutrality. But if one qualifies the abandoning of neutrality or offers a choice between "defending Austria alone" and "defending it together with a group of countries," the majority of Austrians opt for membership in an alliance (Ulram 1999: 154–155).

The Sanctions of the EU-14

The conflict on neutrality was one of the reasons why the Grand Coalition was not continued after the parliamentary elections of October 1999. In these elections, the Social Democrats lost heavily and received only 33.2 percent of the vote. The ÖVP and the FPÖ both earned 26.9 percent and the Greens 7.4 percent. The Liberal Forum did not reach the threshold of 4 percent needed for representation in parliament. After long and tortuous discussions among all political parties, the ÖVP finally opted for a coalition with the FPÖ and nominated Wolfgang Schüssel as chancellor, although the ÖVP had received 415 fewer votes than the FPÖ in the elections. Even before the new ÖVP-FPÖ coalition government was formed, Austria came under pressure by its partners in the EU. Many politicians and commentators in the EU member states and beyond regarded the FPÖ as an extreme right-wing, neo-Nazi party, an accusation more often than not rejected in Austria.[11]

According to the Portuguese EU presidency, the FPÖ and its leader, Jörg Haider, had repeatedly questioned "the values and principles of humanism and democratic tolerance underlying the European project" (statement of the Portuguese EU presidency on February 3, 2000). It therefore enforced the three decisions made by the fourteen EU member states, already announced on January 31, 2000:

> 1. Governments of the 14 Member States will not promote or accept any bilateral official contacts at political level with an Austrian Government integrating the FPÖ.
> 2. There will be no support in favor of Austrian candidates seeking positions in international organizations.
> 3. Austrian Ambassadors in EU capitals will only be received at a technical level.[12]

The main critique of the FPÖ seems to have been based on statements by Haider, who had praised the employment policy of the Nazis and strongly opposed immigration of foreigners. Therefore, the measures were not based on EU law, since the conditions of Article 7 of the Treaty on European Union ("existence of a serious and persistent breach" of EU principles in deeds, not in verbal statements) were clearly not existent. The EU-14 introduced these measures (soon called "sanctions") for their *bilateral* relations with Austria; nevertheless, the Portuguese EU presidency published them on the presidency's website.

In addition, Portuguese prime minister António Guterres was at the same time president of the Socialist International (the world federation of socialist parties). Most of the EU countries had Social Democrats heading coalition governments. This information was used by the ÖVP and FPÖ to suggest a socialist "conspiracy" against the new government, despite the fact that conservative French president Jacques Chirac was one of the prime movers behind the actions of the EU-14.

Inside Austria, in the early weeks after the formation of the coalition, demonstrations in the streets put intensive pressure on the government.

Although these protests dwindled and lost their impact, the measures of the EU-14 were much more serious. Their direct effects were the cessation of high-level bilateral contacts between Austrian officials and Austria's fourteen EU partners. Yet these measures often involved technical levels as well, and one could not distinguish between the refusal of "bilateral" contacts and "normal" EU procedures. Austria's participation in the important preparatory phase of EU decisionmaking was definitely hampered by the EU-14 measures (Böhm 2000).

But there were even more wide-ranging consequences for Austria. Foreign Minister Louis Michel, one of the principal organizers of the measures against Austria, even recommended that Belgians not go skiing in Austria because he considered it immoral (Voogt 2000). This advice and also the very critical reports in the French media (compare the extensive coverage of Austria's "extreme right" in *Le Monde*) probably led to a reduction in tourist visits from these countries to Austria.[13] Cultural, media, and scientific contacts between Austria and other EU countries (in particular Belgium and France) were stopped or reduced for several months. Austrian schoolchildren having exchange programs with French, Belgian, and Portuguese schools were told not to come (Martin 2000). There were stories of Austrians being attacked in EU countries (e.g., *Neue Zürcher Zeitung,* September 16, 2000).

Israel called back its ambassador from Vienna, but among the other non-EU states only the Czech Republic, Canada, and Argentina partook in the EU-14 "sanctions." The United States simply "observed" Austria. Officials in the Central and Eastern European countries, candidates for EU membership, regarded the EU-14 measures with skepticism or outright hostility (Green 2000: 1; Maier 2000: 33).

The European Commission kept normal working relations with Austria, because the EU-14 measures lacked a base in EU law. The commission even helped Austria in situations where such measures potentially violated EU law. One case in point was the starting of an information procedure against Belgium when Belgian authorities prohibited their schools to book skiing courses in Austria (Streitenberger 2000).

If the aim of the EU-14 measures was to topple the ÖVP-FPÖ government, they were ineffective.[14] Surveys showed that these measures were very unpopular in practically all strata of Austrian society. Asked in a public opinion poll in March 2000 about the sanctions, 66 percent of Austrians said that they were "outraged"; only 24 percent showed "understanding" for the measures of the EU-14 (Telefonumfrage 2000). For pollsters, the sanctions were almost a "stroke of luck" for the government, diverting the public from the troubles of the new government, especially the problems with the inexperienced ministers from the FPÖ. The ÖVP increased its support among the public; although the FPÖ did lose backing, the ÖVP and the FPÖ together secured in all opinion polls an absolute majority of Austrians during the initial year of their rule (*Der Standard Aktuell* 2000).

The opposition in Austria, the Social Democrats and the Greens, at first backed the EU-14 measures against the new center-right government. Trips of their party leaders to other EU countries to explain the situation in Austria were criticized by government officials as a "betrayal" of Austrian interests. The party leaders should fight against the "unjustified" measures and not "drink champagne" with French hard-liners. The low popularity of the sanctions among the general public finally obliged the opposition parties also to call for an end to the measures.

The futility of the actions of the EU-14 made some (mostly smaller) EU countries, which only reluctantly had supported the measures in the first place, call for a termination of the sanctions. In particular, the Danish government pleaded for a cessation since the measures threatened to lend support to the opposition in the upcoming referendum on the introduction of the euro in Denmark.

During the first weeks of the bilateral sanctions, the representatives of the Austrian government rather submissively endured various "humiliations" by their colleagues at EU meetings. Ministers did not shake hands with their Austrian counterparts, French and Belgian ministers left the rooms when Austrian ministers spoke, some ministers put on buttons with crossed-out bow ties (Austrian chancellor Wolfgang Schüssel did wear such bow ties—but later, to avoid this embarrassment, he changed styles).

As the disapproval of the sanctions by a large majority of Austrians became obvious, the government started to fight back. The nomination of Horst Köhler as director of the International Monetary Fund (IMF) by the EU was only possible after Germany agreed in March 2000 to a bilateral meeting with Austria's finance minister, Karl-Heinz Grasser (FPÖ), to provide the necessary information to the Austrians (Winestock 2000). The EU summit in Lisbon in March 2000 did not bring the steps toward an end of the measures as the Austrian government had wished.

Hence the Austrian government passed an "action plan" for working against the sanctions. Its eighteenth and final point consisted of a referendum on the "unjust" measures by the EU-14. This referendum was planned for the fall of 2000 if the measures had not been removed by then. The Feira European Council in June 2000 saw the Austrians threatening a veto against an agreement on taxation of nonresident savings. The retracting of this threat was seen as a quid pro quo for a step-by-step ending of the sanctions.[15] The Portuguese EU presidency, which had suffered under the quarrels of the Austrian case, finally succeeded in putting together a possible scenario for ending the EU-14 measures.

The Portuguese presidency asked the president of the European Court of Human Rights, the Swiss Luzius Wildhaber, to appoint a three-man panel to assess Austria's human rights record.[16] Luzius Wildhaber only accepted this mandate under the condition that the Austrian government would consent to the appointment of the "three wise men" by him. The Austrians agreed to this procedure; it was the first time they were at least indirectly involved in a decision of the EU-14 concerning their government. But the Austrians strongly criticized the "mandate" for the three wise men, who were asked to deliver, on the basis of a thorough examination, a report covering the Austrian government's commitment to the common European values, in particular concerning the rights of minorities, refugees, and immigrants and the evolution of the political nature of the FPÖ (quoted from Ahtisaari, Frowein, and Oreja 2000).

The Austrian government especially complained that the sanctions would remain in place (and not be at least suspended) and that there was no timetable for the work of the wise men. Luzius Wildhaber noted in his "acceptance letter" from June 29, 2000, that all fifteen EU member states (including Austria) had agreed to his selecting the panel of wise men. In addition, he admitted that no time frame was laid down by the EU-14, but he would recommend to the wise men that they "should deliver their report as quickly as at all possible."[17]

On July 12, 2000, Wildhaber announced the names of the three wise men: Martti Ahtisaari, the former president of Finland; Jochen Frowein, a German specialist in comparative public law and international law; and Marcelino Oreja, a former Spanish minister of foreign affairs. In fact, these eminent people speedily carried out their mandate. Less than two months later, on September 8, 2000, they presented their report to President Jacques Chirac, France having the EU presidency in the second half of 2000.

Their conclusions concerning the Austrian government were unambiguous:

> [B]ased on a thorough examination, it is our considered view that the Austrian Government is committed to the common European values. The Austrian Government's respect in particular for the rights of minorities, refugees and immigrants is not inferior to that of the other European Union Member States. The legal situation in the three mentioned areas is well up to the standards applied in other EU Member States. In some areas, particularly concerning the rights of national minorities, Austrian standards can be considered to be higher than

> those applied in many other EU countries. (Ahtisaari, Frowein, and Oreja 2000: 32)

Concerning the evolution of the political nature of the FPÖ, the report was critical. There are reasons why the description of the FPÖ as a right-wing populist party with radical elements still appears to be correct (Ahtisaari, Frowein, and Oreja 2000: 32). In describing the FPÖ as basically a "populist" party, the three wise men seemingly adhered to the opinion of many social scientists, who have regarded the FPÖ more as a populist and less as an extreme-right or neo-Nazi party.[18] The three wise men also included a sentence that made a further maintenance of the EU-14 measures, as some French politicians had suggested, practically impossible: "It is in our opinion, however, that the measures taken by the fourteen member states, if continued, would become counterproductive and should therefore be ended" (Ahtisaari, Frowein, and Oreja 2000: 33).

Frantic contacts and phone calls over the next few days among EU-14 officials did not bring a conditional suspension of the sanctions and a monitoring of Austria's government as French and Belgian politicians wanted. Instead, on the evening of September 12, 2000, the EU-14 agreed on an unconditional end of the measures imposed on February 3. A joint statement was published on the website of the French foreign ministry (and not on the EU presidency website, as the Portuguese did in announcing the measures). "The measures taken by the 14 were useful," the statement said. "They can now be lifted." But the statement added: "The nature of the Freedom Party and its uncertain evolution remains cause for serious worry. The 14 consider that a particular vigilance should be exercised with regard to this party and the influence it exerts on the government it is a part of" (quoted from Daley 2000).

"This is a big success for Austria" was the comment of Chancellor Wolfgang Schüssel (ÖVP); Vice Chancellor Susanne Riess-Passer (FPÖ) spoke about a "victory of reason" (Stolz 2000a). Less levelheaded was Jörg Haider, who had already called French president Jacques Chirac a "pocket-sized Napoleon," speaking now of Chirac's "Waterloo" (Le Rider 2000). President Chirac, however, maintained that "the participation of an extremist and xenophobic party in a European government is totally abnormal" (Stolz 2000b).

EU Commission president Romano Prodi had become more and more critical of the EU-14; after the lifting of the sanctions he said that "this will never happen again." The EU would have to accept governments of member states as long as they did not violate the rules of democracy (*Neue Zürcher Zeitung* 2000b).

Analysis and Conclusion

The cases related here on Austria's experiences after World War II point to several conclusions that can be distilled about the foreign policy of Austria. After 1945, the country did not have to worry about its physical survival, as during the interwar period. For several decades its governments conducted a successful foreign policy, giving it for some time more weight than its small size would have warranted. But Austria's foreign policy in a broader sense, including its external economic relations and its integration policy, has not always been consistent or powerful.

Smallness helps—sometimes. The much earlier solution of the "Austrian question" after 1945, compared to the solution of the "German question," had a lot to do with Austria's smallness. Leaving the eastern parts of Austria was not as considerable an issue for the Soviet Union as giving up East Germany. In the same vein, a neutral Austria was not as much a problem for the West as a neutralized Germany would have been. The Austrians also played their cards well, early recognizing the first signs of a "thaw" in East-West relations. The neutrality status they agreed to could be accepted by both East and West.

Still, the Austrian "solution" brought problems. For the Soviet Union, since Austria was an example for the Hungarian freedom fighters and wanted Hungary to become neutral as well, that was just the reason for the Soviet troops to intervene. Neutral Austria, together with Switzerland, put a "neutral wedge" between NATO's central and southern forces and thus hampered connections between southern Germany and northern Italy.

In view of the sanctions of the EU-14, smallness was a handicap. Austria's partners would have thought twice before introducing these unusual measures against a bigger country. German foreign minister Joschka Fischer refused to contemplate similar sanctions against a right-wing government in Italy.[19] This is explained by the different sizes of the countries, since, for example, the differences between the FPÖ and the Italian right-wing Lega Nord are not great (*Kurier Online* 2000). Lega Nord, a regional party in northern Italy, led by its charismatic leader, Umberto Bossi, has agitated since the 1980s against Italian centralism and with xenophobic arguments against southern Italians and immigrants from the third world.

Personal qualities and adequate domestic support enable an active foreign policy—as long as systemic circumstances are accommodating. Chancellor Bruno Kreisky's popularity (as leader of the SPÖ, he achieved in three successive elections, in 1971, 1975, and 1979, an absolute majority for his party) gave him much domestic leeway for his foreign policy activities. They brought him prestige abroad and strengthened his position at home. Henry Kissinger wrote:

> Austria's shrewd and perceptive Chancellor Bruno Kreisky, who had parlayed his country's formal neutrality into a position of influence beyond its strength, often by interpreting the motives of competing countries to each other. . . . He was much traveled; his comments on trends and personalities were invariably illuminating. He had a great sense of humor and far more geopolitical insight than many leaders from more powerful countries. (Kissinger 1979: 1204)

Combined with those personal qualities were circumstances at the system level: détente in East-West relations. In the short term, his activities, in particular in the Middle East, were not successful. In the long term, more than twenty years later, his ideas about direct contacts between the PLO and Israel were adopted by the United States—which reveals the limits of influence small states have on world politics.

In addition, as the tensions between East and West rose in the early 1980s, Austria abandoned its "active neutrality" policy step by step. The resignation of Kreisky and the economic troubles of the mid-1980s changed also the domestic basis of this policy. The opposition parties promptly used this situation to push for more attentiveness for West European politics, that is, integration policy. This was helped by the new dynamics of the EC (completion of the internal market).

Changes in the international system have a significant impact on the foreign policy of small states—but do not always determine it. The increased tensions between East and West in the 1980s obviously reduced the leeway for Austrian foreign policy, ending the era of "global" active neutrality policy. When the conservative ÖVP formed a government with the SPÖ in early 1987, its aim was clearly to establish closer relations with the EU. The ÖVP soon pushed for full membership in the EU, the SPÖ only reluctantly following suit. On July 17, 1989, the membership application was sent to the EU. In a move to appease the SPÖ, Austria's neutrality status was explicitly stated in the application.

This move was made even though it was widely expected that the application would be met by opposition outside Austria. Its partners in the EFTA disapproved of this breaking of the ranks and weakening of the EFTA's position vis-à-vis the EU. The Soviet Union feared that Austria's neutrality status could be changed or abolished.[20] The European Commission saw the application as premature, arguing that the EU should contemplate new applications only after the completion of the internal market in 1993. Some member states, like Belgium, thought that Austria's neutrality status would not be compatible with EU membership (Luif 1995: 150, 173, 198–199).

Despite these obstacles, the ÖVP succeeded in getting the "letter" sent to Brussels. Domestically, the SPÖ had difficulty opposing the move since it could not deny that there would be real (and perhaps also only imagined) problems for Austrian business when being discriminated against on its most important markets. The fall of the Berlin Wall on November 9, 1989, made the obstacles on the systemic level more or less irrelevant. Perhaps the politicians of the ÖVP had rightly interpreted the developments of East-West relations in the second half of the 1980s. The bold move of mid-1989 proved to be the right thing to do, somewhat similar to the attempt to solve the "Austrian question" in 1955. Even if the circumstances in the systemic level are not that favorable, a correct interpretation of the impending changes—or plain luck—can give a small state some room to maneuver.

Still, it has not always been a smooth ride for Austrian foreign policy. Since the end of the Cold War, one of the most obvious inconsistencies in Austrian external relations has been the maintenance of permanent neutrality (even in its reduced scope) when at the same time the EU has become more active in the defense field and at least some of Austria's neighbors have joined NATO. The country thus found itself in an increasingly awkward position. But for domestic reasons, this predicament cannot be changed anytime soon. The electorate and vocal politicians will not permit abandonment of formal neutrality.

As the above analysis has illustrated, looking at the external (systemic) reasons as well as domestic reasons (economic development, governments, parties, persons) for foreign policy stress yields the fullest explanation of Austrian behavior. Sometimes a maverick or shrewd politician can inject his personality into the foreign policy outcome. In general, however, Austria is a small country with strong political institutions. As such, the system and domestic levels best explain Austrian foreign policy.

Notes

1. Quoted from Stourzh 1998: 607. In a strict sense, Austria did not exist at that time, so the demand of the Allies could only mean the contribution of the Austrians for the liberation of their country.

2. In June 1991 the SPÖ, in line with most other center-left parties in Western Europe, renamed itself the Social Democratic Party of Austria.

3. A comprehensive analysis of Austria's foreign policy, with extensive references to the relevant literature, can be found in Kramer 1996.

4. For a comprehensive analysis of Austria's policies vis-à-vis the four Allies, see Stourzh 1998.

5. See the text of the so-called Moscow Memorandum in Verdross 1978: 26.

6. Policy declaration of Chancellor Julius Raab, October 26, 1955, quoted from Mayrzedt and Hummer 1976: 337–349.

7. This was the argument of Raab in the government's policy declaration on March 12, 1960. See Mayrzedt and Hummer 1976: 337–349.

8. Austrian foreign minister Kurt Waldheim on November 7, 1968, quoted from Mayrzedt and Hummer 1976: 145–146.

9. I take the expression "realist foreign policy" from Kramer 1988.

10. On Sweden, see Lindmark 1985, Luif 1987, and Mörth and Sundelius 1993; on Finland, Ruoho 1985; and on Switzerland, Gabriel 1989.

11. See, for example, the statement of the speaker of the Austrian parliament, Heinz Fischer (SPÖ), maintaining that "there is no neo-Nazi party in the Austrian Parliament, since the Austrian Constitution and Austrian laws would prohibit that; the same holds true for the government" (*Neue Zürcher Zeitung* 2000a).

12. These statements were published on the website of the Portuguese EU presidency, www.portugal.ue-2000.pt/uk.

13. According to statistics of Austrian tourism, between May and July 2000 the visits from the French and the Belgians declined by 17 percent and 14 percent respectively compared to the year before (*Die Presse,* August 26, 2000).

14. This was the declared goal of Belgian foreign minister Louis Michel. See Michel 2000.

15. *The Economist* ("The European Union: One Row Settled, Another Festers," June 24, 2000) was quite explicit:

> Each of the 14 claims to be snubbing Austria bilaterally, while doing business as usual within EU institutions. But this polite fiction has fooled no one, and the wonder is that Austria, humiliated at every turn, has put up with it for so long. At [the European Council in] Feira it showed its displeasure by withholding agreement to the tax package until the very end. Even then, it said only that it would not block the agreement. It could not promise changes to its own banking secrecy laws "at this stage." In return, it appeared to expect some concessions from the 14 very soon. Failing which, it is talking of holding an autumn referendum on relations with the Union that could well put the two sides on a collision course.

16. The European Court of Human Rights is an institution of the Council of Europe, not to be confused with the EU's Court of Justice.

17. The quote from Wildhaber's letter to the EU presidency is from *Neue Zürcher Zeitung,* June 30, 2000: 2.

18. See, in particular, Kitschelt and McGann 1997: 177; Mény and Surel 2000: 308; and Decker 2000: 121. On the opposite position (the FPÖ is an extreme-right party), see Bailer-Galanda and Neugebauer 1997: 51–52.

19. In an interview with the Italian daily *Corriere Della Sera,* German foreign minister Joschka Fischer said that "the political geography of a parliament

and the formation of a government are to a very high degree domestic politics questions; one must not interfere in these matters." Quoted from Ortner 2000.

20. In 1988 the Soviet reactions on the planned membership application were very critical. But comments by Soviet officials on the actual letter were rather restrained; see Luif 1995: 199.

7

Gambia: The Military and Foreign Policy

Abdoulaye Saine

This chapter analyzes Gambia's foreign policy from the 1994 coup d'état to 2001. The coup effectively brought to power Lieutenant Yahya Jammeh, who headed the Armed Forces Provisional Ruling Council (AFPRC) from July 1994 to September 1996, when the AFPRC was dissolved. Jammeh, having earlier resigned his commission, subsequently founded the Alliance for Patriotic Reorientation and Construction (APRC) party, contested and won the disputed presidential election of September 26, 1996.

Gambia is a former British colony of 4,000 square miles located in West Africa. It has a population of 1.2 million and is virtually surrounded by its much larger neighbor, Senegal. Since gaining independence in 1965, Gambia remained one of four democracies in Africa until the coup d'état of July 22, 1994. The coup, therefore, simultaneously ended the longest continuously surviving multiparty democracy in Africa and the reign of Sir Dawda Jawara, who at the time was the longest-serving head of state on the continent. With the AFPRC in place, the constitution was suspended, politicians and political parties were banned, and all semblance of the rule of law ended.

Combined international economic sanctions and domestic protests, however, led to a two-year timetable back to "civilian rule." This culminated in presidential and National Assembly elections in 1996 and 1997, respectively. The presidential election was neither free nor fair, because the electoral process was engineered from the very beginning to enable the incumbent, military-turned-civilian leader, retired Colonel Yahya Jammeh, to win. In July 2001, combined international and domestic pressure forced Jammeh once more to annul Decree 89 to enable previously banned political parties and politicians to contest the October 2001 presidential election. While voting on election day proceeded peacefully, violence and intimidation marred the three-month campaign and post-election periods. Jammeh won a disputed second term because of allegations of cross-border voting by Jammeh's ethnic Jola kin from Senegal's neighboring province of Casamance.

Thus, in spite of Gambia's return to "civilian rule" since 1996, the country continues to be run by a "civilianized" military cadre. Predictably, human rights protections have deteriorated. This has led to the deaths of many citizens, including the tragic killing of fourteen students shot while peacefully protesting government policy in April 2000. The National Intelligence Agency (NIA), the repressive arm of the state, engages in torture of dissidents and opposition leaders. Accordingly, the judiciary and other branches of government are not generally regarded as independent and serve the primary purpose of enforcing draconian laws and military decrees. Also, the press remains severely constrained, as journalists are often subjected to brutal beatings and torture. The "civilianized" military leadership has effectively excluded the role of civil society and other governmental institutions in the foreign policy decisionmaking process. While APRC foreign policy appeared chaotic in the aftermath of the 1994 coup d'état, it took on a form that was both anti-Western and assertive in its support of "rogue" states like Libya and Iraq in subsequent years. This represented a major departure from Gambia's historically strong ties with and goodwill toward the West. What remains constant, however, is the preponderant role of the president in foreign policy decisions.

The regime prides itself on the numerous schools, hospitals, clinics, and roads it has constructed since 1994. The regime also refurbished the national airport and government-owned radio station, in addition to building the country's first university and television station. This is a remarkable achievement in which many Gambians take pride. On this score, the regime performed better than the civilian regime it replaced. Notwithstanding these improvements, the economy remains sluggish, in part because of a cessation of economic aid from the country's main European donors on whom Gambia depends. The major consequence has been a deepening poverty for the bulk of Gambia's people. It is against this backdrop of anti-Western rhetoric by the regime, repression, growing political tension between the regime and opposition actors, weak institutions and civil society, and deepening economic malfeasance that Gambia's foreign policy from 1994 to 2001 must be situated and analyzed.

This chapter is concerned with Gambia's foreign policy since the 1994 coup d'état. I seek to answer three central questions: (1) What external policies did the AFPRC adopt to achieve its objectives? (2)

What effects did the foreign policies of the AFPRC and the ruling APRC government have on the national economy and Gambians? (3) Is there continuity or change in Gambia's foreign policy goals and orientation under Jammeh? In answering these questions, the reinforcing effects of the international, state, and individual levels of analyses are used as analytical tools to explain Gambia's foreign policy.

Foreign Policy History

An appraisal of the content and conduct of Gambia's foreign relations since the coup of 1994 must take into account what transpired during the Jawara years (1965–1994). It is generally agreed that the search for outside resources to maintain domestic power structures was central to the foreign policies of the great majority of African states (Clapham 1996: 63). The way in which this search was conducted, however, varied appreciably according to the nature of the government concerned and the domestic and external threats it faced. The literature on Gambia's foreign policy indicates convincingly that at independence in 1965, and until the coup in 1994, it was driven by two overarching objectives. The first was the continuing desire to maintain territorial sovereignty in the face of a perceived threat of assimilation by neighboring Senegal (Wiseman 1996: 924). The second had to do with attracting external economic resources to support the development agenda of the People's Progressive Party (PPP), which in turn helped to enrich Gambia's political and bureaucratic class. In so doing, the PPP government under Jawara succeeded in attracting considerable economic and political support from the outside, principally because of his pro-Western, anticommunist, and strong human rights record. Also, Gambia's cordial relations with oil-rich Arab and Gulf states proved financially rewarding in Jawara's bid to diversify Gambia's funding sources in order to reduce the country's dependence on the UK.

Gambia's relations with Senegal have occupied center stage since independence in 1965. It is a relationship often characterized by cycles of relative calm and turbulence. Cooperation was evident in the now defunct Senegambia Confederation (Hughes 1992; Senghore 1982), but also in border closures to stem Gambia's reexport trade into Senegal and neighboring states. In the immediate aftermath of the July 1981 aborted coup (Hughes 1991: 98), led by Kukoi Samba Sanyang, Gambia agreed to join Senegal in a loose confederation, which Senegal hoped would lead ultimately to full political union. The confederation was, however, marred from the outset by Gambian fears of being disadvantaged and the confederation's "shotgun-wedding" character (Hughes 1991: 105). The confederation ended in 1989, in particular over the issue of a rotating presidency, which Jawara would have liked, but which Abdou Diouf of Senegal opposed. Predictably, with the 1994 coup against Jawara, Senegal refused to intervene but offered the former president and his entourage political asylum immediately. In fact, poor relations with Senegal after 1989 and, in particular, Senegal's border closure contributed to both the causes and the success of the coup. The immediate causes of the coup, however, lay more concretely in the social, political, class, and generational problems that built up in the long years of PPP rule and within the army as well (Saine 1996: 102–103).

Gambia's political history under Jawara resembles a plateau occasionally marred by volcanic eruptions. The general image, as projected perhaps too often to the world outside, was of a ministate adept at survival, able in spite of underdevelopment to run an open society with a multiparty democracy and encapsulating both the problems and the opportunities of small states (*West Africa* 1995a: 201–211). In this picture the putsch in 1981, and for that matter the coup of 1994, were portrayed as aberrations. On the economic front, despite years of claimed economic success, Gambia under Jawara continued to have one of the lowest living standards on the continent and ranked 166th in the world out of 173 countries according to the UN Development Programme (UNDP) Human Development Index. In spite of very generous financial assistance after the 1981 attempted coup (Cooke and Hughes 1997; *West Africa* 1995b: 11, 25), approximately 63 percent of Gambia's population still lives under the poverty line (Economist Intelligence Unit 1998a: 29). Thus Gambia's paradox under Jawara lay in the fact that here was a ministate whose independence was in question and in spite of the odds managed to build a relatively open economy and a functioning democracy, yet achieved a very low level of development (Economist Intelligence Unit 1998a: 29). Clearly, while part of the problem lay in elite corruption and enrichment, the overriding cause more generally was the poor performance of public institutions. Poor factor endowments compounded human shortcomings, which in addition to a tiny size, limited natural resources, and recurrent droughts in the 1970s, exacerbated existing problems.

Regionally, Jawara maintained good relations with neighboring states and played the elder statesman, seeking to resolve the Liberia conflict. At the continental level, Gambia under Jawara supported the Organization of African Unity (OAU) and its efforts to end racism and apartheid in South Africa. What at first started out as good relations with Libya quickly deteriorated in the early 1980s because of Muammar

Qaddafi's alleged support of Kukoi Samba Sanyang, who led the unsuccessful coup against Jawara in 1981. By the time he was overthrown, Jawara had received international acclaim for his commitment to human rights, democracy, and the rule of law, especially within the Commonwealth. Consequently, the condemnation and the subsequent sanctions imposed by the Commonwealth and Western institutions on the AFPRC following his ouster were to have a chilling effect on the coup and Gambia's economy. Therefore, Gambia's foreign policy during the First Republic was driven by the need to protect national sovereignty and the procurement of external financial support.

The AFPRC's External Policy Pronouncements, 1994–1996

The primary concern of the AFPRC following the coup was the survival of the regime itself in light of two alleged attempts to overthrow it, in November 1994 and January 1995. Three violent incidents against the Jammeh regime at army camps, in Farafenni, November 1995; Kartong, July 1997; and Bakau, January 2000, are cases in point (Hughes 2000: 43). Second was the need to ensure Gambia's economic survival in the face of mounting Western and, in particular, Commonwealth displeasure and threats of economic sanctions. These threats were not taken lightly by the AFPRC. The fact that 80 percent of Gambia's national development budget was at the time funded by the European Union (EU), Japan, the United Kingdom, and international financial institutions (Economist Intelligence Unit 1998a: 29) meant that the severing of aid would have disastrous economic and social consequences. Until 1972, Britain provided the bulk of foreign financial assistance to Gambia and by 1981, EU aid to Gambia rose from U.S.$500,000 in 1976 to U.S.$13 million, making it the largest multilateral donor in that period. Although the volume of aid declined in subsequent years, the EU maintained its lead as Gambia's principal multilateral donor until 1986 (Cooke and Hughes 1997: 107; *West Africa* 1995b: 11–27). In that year, the International Development Agency, a World Bank affiliate, took the leading position. In 1987–1990, EU assistance to Gambia amounted to some U.S.$30 million. A large part of this came in the form of balance of payments assistance.

Furthermore, U.S. withdrawal of $10 million in aid, coupled with Japan's and the UNDP's freezing of all development aid, meant that Gambia's external reserves, scant as they were, would become a major source for financing the balance of payments deficit. A travel advisement by the British foreign office on November 23, 1994, four months after the coup, that "Banjul is calm but the political situation in The Gambia remains uncertain and could deteriorate quickly" almost destroyed the tourist industry (*West Africa* 1995a: 386–387). This travel advisory was quickly followed by similar Swedish and Danish announcements cautioning potential tourists not to visit Gambia because of political instability. Since the mid-1970s, tourism, second only to groundnuts, had become a major source of foreign exchange and constituted 12 percent of the gross domestic product (GDP). It employed approximately 10,000 workers, many of whom were heads of households supporting on average ten individuals (*West Africa* 1995a: 337).

Combined Western sanctions came into effect following the alleged coup attempt on November 11, 1994, in which as many as thirty soldiers were said to have been summarily executed (Yeebo 1995: 82–88; Saine 1996: 106; Economist Intelligence Unit 1995b: 20, 1994b: 22). Also, the dismissal of Bakary Dabo, the minister of finance, for his alleged involvement in the foiled coup triggered a swift and severe Western reaction (Economist Intelligence Unit 1994b: 16–20). Dabo, who was at one time Jawara's minister of finance, also held the same portfolio in the new regime. He subsequently fled the country out of fear for his life. The EU froze all balance of payments support, and suspended all but humanitarian aid by the United States and Japan, pending the announcement of a program to return the country to democratic rule. With sanctions in place, government coffers were quickly being depleted, and the average Gambian's standard of living fell even lower. The failed coup combined with Western sanctions to create an atmosphere of growing AFPRC insecurity.

Suspended bilateral aid and balance of payments assistance provoked two main reactions. The first was a defensive reaction from the AFPRC itself, that "with or without aid, The Gambia would maintain an independent state, run by Gambians in the interest of Gambians" (*West Africa* 1995a: 11). The second came generally from government officials and the public at large, who felt that the sanctions were unjustifiable. All, however, were concerned with Gambia's economic future in the face of these sanctions. The sanctions also affected projects outlined in the transition-period development programs. Indirectly, they led to lower tax revenue for the AFPRC, due in part to dislocation of trade caused by foreign currency shortage. Jammeh criticized the International Monetary Fund (IMF) and the World Bank for the negative effects structural adjustment had on Gambia's poor and vowed that the burden of such policies would be borne by the rich as well. He also rejected forthwith the linkage between Commonwealth support and IMF and World Bank aid resumption to Jawara's return to Gambia. He castigated Jawara for presiding over a corrupt democracy and promised to recover money embezzled by officials of the previous regime. In so doing, the AFPRC created Commissions of Inquiry, which ultimately uncovered graft at multiple levels of government. These ranged from ghost workers, whose salaries went to top government officials, to cases of theft in the Gambia Cooperative Union (GCU).

Perhaps the earliest and most significant demonstration of goodwill toward the AFPRC came from Libya. Following the withdrawal of Western bilateral aid in November 1994, Libya stepped into the void with a U.S.$15 million grant (Wiseman 1996: 932). In November 1994, full diplomatic relations with Libya were restored after fifteen years of hostile relations between Jawara and Qaddafi. Chinese support and goodwill in the form of a U.S.$23 million grant for agriculture followed. Chinese assistance was to cease immediately, however, following the AFPRC's resumption of diplomatic relations with Taiwan on July 13, 1995, after a twenty-one-year break (Economist Intelligence Unit 1995b: 23). The Jawara government had earlier in 1968 established diplomatic relations with Taiwan, but broke them off in 1974 in favor of China. Outraged by the APRC policy change, China severed relations with Gambia on July 25, 1995. Since then, Taiwan has been a staunch supporter of the AFPRC and the subsequent APRC government, with an initial loan of U.S.$35 million (Economist Intelligence Unit 1996a: 59). Today, Taiwanese aid has totaled more than U.S.$100 million (Economist Intelligence Unit 1995b: 22; *West Africa* 1995b: 217). Clearly, because of ongoing difficulties with the mainland, Taiwan has tried to make friends and win support for its position internationally.

The AFPRC's efforts to make friends and hence stem international isolation also led to the dispatching of several government delegations to Nigeria and Sierra Leone, and to Jammeh making his first trip to Senegal on September 22, 1994, to meet with President Diouf (Hughes 1991: 98). Diouf promised support for the new regime, aware of Jammeh's potential role in the civil war in Senegal's southern province of Casamance. Senegal's border closure before the coups, together with the impact of Western sanctions, was already endangering Gambia's economy (*West Africa* 1995b: 30).

At this point Nigeria became Gambia's benefactor and proved critical to its economic survival. Yet relations between the countries were ambivalent, as Jammeh had often been critical of the Nigerian military training mission to Gambia. In fact, resentment by Gambian junior officers against Nigerian senior officers by the end of Jawara's rule was a major cause of the coup (Saine 1996: 105). This lingering resentment in turn pushed Jammeh to cultivate more enduring ties with President Jerry

Rawlings of Ghana (Hughes 2000: 51; Yeebo 1995: 55–58). Surrounded by Senegal and other French-speaking countries, Gambia under Jawara maintained warm and cordial relations with its larger and more populous protector, and thus supported Nigeria's military role in Liberia by way of Gambian troops. The latter was to have a contributory effect, albeit indirectly, to the ouster of Jawara in 1994. With the demise of the Senegambian Confederation in 1989, Gambia sought and received a military training mission to replace the British force. Following the coup in 1994, however, Jammeh became a protégé and ally of the late Nigerian president General Sani Abacha. Both regimes were considered "outcasts" because of their poor human rights record. At the Commonwealth's thirtieth heads of government meeting in New Zealand in November 1995, Jammeh stood by Nigeria when the latter was under fire for the execution of Ken Saro-Wiwa and six human rights activists of the Ogone. In fact, recent court disclosures in Britain reveal that Abacha gave Jammeh a free tranche of 20,000 tons of Nigerian oil in return for his support at the New Zealand Commonwealth summit. The money, of course, ended up in a Swiss bank account, rather than the Central Bank of Gambia (Economist Intelligence Unit 1996b: 22). It was used to finance Jammeh's private economic and political activities. In fact, Jammeh cut short a regional tour to Mauritania, Cape Verde, and Guinea on learning of Abacha's death in June 1998. Jammeh maintained cordial relations with Nigeria's military president and successor to the late Abacha, General Abdusalami Abubakar, who visited Gambia in early 1999. With Nigeria's newly elected civilian government now in power, it is likely that such relations with President Olusegun Obasanjo will continue for geopolitical reasons. Since coming to power in early June 1999, however, Obasanjo has begun a purge of many senior military officers in Nigeria's army.

The severe reduction and in some cases freezing of aid compelled the Jammeh regime to seek alternative sources of development funding to keep the economy afloat. In January 1995, Jammeh held talks with President Joao Bernardo Vieira of Guinea-Bissau and held similar meetings with Captain Valentine Strasser of Sierra Leone and President Rawlings of Ghana. A visit to Mauritania in the summer of 1995 and various delegations to Egypt and Nigeria and promises of financial support and cooperation eased, at least temporarily, AFPRC isolation. At the same time, however, Commonwealth, IMF, and World Bank pressure to hand power over to a civilian government was mounting and the sanctions were having a detrimental effect on business activity.

By the end of October 1994, three months after the coup, Jammeh announced at a rally in Banjul that the AFPRC would return the country to civilian rule in December 1998 after free presidential elections. This meant that the AFPRC would be in office for nearly four and a half years. The length of the transition was condemned both nationally and internationally. Chief Emeka Anyaoku, the Commonwealth secretary-general at the time, issued a statement in London rejecting the four-year delay as "unacceptable" and called for elections within three to six months. Aware of mounting domestic and international pressure against the four-year timetable and responding to the recommendation of the National Consultative Commission (NCC), the AFPRC agreed to a two-year timetable to culminate in presidential elections in June 1996. The AFPRC, however, rejected the NCC's proposal for an interim civilian government to be headed by Wally Ndow, a UN official, or Lamin Sanneh, a Yale University professor of religion (Saine 1998: 165).

Following the two-year term limit announcement, AFPRC foreign relations assumed a more assertive stance with Jammeh visiting Egypt in June 1995, where he met President Mubarak and PLO leader Yasser Arafat. At the thirty-first OAU heads of state meeting in Addis Ababa, Jammeh pledged to pay, in full, Gambia's overdue contributions to the organization. This earned him needed recognition. But perhaps the regime scored its greatest foreign policy success when in July 1995 it hosted President Rawlings of Ghana as the guest of honor during the first anniversary of the coup. In fact, the ties between Rawlings and Jammeh were to prove enduring and substantive (Saine 2000: 199). Gambia's transition program, which culminated in the election of Chairman Jammeh as Gambia's second president in September 1996, closely replicated Ghana's in 1992. Chairman Rawlings's delayed lift of the ban on political activity, the guessing game inspired by his late announcement of his candidature for the presidency, and his liberal use of state resources, including the media, reemerged four years later in Gambia. Only in the case of Gambia, Chairman Jammeh banned all the major precoup parties and politicians, and allowed the newly created opposition parties barely three weeks to contest the presidential elections (Saine 1998: 162). Also, the official opening of the mosque at the State House, in the summer of 1995, by the imam of Mecca, had an important symbolic effect on a predominantly Muslim country, in addition to cultivating support and goodwill with the oil-rich Arab and Gulf states. Jammeh's ostentatious adoption of a Muslim public image had as much to do with building up domestic and external support as it did with personal belief. His insistence to Muslim leaders in Gambia that they form a Supreme Islamic Council, in particular, was motivated primarily by his desire to "attract a lot of foreign assistance, including funds for development projects as well as the construction of mosques around the country" (Mendy 1998: 1).

In time, the AFPRC cultivated and maintained cordial relations with these states and in August 1996 Iran pledged to improve relations with Gambia and to cooperate in the agriculture and fishing sectors (Economist Intelligence Unit 1996b: 25). By the time the AFPRC celebrated its second year in office in July 1996, it had succeeded in spite of the sanctions to make friends and earn the financial support it needed to undertake its development projects. A U.S.$20 million loan from the African Development Bank to refurbish Banjul's international airport is a case in point. This was indicative of the slow but growing acceptance of the regime in some circles, in part because of its putative objective of improving living conditions for the average Gambian. A visit by President Abdou Diouf of Senegal earlier in January was also a sign of Senegal's approval of the AFPRC. The resumption of some financial aid from the Commonwealth, in preparation for the impending presidential elections now slated for September 1996, suggested some shelter from the storm. In fact, during his address at the second-anniversary celebration of the coup, two months before the elections, Jammeh singled out Taiwan, Egypt, Libya, Nigeria, Sierra Leone, the Philippines, Malaysia, and Indonesia as "true friends." He also spoke warmly of the improved relations with Senegal (Economist Intelligence Unit 1996b: 25).

In retrospect, it seems that the AFPRC succeeded in maintaining the economy, albeit marginally, with funds made available by friends abroad. In fact, by March 1996, Gambia's external reserves stood at U.S.$140 million compared with U.S.$90 million at the end of June 1995 (Economist Intelligence Unit 1996b: 26). The generally held belief that the economy would ultimately collapse in the face of reduced development aid, balance of payments support, and reduced revenue because of the British travel advisory was not realized (*West Africa* 1995a: 1963). While all these were inevitably affected, Gambia's macroeconomic framework under the supervision of the Central Bank and the Ministry of Finance averted major economic dislocation. That the AFPRC initiated several development projects, including two high schools, a hospital in Farafenni, and salary increases, was indeed remarkable given the adverse international environment.

The consequences of donor sanctions were far-reaching, nonetheless. They undermined business confidence and activity, created mass unemployment in tourism, and raised the price of essential commodities. Personal income, not to mention government and corporate revenue, plummeted. It is estimated that the sanctions resulted in a U.S.$100 million loss in aid and a U.S.$10 million loss in direct foreign investment by the end of 1995 (Economist Intelligence Unit 1995b: 19). While the sanctions targeted the AFPRC, in hindsight they hurt the average Gambian economically.

The APRC and Gambia's Foreign Policy, 1997–2001

Gambia's transition to "civilian" rule culminated in the election of retired Colonel Yahya Jammeh as president of the Second Republic on September 26, 1996, and the holding of National Assembly elections on January 2, 1997 (Saine 1998: 157; *West Africa* 1996a: 1540). Jammeh resigned his commission shortly before the presidential election, formed the APRC party, and manipulated the rules to favor him after banning his major political opponents (Saine 2000: 192). Jammeh doctored the constitution by eliminating the age and term limit clauses, required high deposits of candidates, and then held snap elections. Predictably, the Commonwealth condemned both the results and the process, in which all the major contestants were excluded from participation. Jammeh responded "that the West wanted democracy to be restored in The Gambia. Now they have it and as an added bonus an olive branch as a sign of goodwill." He further argued that there was no reason to "ostracize the regime and no justification for maintaining the economic sanctions on the country" (*West Africa* 1996b: 1640). In early November 1996, Libya expressed strong support for the new government and urged Gambians to "live in dignity and freedom under its youthful revolution" (*West Africa* 1996b: 1682). Thereafter, Jammeh paid a four-day visit to Libya and in a communiqué called on OAU member states to work together and called for the end "to unjust sanctions imposed on the Libyan people" (*West Africa* 1996c: 1908; Economist Intelligence Unit 1997: 27). On January 22, 1997, Taiwan announced a U.S.$411,500 grant to enable the Jammeh government to pay the salaries of Cuban, Nigerian, and Egyptian doctors and healthcare workers (Economist Intelligence Unit 1997: 28). Aware of the fact that his regime was not looked upon favorably by its main aid donors and by the Commonwealth in particular, Jammeh determined to cultivate productive alliances and support elsewhere. He made several trips to the Middle East and performed the pilgrimage to Mecca in 1997. Thus, with Jammeh in power and wielding control over the National Assembly, the APRC's diplomatic flurry sought to consolidate preelection friendships and the creation of new ones. In fact, Jammeh's wedding to a Moroccan in early 1999 further strengthened Gambia's relations with Morocco.

The meeting in Gambia on September 11, 1997, of the nine member countries of the Permanent Interstate Committee on Drought Control in the Sahel (CILSS) accorded the new regime much needed recognition and prestige regionally. Serving as the CILSS chairman gave Jammeh a forum to showcase his development programs, especially the newly refurbished airport and new television station, not to mention the triumphal July 22 Arch. The APRC gained more international recognition when Gambia became a nonpermanent member of the UN Security Council on January 2, 1998, for a two-year term. Jammeh has used his newly found status to support friends like Taiwan, Libya, and Iraq. On May 14, 1998, Iraq's foreign minister visited Gambia to seek help in lifting UN-imposed sanctions. Similarly, Jammeh has called for the end of UN-imposed sanctions against Libya at the OAU and the UN respectively. It appears that Jammeh's international image is improving with Gambia's presence in the Security Council. In February 1998, Jammeh paid visits to France and Italy, chaired the UN Security Council in March, and held talks with leaders in Saudi Arabia, Iraq, and Nigeria in April and May.

Regionally, Jammeh's government successfully mediated the conflict in Guinea-Bissau. Gambia's foreign minister, Lamin Sedat Jobe, tirelessly shuttled between Banjul and Bissau to negotiate a cease-fire between the warring military factions. Jammeh himself was instrumental in the cease-fire agreements that were signed in Abuja, Nigeria, in early 1999. This was a major accomplishment for the regime and a sign of successful diplomacy. The APRC has also offered its good offices in the civil war between Senegal's government and the rebels of the Movement for a Democratic Casamance (MFDC). Clearly, this has enhanced Jammeh's sense of confidence, even if Senegal's current president, Abdoulaye Wade, has excluded Jammeh from continuing his once active role in resolving the conflict. Thus, Jammeh, like Jawara before him, has emerged as a peace broker in part to ward off these conflicts from destabilizing his regime. Already, Gambia is home to over 9,000 refugees from Senegal's neighboring province of Casamance, Guinea-Bissau, and Sierra-Leone (Economist Intelligence Unit 1998a: 31). The need to attract foreign resources for his own and AFPRC survival, support for the regime's development agenda at home, and to maintain Gambia's territorial integrity are the driving forces for Jammeh's numerous missions abroad.

Gambia's foreign policy successes are also attributable to the work of career diplomats, notwithstanding the frequent changes at the foreign minister level. Since the coup, Bolong Sonko, Baboucarr Blaise Jagne, Omar Njie, and Lamin Sedat Jobe have held this position. The reasons for such a rapid turnover of foreign ministers are unclear. It appears, however, that Jammeh terminates these ministers and others when they no longer serve his political ends. He has also been known to use his ministers as scapegoats when problems arise for which he has no solutions, as in the ongoing crisis in the purchase of groundnuts. Musa Mbenga (Economist Intelligence Unit 1998b: 23–24) and Fasennay Dumbuya were both terminated as ministers of agriculture, allegedly for failing to increase food production and not having the funds to purchase a bumper groundnut harvest in 1999, respectively. These officials had little or no control over a deteriorating economy, and even less control over declining aid flows. Western-imposed economic sanctions after the coup were largely responsible for these economic difficulties. Also, AFPRC financial mismanagement and overspending on "feel-good" development projects, like the July 22 Arch, also contributed to the state's inability to purchase groundnuts or increase food production.

Together, however, these foreign ministers have given leadership, coherence, and direction to Gambia's foreign relations. The appointment of seasoned diplomats like Njogu Bah, who served as ambassador to France, is indicative of France's growing importance and source of support for Gambia (Economist Intelligence Unit 1998c: 26–29). Bah, who studied in Senegal and France respectively, first served as ambassador to Senegal and he was also accredited to several European countries. Former minister Sonko has since joined the major opposition party, the United Democratic Party (UDP). As in most countries, ambassadorial appointments under Jammeh have often been political. The accreditation of Crispin Grey-Johnson as ambassador to Washington was greeted with enthusiasm. Though not a career diplomat, Johnson, by most accounts, performed well as ambassador, though he has since been recalled to Gambia with the official reason that his two-year term was later posted to Sierra Leone (Ceesay 1998: 3).

It seems likely that Gambia's increasingly assertive foreign policy may begin to restore the goodwill of its main donors and the Commonwealth and reverse what once was an antagonistic relationship. After almost a four-year absence, the World Bank resumed lending to Gambia with an initial loan of U.S.$18 million in April 1998. The IMF at the end of June 1998 also approved a three-year loan to the regime under an enhanced structural adjustment facility (ESAF) of U.S.$27 million. The UNDP and the United States have also resumed some aid. The EU as well has promised U.S.$100 million over a three-year period. The African Development Bank made an additional U.S.$13 million loan in 1998 to complement the U.S.$14 million in aid given in 1997 (Economist Intelligence Unit 1998b: 23). The money is to be used toward health services and population and poverty reduction measures (Economist Intelligence Unit 1998d: 23). While the UK, Sweden, and Denmark have reversed their travel advisory to tourists and resumed some aid, it has yet to reach precoup levels.

Jammeh's commitment to democracy and human rights will be the basis upon which Western aid and support will continue. Yet, with tourist bookings approximating precoup levels, the economy could receive a needed boost. These loans and added revenue could give the regime the needed stamp of approval to attract more loans and support. Also, the resumption of aid to almost precoup levels could give the regime a new lease on life. Jammeh's conciliatory gesture to the diplomatic community in Gambia in January 1998 seeks to forge a "new era of partnership and cooperation" with its development partners and the World Bank in particular. What is worrisome, however, is Gambia's growing external debt of over U.S.$482 million. In 1997 alone Gambia's external debt rose to U.S.$452 million, up from U.S.$423 million the year before (Economist Intelligence Unit 1998d: 30). With more than three-quarters of the country's total external debt owed to multilateral institutions, Gambia has benefited from debt cancellation schemes.

"Jubilee 2000," a debt cancellation scheme initiated by the rich for the poorest countries of the world, has also meant added debt relief for Gambia. In spite of the resumption of some aid and returning tourists, however, the economy remains vulnerable to external shocks. The APRC's growing repression of opposition leaders, parties, and the press could deteriorate into instability with potential spillover into the army and civil society. It seems the donor community and the Commonwealth will keep a watchful eye over Jammeh's commitment to principles of good governance and human rights. Jammeh's victory in the 2001 presidential elections has given him more legitimacy in the eyes of the international community and those at home. This bodes well for added support from the West, especially in light of his national reconciliation overtures to the opposition and the country at large.

Jammeh's growing acceptance by the international community may realign Gambia's foreign policy with that of the precoup years of Jawara. This appears unlikely in the immediate future, however, given the regime's expulsion on January 2002 of Marc Andre, the EU chargé d'affaires in Banjul. Yet the gradual strengthening of civil society and the reintroduction of democratic norms could enhance the role of political parties and their leaders, the media, religious leaders, and other actors to impact not only the conduct but also the content and decision-making process of Gambia's foreign policy. If this were to occur, the EU could once more act kindly toward Jammeh and Gambia.

Analysis

The Individual

Gambia is a small state that fits the conventional wisdom to the extent that the executive branch, especially the leader, dominates foreign policy. This has been true under both Jawara and Jammeh, who both put their personal imprint on Gambian foreign policy behavior. Jammeh has succeeded in increasing international acceptance of him personally and of Gambia, owing in large part to his tenacity and skill in international affairs. A second important component of the individual level's explanatory impact in Gambia concerns its effective diplomatic corps. In this area Gambia is an exception to the rule, as most small, less developed states suffer from underfunded and little-experienced diplomats. But Gambia's seasoned diplomats have been especially important in forging regional alliances that aid the APRC's ties within Africa.

Individual-level factors are potent in explaining Gambian foreign policy. The executive and his diplomatic corps personally design all foreign policies, unencumbered as they are by most domestic political groups. And in the face of limited diplomatic representation overseas, the role of the president in defining the content and conduct of foreign policy is further enhanced and magnified. Yet the role of seasoned diplomats in the Ministry of External Affairs cannot be underestimated, as they have provided, because of their training and experience, direction and cohesion to the country's foreign relations. This notwithstanding, the role of the president is without doubt more prominent.

The State

Much of Gambian foreign policy is driven by its great domestic needs. These include territorial sovereignty, especially but not limited to the years under Jawara. Gambia's unique geographical position, surrounded by Senegal, means that it has to worry about its territorial integrity more than many other African states, many of whom are also troubled by postcolonial border concerns. Equally crucial has been to attract economic aid and other financial resources aimed at improving Gambians' way of life. As a poor country, and especially one that has been ostracized globally, Gambia has prioritized economic survival as a foreign policy goal. Many of its alliances are created specifically to promote economic aid. This was true under Jawara, whose pro-Western, anticommunist stance helped to earn millions in support of Gambia. It has also been true under Jammeh. Perhaps even more pressing is the need to consolidate the rule of shaky regimes. As much as Jawara employed foreign aid for the good of the country, he also used it to prop up the PPP. Jammeh's recognition of Taiwan, a policy that contradicts the vast majority of the world's attitude toward the two Chinas, instantly won millions for Gambian development and for Jammeh's political standing. Especially because of questionable democratic practices, Jammeh has used foreign policy as a tool toward regime legitimacy, very much a state-level concern.

Because of the government's suppression of the press, civil society, and political parties, the type of pluralist democracy operating in the West has not taken hold in Gambia. This absence of domestic political actors contributes to the executive-dominated foreign policy decision-making process described above. In other words, it is precisely because of a state-level feature—a flawed democracy—that Gambia's foreign policy is so personalistic and controlled from the top.

The System

The system level accounts for much of the foreign policy agenda and content exhibited by Gambia during the period under study. In contrast to those of many less developed states, Gambia's regime legitimacy problems were driven by external forces, rather than emerging from internal challenges to authority. Military regimes and questionable democratic practices led to Gambia's being isolated by key international actors, such as the Commonwealth. To manage this problem, Gambia turned to new trading and diplomatic partners, not only for commerce, but also for legitimacy that could undercut the effects of diplomatic isolation. The second driving theme of Gambian foreign policy—the search for economic aid and development—also emerges from a system-level factor: Gambia's colonial history and its limited resources when compared with its neighbors.

System-level features also gave Gambia space within which to display its foreign policy activity and skill. Regional armed conflict in Africa created an opportunity for Gambia to shine diplomatically and to gain regional support. Had Gambia's neighbors been more democratic and peaceful, the regional and global spotlight on Gambian lack of democracy would have been all the more intense. Instead, regional conflict deflected that attention and provided Gambia with a chance to highlight its own relatively pacific internal system and its regional diplomatic offices.

Like the domestic system, the international system is a key part of the structure within which Gambian executives create and implement foreign policy. The individual level best explains specific choices, as well as foreign policy style. But the system and state levels generate the foreign policy problems, needs, and menu of choices from which those executives choose.

Conclusion

Gambia's foreign policy since the coup d'état of 1994 has been remarkably innovative and effective in attracting needed funds from alternative sources abroad to support domestic programs. In this regard, AFPRC/APRC foreign policies are a continuation of Jawara's foreign policy and strategy. Jammeh and his ministers wasted little time in cultivating new friendships and consolidating old alliances outside the Western sphere of influence. Thus, following the coup, AFPRC policy had the dual objectives of making friends and securing alternative sources of financial assistance. In so doing, AFPRC policy succeeded partly in circumventing growing international isolation and the negative impact of Western-imposed economic sanctions. Under the APRC, Gambia's foreign policy also has a dual strategy of partly appeasing the West and lending institutions in order to attract needed funds, and to lend support for so-called rogue states like Libya and Iraq. Gambia's nonpermanent membership in the UN Security Council, however, broadened the scope and conduct of its increasingly assertive foreign policy. This engendered a growing sense of confidence for President Jammeh, leading him to play an important role in conflict mediation and resolution, regionally and internationally.

Gambia's growing assertive foreign policy has also begun a gradual reversal of Western-imposed economic sanctions and its international isolation. The combined roles of the president as peace broker and fundraiser underscore the three central objectives that have driven Gambia's foreign policy historically: territorial independence, procurement of external financial resources for internal development, and more important, regime/leadership survival and legitimization. In this regard, Gambia's foreign relations have remained remarkably consistent since independence. This is what links Jammeh to Jawara and explains to some extent why both men use foreign travel in part to fulfill these objectives. The fates of geopolitics and limited resource endowments have conspired to keep it this way. Omar Touray (1994: 334–334) and Fatma Denton (1998: 291) in particular have arrived at a similar conclusion. Future presidents are not likely to deviate significantly from this path.

Perhaps this realization, coupled with Jammeh's slow, albeit growing acceptance in the international community, has led him to temper his once defiant and defensive posture toward the Commonwealth and multilateral institutions. He has, as a result, become more conciliatory, like Jawara before him, in order to gain Western support and financial assistance, with occasional criticism of the West. This indicates a shift from a defensive to an assertive foreign policy. However, this changed strategy has not led to full resumption of aid. Jammeh therefore finds himself in a difficult mediator role as he seeks to balance Western capitalist interests, and adverse effects of structural adjustment, on the one hand, and the welfare of a poor and growing population, on the other.

This systemic tension, perhaps conflict, is likely to sow the seeds of discontent and instability in the army and civil society. While Gambia's foreign policy under the AFPRC and APRC succeeded in attracting external financial assistance, the question remains whether this would translate into tangible welfare improvements and benefits for Gambians. Foreign policy under Jawara, successful as it was, only marginally improved the lives of Gambia's poor, and notwithstanding APRC projects and the good intentions of the donor and lending community, the logic of IMF and World Bank policies often fails to ameliorate or reduce poverty levels. David Cooke and Arnold Hughes (1997: 93), however, provide a more positive evaluation of IMF/World Bank activity in Gambia.

Jammeh's commitment to human rights and democratic principles will be the basis upon which Western aid and support will be continued. The appeal by Jammeh to traditional African principles and practices of democracy as possible alternatives to a more inclusive and participatory type of democracy is not likely to bring aid to precoup levels. Insistence by Jammeh on maintaining the status quo may not in the end elicit desirable outcomes. Consequently, an enabling political and economic environment that has at its root individual freedoms and opportunity for self-improvement, especially for women and the rural poor, must accompany the drive to political maturity. Despite some obvious flaws, "Vision 20/20" is a good start in this direction (Saine 1997: 97). These strategies, combined, could go a long way in releasing and further developing both the creative and entrepreneurial qualities of Gambians. However, when stifled they deepen underdevelopment and mediocrity and no amount of external funding or successful foreign policy per se can begin to reverse this process.

Gambia and Gambians stand to gain from globalization if it is far-reaching and if comprehensive economic and political reforms are undertaken. Global economic trends, of which increased globalization and integration are manifestations, do not necessarily portend disadvantages for relatively resource-strapped small state economies. By mobilizing local resources, defining strategic needs and interests with strategies to achieve them, countries like Gambia could carve a niche in the global economy. The alternative, however, could spell further misery, poverty, conflict, and increased marginalization for this once improbable African ministate.

8

Jordan: The Politics of Alliance and Foreign Policy

Curtis R. Ryan

In the often tumultuous politics of the Middle East, the Hashimite Kingdom of Jordan has long been seen as a survivor against great odds, from repeated wars to internal unrest. Under King Hussein (1953–1999) and King Abdullah II (since 1999), Jordan has steered a cautious and ultimately successful course in international relations, largely by relying on a conservative foreign policy and the support of international allies. This chapter examines Jordan's foreign policy decisionmaking and its alliance politics in an attempt to explain the dramatic shift in Jordanian relations from alliance with Iraq to peace and full alignment (if not formal alliance) with Israel. Linked to this realignment are Jordan's ever warmer relations with the United States, Turkey, and even the North Atlantic Treaty Organization (NATO). This chapter examines the sources of Jordanian foreign policy in an effort to move beyond explanatory models that see Jordanian foreign policy as either a pawn of the great powers or simply the whim of a king.

Theoretical Approaches to Jordan's Alliances and Foreign Policy

The empirical analysis in this chapter explains Jordanian policy at the individual, domestic, and system levels.[1] Taking all these factors into consideration moves us beyond the neorealist approaches to alliances that predominate in international relations theory. These traditional perspectives tend to emphasize external security issues as of paramount importance to states, resulting in a strategy in which states use alliances to balance against external threats (Waltz 1979; Walt 1987).

But in the Arab state system, and indeed throughout much of the postcolonial world, security may be more multifaceted than it is for developed postindustrial states in the West (Korany, Brynen, and Noble 1993). This is because threats in many developing countries are as likely to come from within as they are from without. And "security" itself tends to be seen as a far more broad-based concept than that utilized in many Western theories of alliances and alignments (Azar and Moon 1988; Job 1992; Thomas 1987). Security for developing postcolonial states, in short, has economic as well as military components, and often the threat of economic collapse is of far greater concern to "third-world" regimes than is the threat of external invasion (Ayoob 1991, 1995; Ball 1988).

For theories of foreign policy and alliances to be useful in non-Western contexts, therefore, it may be necessary to consider more complex meanings even for such basic issues as the "state," "security," and "alliance." In the Arab regional context, for example, alliances tend to be informal, while formal defense pacts such as NATO are rare. Since these regional alignments are rooted more often in expectations of political and economic (rather than military) support, they can in some ways be viewed not just as state-state linkages, but as transnational support coalitions between governments. In this chapter, I examine the state as a ruling regime, rather than making holistic assumptions about the state-as-country. Once we focus on the regime as the locus of foreign policy decisionmaking—and as the nexus of the individual, domestic, and system levels of analysis—it becomes clear that the security concerns driving policy (including international alignments) are not just those of the country as a whole, but more importantly those aimed at preserving the ruling elite and the regime itself. Thus in what he terms "omnibalancing," Steven David (1991) argues that the real balancing act for developing countries is that between internal and external security concerns. Alliance choices, he argues, are intended to shore up the state's position in both domestic and international spheres. Similarly, Michael Barnett and Jack Levy (1991) have underscored domestic factors combined with economic constraints as decisive in international alliance behavior.

Studies of Jordanian foreign policy more specifically have emphasized the profound vulnerability of the kingdom as a key factor in understanding its international relations (Dessouki and Aboul-Kheir 1991). Laurie Brand (1994), for example, has argued that economic factors are paramount in Jordanian policy, so much so that "budget security" is the guiding force in Jordan's foreign policy and its alliance choices. Marc Lynch (1999), in an application of constructivist theory to Jordanian policy, has argued that domestic politics is particularly important, including public opinion, in changing the nation's sense of identity at domestic, regional, and global levels of dialogue and in turn changes Jordanian policy. Changes in the very nature of national identity, for Jordan and for the Arab system, have in turn changed the constraints on decisionmakers and changed their policies. In many respects, Lynch's approach is virtually the opposite of the neorealist assumption of the timelessness of the balance of power in explaining state policy and alliances. For Lynch and other social constructivists (e.g., Barnett 1998; Wendt 1992, 2000) state interests are not constant but rather are variables to be explained.

I draw on the above critiques and on three levels of analysis (system, state, individual) in analyzing Jordanian alliance behavior and foreign policy choices since 1990. By focusing on the regime and its multiple security concerns—internal and external, economic and military—we can better understand the foreign policy and especially the alliances of a small state such as Jordan. That does not imply, however, that all these aspects and factors are equally important. Based on the empirical analysis in this chapter, I argue that the core factors guiding the Jordanian state are rooted far more in domestic politics and political economy than they are in external security or military concerns, even in the Middle East, and even for one of that region's smallest and weakest states. This chapter provides an overview of Jordanian foreign policy from 1946 to 1990. It then examines the system-, state-, and individual-level factors affecting Jordan's foreign policy transitions from 1990 through 2002, including the kingdom's wholesale realignment (both domestically and internationally) as it has come to grips with globalization and the post–Cold War, post–Gulf War, and post–King Hussein world.

Jordanian Foreign Policy, 1946–1990

In many respects, the Hashimite Kingdom of Jordan is the classic "small state." It has a population of 5 million people and a small landmass. It is a developing country with limited resources and a weak economy, and it has historically depended on financial aid from various external patrons. The kingdom is surrounded by more powerful neighbors Israel, Iraq, Saudi Arabia, and Syria. Despite being weaker politically, economically, and militarily than any of its neighbors, Jordan's strategic position and its geopolitical importance to regional and global powers have led the kingdom to play a role in international politics that belie its small and weak status. Hackneyed though the term may be, Jordan was long regarded as "pivotal," especially by Western powers in the Cold War, in the Arab-Israeli conflict, and in the Middle East peace process (Madfai 1993).

The modern state of Jordan first emerged from the imperial machinations that divided the Middle East following the collapse of the Ottoman Empire in World War I. After the war, Britain carved out Jordan's borders and set up the Hashimite regime under the emir Abdullah. The Hashimite family had previously ruled Mecca in Western Arabia, before being defeated and expelled by the rising power of the Saudi family and its allies. Britain shortly thereafter established Hashimite monarchies in the newly emerging states of Jordan and Iraq. From that point onward, Britain maintained close strategic ties to the kingdom (Wilson 1987). After World War II, and with the onset of the Cold War, the United States also established strong links to Jordan, as the Western powers came to view Jordan as a conservative bulwark against communism and radical forms of pan-Arabism, and as a potentially moderating element in the Arab-Israeli conflict. From its beginning, then, Jordan has held close ties to powerful Western states and has in fact depended heavily on foreign aid from these countries to keep the kingdom afloat (Stephens 1983; Brand 1994: 39–83).

But Jordan's very centrality has also carried a strategic vulnerability. In the 1950s, when the kingdom was still young and viewed by many pan-Arab nationalists as a "paper tiger," some Jordanian officials feared that another regional conflict might eliminate the Hashimite state altogether. Jordanians did not want to become the "Belgium of the Middle East." And they had in mind here not the strong and independent Belgium that today serves as headquarters to the economically powerful European Union, but rather the vulnerable Belgium of 1914 and 1940—a battleground for more powerful neighbors.

Three major wars with Israel underscore Jordan's strategic concerns. The kingdom actively participated in the first of the Arab-Israeli wars in 1948. In that hard-fought campaign—a defeat for the Arab forces—Jordan's Arab Legion held on to East Jerusalem and the West Bank. Following the war, Jordan's King Abdullah made the still-controversial move of annexing the West Bank to the Kingdom of Jordan. The debate ever since has turned on whether Abdullah's move preserved Arab territory from complete Israeli control or whether he had foreclosed the possibility of a smaller Palestinian state by annexing the territory (Shlaim 1988). Abdullah paid for that decision with his life, when he was gunned down in East Jerusalem by a Palestinian nationalist in 1951. Standing beside him that day was his grandson and the future king, Hussein. He too had been hit by the assassin's bullet, which amazingly ricocheted off a medal on the young Hussein's chest (Lunt 1989). After a brief transitional period in which his father, Talal, was judged mentally unfit to rule, Hussein became king in 1953. Thus for most of

Jordan's modern history (1953–1999) it knew only one king as architect of the kingdom's domestic development and of its foreign policy. Hussein—like his country—developed an international reputation as a survivor. He consolidated the Hashimite regime in Jordan and defended it against internal and external challenges, neither of which were in short supply (Satloff 1994).

In the 1950s, Arab politics became intensely radicalized, with the Cold War and Arab-Israeli conflict looming large in political discourse. Radical trends from communism to pan-Arab nationalism (of both Ba'thist and Nasserist varieties) were at their peak, challenging the legitimacy of Western-leaning conservative monarchies like Jordan (Kerr 1970). In 1958, Hussein headed off an attempted coup d'état and used the opportunity to solidify Hashimite royal control, largely nullify the Jordanian parliament's power, and ban political parties. That same year, a bloody military coup overthrew the Hashimite monarchy of King Hussein's cousin, Faisal, in Iraq. The new regime in Baghdad killed the king and his family before consolidating control over the country. Only months earlier, the two Hashimite monarchies had briefly allied with one another, in a failed effort to enhance their security. But it was the seemingly stronger of the two, in Iraq, that was gone by the end of the year (Dann 1989). With that event in mind, the Hashimite regime in Jordan showed little tolerance for pluralist politics or domestic opposition.

By the late 1960s, however, the regime was forced to focus outward once again, as regional tensions escalated especially between Israel and the regime of Gamal Abdul Nasser in Egypt. Those tensions soon led to the defining event of the decade: the disastrous 1967 Arab-Israeli war. The conflict began when Israeli forces launched what they viewed as a preemptive strike on Arab forces in Egypt and Syria, effectively destroying them on the ground. With no air support, the land battles that followed produced an overwhelming Israeli victory not only against Egypt and Syria, but also against Jordan, whose forces had joined the war effort to aid its Arab allies (Mutawi 1987).

That fateful decision and the complete failure of the Arab war effort led to Israeli occupation of the Sinai from Egypt, the Golan Heights from Syria, and East Jerusalem and the West Bank from Jordan. In less than six days, Jordan had lost some of its most prized territory, including the agriculturally rich West Bank and the religiously significant East Jerusalem. East Jerusalem includes all of the "old city" of Jerusalem, which in turn comprises the Muslim holy sites of the Dome of the Rock and the Al-Aqsa Mosque, in addition to the Western Wall of the ancient Jewish temple and the Christian Church of the Holy Sepulcher. The loss of this city and even the entire West Bank was not, however, the only concern for the Jordanians. For as in the war of 1948, tens of thousands of Palestinian refugees poured across the border into Jordan in June 1967, changing the demographics and ultimately the domestic stability of the kingdom (Bailey 1984).

That uneasy situation collapsed in September 1970, when guerrilla forces of the Palestine Liberation Organization (PLO) fought the royalist forces of the Hashimite government. This Jordanian civil war, called "Black September" by Palestinian nationalists, resulted in a bloody Hashimite victory and the expulsion of PLO guerrilla forces from Jordan. What looked like a particularly vicious internal struggle became internationalized, however, when Syrian forces launched an unsuccessful invasion of northern Jordan in support of the PLO. Many feared that Israeli or U.S. intervention would also soon follow, but those very threats, coupled with the efforts of the Hashimite armies, repelled the Syrians and defeated the PLO (Bailey 1984; Day 1986: 75–78; Salibi 1998: 231–241). For some Palestinians and Jordanians, the bitterness of that conflict still remains.

What is perhaps most amazing about those years is that Jordan survived at all as a state and as a Hashimite monarchy despite international wars, civil war, and revolutions toppling monarchies in neighboring countries. Awareness of this strategic vulnerability led Jordanian policymakers to focus on ensuring international allies and domestic military prowess (Cordesman 1983). Yet since the early 1970s, Jordan's vulnerability seemed to decline. With the Hashimite triumph in the 1970–1971 Jordanian civil war, PLO military forces were expelled from the kingdom, thereby eliminating the threat of a second PLO-Hashimite struggle over the kingdom itself. Similarly, Egypt's 1979 peace treaty with Israel changed the strategic equation by limiting the possibility for another full-scale Arab-Israeli war. Egypt had made peace with Israel; Jordan had no interest in renewed hostilities; and Syria, which desperately desired to retrieve the Golan, was not in a position to go it alone against Israel (Taylor 1982). Although Jordan was widely regarded as a "moderate" state in Middle East politics, it did not follow the Egyptian lead and conclude its own peace treaty with Israel. Domestic and regional constraints proved too great, and thus the Hashimite regime drifted away from Egypt and instead aligned more closely with Iraq and Saudi Arabia, both highly critical of Egypt's separate peace (Taylor 1982).

In the 1980s the Jordanian regime appeared far more concerned with the strategic and perhaps internal challenges posed by the new revolutionary regime in Iran. Certainly, distant Iran posed no direct military threat to Jordan. Hussein focused instead on Iran's potential threat to Jordan's domestic politics and economic stability. Domestically, Iran was a successful example—and indeed an active supporter—of the overthrow of conservative pro-Western monarchies. This perception of a threatening and hostile revolutionary Iran was one reason why the six Arab Gulf monarchies formed themselves into an alliance in 1981, the Gulf Cooperation Council (GCC). Any threat to these oil-wealthy kingdoms indirectly affected Jordan, since the GCC states were major suppliers of financial aid and oil. Thus when Iraq invaded Iran in 1980, King Hussein's regime supported Baghdad for all eight years of the war, and indeed Jordan came to serve as Iraq's main supply source through its port of Aqaba and its overland trucking routes (Terrill 1985).

Despite the regime's continuing concern with security threats, these no longer seemed to include serious fear of invasion or war on any of Jordan's borders. By the early 1980s, the external-military dimensions declined in importance relative to concerns for the economic security of the regime and concurrently for Jordan's domestic stability.

The transition to the 1990s, however, was by no means smooth. In 1989 an economic austerity program initiated under the aegis of the International Monetary Fund (IMF) triggered domestic unrest. A year later, in 1990, Iraq invaded Kuwait. But Jordan managed to survive both the internal and the external upheavals, and by 1994 had made peace with Israel and even reestablished its alliances with Britain and the United States, while also slowly reaching rapprochement with the Arab Gulf monarchies. Despite the many challenges of the 1990s, Jordan in the early twenty-first century—and under a new king—finds itself more secure in the regional system than ever before.

Shifts in Jordanian Foreign Policy Since 1990

In the 1990s, Jordan made several major foreign policy changes. Particularly in 1994, Jordan signed a full and formal peace with the state of Israel. This soon affected Jordan's other alignments. Within two years, Jordan's long-standing alliance with Iraq began to rupture, leading to a de facto Jordanian dealignment from Iraq and to a realignment toward such non-Arab countries as Israel and even Turkey (Ryan 2000b).

It is worth considering just how dramatic these shifts really are—both in Jordan's foreign relations and indeed in the Middle East regional alliance system as a whole. For just a few years earlier, in 1991, a U.S.-led coalition had attacked and defeated the forces of Saddam Hussein following the August 1990 Iraqi invasion and conquest of Kuwait. The Iraqi invasion had triggered a regional crisis resulting in a massive realignment. Most Arab states opposed Iraq and joined the coalition, including Egypt, Syria, and all the states of the GCC (Garnham 1991). Noticeably absent from that coalition was Jordan. The Jordanians had remained out of the war, urging a peaceful solution that was not to be.

While the kingdom declined to join the U.S.-led coalition, Jordan nonetheless called for Iraqi withdrawal, maintained its recognition of the Al-Sabah government of Kuwait, and rejected the Iraqi claim of annexation. Many individual Jordanians volunteered to defend Iraq, but the Jordanian armed forces remained strictly neutral and did not fight alongside the Iraqi army. The regime's cautious stance kept King Hussein's domestic popularity intact, but Jordan suffered severe economic repercussions from the United States and also from the GCC states. The United States, Kuwait, and Saudi Arabia each abruptly halted all foreign aid to Jordan. Exports to and from most Arab countries also declined rapidly. The port of Aqaba was eventually all but shut off to commercial traffic, leading to a sharp decline in port revenues as well as in goods entering the country. Jordan's much needed tourism income effectively evaporated. Finally, angry Gulf states—first Saudi Arabia and then liberated Kuwait—expelled several hundred thousand Jordanians and Palestinians working in their countries.

Largely isolated regionally and globally, Jordanian policymakers realized that the kingdom's road to recovery lay in the usual place: its geostrategic role and its importance to any hope for Arab-Israeli peace. In 1991, in the immediate aftermath of the Gulf War, Jordan quickly agreed to participate (in a joint delegation with Palestinians) in the regional peace conference in Madrid. But having used that political compromise to begin the multilateral negotiations, Jordanians and Palestinians soon formed separate delegations for further bilateral and multilateral talks. The key departure point came in 1993 with the surprise announcement of the Oslo Accords between Israel and the Palestinians. The two sides had negotiated secretly to reach the accords, setting the stage for direct talks thereafter. The 1993 Oslo Accords between Israel and the PLO initially surprised and angered the Jordanian government. If Oslo amounted to a breakthrough for the Palestinians and Israelis, it also seemed to be a blow to Jordan's role in the peace process. Before Oslo, Jordan diplomatically benefited from its role as sometime-spokesperson for the Palestinians. Since the United States and Israel refused to talk with the PLO, Jordan had remained a major interlocutor (although not without considerable Palestinian resentment of the continuing Jordanian role). Many on the right wing of Israel politics continued to view Jordan, by virtue of its large Palestinian population, as a de facto Palestine, notwithstanding both Hashimite and PLO hostility to that notion (Klieman 1998).

Jordanian decisionmakers feared that their regional importance might have been compromised in the stroke of a pen at Oslo. Unlike Egypt and Syria, Jordan was not a major player involved in the peace process in large part to gain back territory lost in the disastrous 1967 war. Quite the contrary, Jordan had renounced its claims to the West Bank in 1988 and was not viewed as a serious military threat to Israel. The Jordanian response to Oslo was swift and stunning. By 1994, Jordan had concluded not simply a set of accords, but a full and formal peace treaty with Israel (Lukacs 1997). Thus for the first time since 1948, Jordan and Israel had conclusively moved from a status of official belligerency toward a legalized peace.

Following the signing of the 1994 treaty, the Jordanian government grew steadily more critical of Saddam Hussein's regime. By January 1996 the government allowed Iraqi opposition groups to open offices in Amman. King Hussein and Jordanian officials met with Iraqi opposition leaders in London in early 1996, and the king met personally with leaders of the Patriotic Union of Kurdistan (PUK) and the Kurdish Democratic Party (KDP). The kingdom also granted political asylum to Iraq's highest-ranking defectors, including daughters and sons-in-law of Saddam Hussein. Some of these defectors, like the Kamil brothers, shocked Jordan by returning to Baghdad, where they met a grisly end. But less than a month later, Jordan granted asylum to another high-level defector, General Nazar Khazraji, who had served as chief of staff for the Iraqi army in the late 1980s (North 1996: 13).

In 1997, Jordan reinforced its new international alignments and further distanced itself from Iraq, by becoming the only Arab country to send observers to joint U.S.-Israeli-Turkish naval exercises. President William Clinton praised Jordan's new anti-Iraq stance and announced that U.S. fighter squadrons would be deployed in Jordan to monitor the "no-fly zone" in southern Iraq (North 1996: 10–11). Jordan developed closer bilateral ties with each of the three states in the U.S.-Israeli-Turkish strategic alliance. Indeed, in November 1996 the U.S. government announced that Jordan would henceforth be regarded as a "non-NATO ally," an unusual status in effect granting Jordan "priority consideration" for future arms and military aid requests (Kamal 1996: 11). The kingdom further extended its bilateral military ties with Turkey, while vociferously denying that military cooperation with Turkey amounted to a Jordanian-Turkish alliance. In 1999, Jordanian troops participated in Egyptian and NATO military exercises in the western desert of Egypt. By 2000, Jordan had also gained admittance to the World Trade Organization (WTO) and achieved "association status" with the European Free Trade Association (EFTA).

Jordan's policy shifts since 1990, in short, have been nothing short of dramatic—from the Gulf War, to peace, to realignment again. During the 1990–1991 Gulf War, as the region experienced one of the most comprehensive realignments ever, Jordan stood firm as one of the few states not to realign. It is for that reason that the kingdom's later decisions are particularly striking. A global crisis and regional war had not persuaded the kingdom to budge, yet less than four years later it signed a full peace treaty with Israel. By 1996, the Jordanian-Iraqi rift was so great that Iraqi opposition groups were allowed to set up headquarters in Amman and high-level Iraqi defectors were entertained in Hashimite palaces. And yet by the end of the decade, Jordanian policy had shifted once again toward full rapprochement, not only with Iraq, but also with Syria.

Even before returning to warmer diplomatic ties, Iraq and Jordan returned to functional and pragmatic economic cooperation. By the late 1990s, the lack of an economic windfall from Israel had pushed Jordan and Iraq back together at least at the economic level. Jordan's port of Aqaba remained practically Iraq's sole lifeline to the outside world while the UN sanctions continued (Nimri Aziz 1997: 18–19). Thus the economic symbiosis between the two states, while problematic for several years, managed to survive the Israeli peace treaty after all. Following the succession in the Jordanian monarchy, King Abdullah called—in his first speech before parliament—for an end to the United Nations embargo on Iraq. In 2000, Jordan became the first Arab country officially to break the embargo by sending medical supplies and, later, high-level government delegations to Baghdad. While the improved Jordanian-Iraqi relationship did not amount to a full alliance, it nonetheless signaled an end to the period of hostility that had marked the late 1990s.

Jordanian-Syrian relations had been strained for years, with little love lost between King Hussein and Syrian president Hafiz al-Asad. Following the death of King Hussein in 1999, however, the two countries' bilateral relations began to improve. To the surprise of many in Jordan and elsewhere, President Asad made a rare journey to Amman to attend King Hussein's funeral, while also making a point to speak at some length with Hussein's son and heir. After President Asad himself passed away in June 2000, his son and heir apparent President Bishar al-Asad exchanged state visits with King Abdullah, thereby pushing the warming trend still further. As the twenty-first century began, with the tumultuous 1990s finally behind them, the Jordanians had achieved greater stability in foreign relations than ever before.

Explaining Shifts in Jordanian Foreign Policy

Having described Jordan's major foreign policy and alliance shifts since 1990, I now turn to an examination of the two most dramatic turning points: the 1990–1991 Gulf War and the 1994 peace treaty with Israel. In each case, I examine the policy shift from the system, state, and individual levels of analysis.

The System

The August 2, 1990, Iraqi invasion of Kuwait jolted not only the Persian Gulf but also the entire regional system. In many respects, the invasion itself brought a violent end to a local crisis between Iraq and Kuwait, and instead immediately triggered a much larger global crisis as well as the most dramatic regional realignment since Anwar Sadat signed the 1978 Camp David Accords with Israel (Ryan and Downie 1993; Garnham 1991).

One might have expected that Jordan, particularly as a small and militarily vulnerable state, would have balanced against the power of Iraq. Saddam Hussein's military had just invaded a small Arab monarchy and conquered it within a day. There was, furthermore, only one other small monarchy bordering Iraq, and that was Jordan itself. But the kingdom maintained its alignment with Iraq, refusing to join the U.S.-led coalition. Jordan's actions clearly did not amount to balancing. Nor was it maintaining its alignment with Iraq in order simply to balance against a more threatening Israel. In sum, Iraq was not seen as threatening because it was Jordan's closest ally, while Israel was not threatening because the two states had been at peace since 1973, and Israel clearly viewed Jordan as a moderate and fairly friendly state (Garfinkle 1991; Lukacs 1997). The only real threat at the system level was the threat of direct Israeli-Iraqi confrontation, which presumably would be fought in Jordan. Fear of becoming an Israeli-Iraqi battleground did in part lead the Jordanian regime to try to avoid a regional war over the Gulf crisis.

In terms of regional alliances, the bloc of six Arab Gulf monarchies—the Gulf Cooperation Council—coalesced against Iraq, with Saudi Arabia in particular calling for and receiving U.S. military help. One of the other regional alignment blocs, the Arab Cooperation Council (ACC), had been formed largely through Jordanian efforts just over a year before the invasion. The ACC included Egypt, Iraq, Jordan, and Yemen, and was designed to facilitate political and economic cooperation (Wahby 1989). The ACC had barely broached the subject of more meaningful security cooperation when one of its members invaded Kuwait and neglected to inform the others of its belligerent designs (Ryan 1998b). While the Egyptians renounced the alignment, sided with the United States and the GCC, and sent combat troops to Saudi Arabia, Jordan attempted to hold the ACC together. But even Syria, a state not known for its pro-Western policies, had joined the coalition against Iraq and sent troops to the Gulf. Ultimately the ACC collapsed and while many Arab states joined the coalition, Jordan steered a middle course that ultimately alienated the kingdom from its allies in the United States, the United Kingdom, and the Gulf states.

The context of these decisions is vital to understanding the Jordanian position, especially the key Jordanian role in forming the ACC. In addition, it is important to note that the ACC itself built on the already-existing Jordanian-Iraqi alignment, which had begun as early as 1978 (Baram 1991; Taylor 1982). By the time of the August 1990 invasion, Iraq had become Jordan's most vital ally, especially in economic terms. During Iraq's eight long years of war with Iran, Jordan had served as Iraq's major gateway for supplies (Terrill 1985). Jordan's economic linkages to Iraq had become so deep that they ultimately acted as strong constraints on the regime's room for maneuver. By 1990 Iraq was the largest source of Jordan's imports (17.3 percent) and the main destination for its exports (23.2 percent) as well as its main source of oil, most of which was sold to the kingdom at well below market prices (Economist Intelligence Unit 1991: 28). Jordanian decisionmakers were certainly constrained by the public response in favor of Saddam Hussein in Jordan's streets, but they were also concerned that turning against Iraq would mean losing the country's largest local ally, its largest trading partner, and its main source of oil imports (Brand 1991).

While these external links continued to pull Jordan toward Iraq, other ties nonetheless pulled in the opposite direction. For by maintaining alignment with Iraq, the kingdom alienated its other key economic allies, each of which delivered a sharp economic blow: the United States ceased its foreign aid to the kingdom temporarily, while Saudi Arabia and other GCC states cut off aid and oil supplies, and then deported hundreds of thousands of Jordanian and Palestinian laborers. Thus the economic constraints were severe, but they cut in both directions and were not in and of themselves determinate in Jordan's foreign policy decisions in the Gulf crisis. Thus the decisive factors remained largely on the state and domestic political levels.

In the immediate aftermath of the 1990–1991 Gulf War, Jordan found itself in unaccustomed isolation. Its only remaining ally lay largely in ruins. While the United States resumed aid flows to the kingdom, Jordan's relations with Egypt, Syria, and the six GCC monarchies ranged from cold to hostile. The 1991 Madrid peace conference therefore provided the Jordanians with a crucial opportunity. The kingdom was eager to participate and played on its geopolitical status as vital to Arab-Israeli peace. The peace conference, in short, served as Jordan's conduit to return to the regional system and recoup some of its diplomatic and economic losses. But the more dramatic turning point came, of course, in 1994, when Jordan moved well beyond the loose multilateral discussions at Madrid and concluded a full peace treaty with Israel.

Several external factors appeared to influence the nature and timing of the Jordanian decision to make peace with Israel.[2] First was the 1993 Israeli-PLO accord, which at first appeared to leave the Jordanians on the sidelines but was soon grasped as offering an opportunity for them to make their own, more comprehensive agreement. The presence of the Israeli-PLO negotiation muted previously dominant domestic and regional constraints on the regime's ability to conclude a full peace treaty. Second, Jordanian willingness to press further ahead in the peace process was propelled along still further by U.S. political pressure coupled with economic incentives to achieve a major breakthrough on the Jordanian-Israeli track. Third, the regime had concluded that the above opportunities would lead to tangible material gains from Israel and from Western allies that would, in turn, serve to mollify any domestic skepticism or criticism as well as outweigh any hostility from Syria.

These external factors each may have contributed to the Jordanian decision to break from its well-established pattern of tacit understanding with Israel, and to turn instead toward full and formal peace between the two countries. It is worth noting, however, that none of these external factors amounted to an actual external threat, and thus a "balance of threats" approach cannot explain Jordan's realignment decision toward Israel. Rather, the zeal with which the Hashimite monarchy strode toward a full treaty was strongly influenced by the economic needs of the kingdom and hence of the domestic stability of the regime.

The State

Domestic factors are vital in explaining Jordan's decision both in war in the Gulf and in peace with Israel. But these factors were significant in different ways. The 1990–1991 war occurred in the context of severe domestic vulnerability for the Hashimite regime, while by 1994 the kingdom had managed to solidify its domestic support base and then used that to achieve peace with Israel as a virtual fait accompli.

In many ways the 1990–1991 Gulf crisis could not have come at a worse time for the Jordanian regime. On the domestic front, the kingdom had been rocked by political upheavals following the implementation of an IMF adjustment and austerity program. The IMF riots certainly underscored the regime's economic and domestic political vulnerability. But that negative event also yielded something positive: the initiation of a program of political liberalization that led to parliamentary elections and looser restrictions on the media. As a result, Jordan's position during the 1990–1991 Gulf War was deeply rooted in economic problems and domestic politics—including its nascent "democratization" program (Harknett and Vandenberg 1997). This included loosening restrictions on the press and allowing for parliamentary elections in which opposition Islamist candidates fared well. Both the parliament and the Jordanian public adopted far more clear and unequivocal pro-Iraq positions than did the monarchy during the Gulf crisis. Thus while foreign policy remained the province of a small clique, the regime appeared to have been affected by domestic public opinion. Jordanian policymakers felt that they had few choices, and that dealignment away from Iraq was not among them.

The new domestic political constraints had been brought on by the liberalization process itself. The context had changed from people in the streets in 1989 calling for major changes in the government and its policies, to people in the streets in 1990 calling for the regime to stand by its ally, Iraq, against a coalition of foreign forces. Numerous street demonstrations, speeches on the floor of the parliament, and articles in newly established newspapers and magazines all indicated popular enthusiasm for Saddam Hussein. Jordan's foreign policy decisions must, therefore, be seen against this backdrop of change. Domestic opinion, now more vocal than ever before, was in large part supportive of Iraq against any outside coalition (Lynch 1999).

The 1990 Gulf crisis had come at a particularly vulnerable time for the regime. But in the end, the regime had emerged with a far more solid base than before, and the king's stance during the crisis, while vilified in the Gulf and the West, had gained the monarchy popularity and legitimacy at home (Brand 1991). It was from this strong domestic foundation that King Hussein's regime turned toward the post–Gulf War resuscitation of the Arab-Israeli peace process. Jordan was able to reestablish some of its economic and political ties to the United States, but not to the Gulf states. The kingdom's chronic deficit suggested the need for a longer-term solution. The connection between economic well-being and political stability was not lost on government officials, particularly since the unrest of 1989. They knew, in short, that the atmosphere of positive feeling toward the monarchy following the Gulf War would not last forever unless the economic situation improved. Despite Jordan's continuing economic interdependence with Iraq, alignment with a now isolated Baghdad would not solve Jordan's economic dilemmas. And Saddam Hussein's reckless invasion of Kuwait made Iraq appear a less-than-reliable ally upon which to rest Jordan's hopes for the future. The Jordanians therefore sought a real breakthrough in the peace process not only for its own sake, but also for the economic windfall that they believed would follow from peace.

The treaty was indeed expedited by the Hashimite regime itself, but with little warning or preparation within Jordanian domestic politics. Even today the treaty appears to have far more critics than supporters within Jordan and it remains a sore point in the struggle between state institutions and Jordan's emerging civil society of independent interest groups and parties (Lynch 1999). But despite this resentment of both the treaty itself and the exclusive nature of the decisionmaking that had led to it, the regime argued then—and argues now—that formalizing peace between countries that had not actually fought in decades was long overdue.

Palestinian opposition (both within the kingdom and without) had long been cited as the key obstacle preventing King Hussein from making peace. But Oslo institutionalized direct Israeli-PLO negotiations, and for the Jordanian regime this served as something of a green light. The PLO no longer criticized any Israeli-Jordanian collusion, and the Hashimite regime had as early as 1988 renounced its own ties and claims to the West Bank (thereby removing the thorniest issue from the table, but depositing it directly in the middle of the Israeli-Palestinian track). Thus little except domestic opposition seemed to hold the Hashimites back. And that opposition only mobilized once the process appeared to be largely complete. Having secured its treaty with Israel, Jordan then sought to market it as the source of a new economic boom in Jordan. A windfall of economic growth and prosperity, it was hoped, would mollify critics of the regime and of the peace treaty (Astorino-Courtois 1996).

Indeed, the regime appeared to have used the upsurge in its domestic popularity from the Gulf War to push through the peace treaty with Israel, over the objections of most political parties and many professional associations. This in turn suggested that despite political liberalization, foreign policy remained largely an area of royal privilege. The expected great upsurge in economic well-being, however, never materialized and opposition to the treaty festered. While some elite constituencies such as the military enjoyed the fruits of enhanced military linkages to the United States and even to other NATO countries, many Jordanians saw no benefits from peace and in fact resented Jordan's closer ties to the United States, Israel, and Turkey. Jordan's vocal opposition presses, its political parties, and its professional associations could not stop the treaty, but they did mobilize to stall or prevent normalization of relations between Israeli and Jordanian society. The regime responded not so much by joining the debate but by issuing new and restrictive press laws in 1997. In the parliamentary elections later that year, the eleven-party opposition coalition boycotted the polls, yielding a relatively pliant but unrepresentative parliament for 1997–2001 (Ryan 1998a).

In a move that may hold more than symbolic importance, King Abdullah II, in one of his first acts, met in 1999 with many of the opposition leaders to establish what he termed a "national dialogue." That may provide the starting point for a more meaningful debate and even reconciliation within Jordanian politics. Thus although King Abdullah agreed with his father on many political issues, his personal approach and style were notably different, leading many to hope for a return to political liberalization at home and a stabilization of Jordan's relations abroad.

The Individual

Given the nature of the Jordanian political system, the most critical individual-level factor in Jordanian foreign policy is, of course, the role of the king. From 1953 to 1999, King Hussein ruled the Hashimite Kingdom of Jordan and served as the main decisionmaker in Jordanian foreign policy. And indeed of all policy areas, foreign affairs remained the most solidly based in royal hands throughout his long tenure. Under Hussein, Hashimite Jordan maintained a conservative and cautious foreign policy that included reliance on powerful Western states, especially the United States and the United Kingdom. In addition, while he professed to be committed to pan-Arab and pan-Islamic unity, Hussein was not remotely sympathetic to radical versions of either Arab nationalism or Islamism. His commitment to the Muslim holy places in Jerusalem, however, was genuine. And Hussein believed that the Hashimite royal house, direct descendants of the prophet Muhammad, had a special responsibility to Jerusalem (Hussein 1962; Lunt 1989). There were many times, of course, when that very conviction proved an irritant to both Israel and the PLO.

In the Cold War, Hussein ensured that Jordan would remain solidly in the Western camp, opposed to the Soviet Union and to ideological movements from communism, to Ba'thism, to Nasserism, to Islamism. Hussein and many Jordanians saw his grandfather, King Abdullah I, as the founder of the nation, and Hussein as the builder of the modern state (Satloff 1994). And thus the core goal of Jordan's foreign policy—especially as a small, economically poor, and militarily weak state—was the preservation and survival of the Jordanian state and its Hashimite monarchy, often with strong emphasis on external allies and on alignment decisions in the midst of assorted crises. Jordan's policy during the Gulf War was, for example, not about realignment, but about attempting to maintain all of

Jordan's alignments, including with Iraq. In the 1980s, when King Hussein first made clear that Jordan would back Iraq in its war with Iran, he ran against the grain of Jordanian public opinion, at least initially. Many viewed the new Iranian regime with approval, having toppled an authoritarian monarch seen as too close to the West. For Hussein, the Khomeini regime was an enemy of moderation, monarchy, and pro-Western policies, and now an enemy to Jordan's most powerful Arab ally, Iraq. King Hussein persuaded his advisers, and eventually public opinion went along with him (Rifai 1993).

By 1990 that same ally had triggered a regional and global crisis. Given Jordan's economic dependencies, its domestic vulnerability, and clear signals of public opinion, Hussein may have felt that few choices remained. The key issue in his personal approach seemed to rest on the future of the state itself. The fear of war escalating beyond the Gulf was very real, and Hussein feared for the nation. But given the violent unrest at home just a year earlier, he may also have feared for the monarchy. In the end, he chose to run with, rather than against, the tide of public opinion, with a view to preserving the Hashimite state.

Hussein used his personal diplomacy in unsuccessful bids to thwart a major conflict, shuttling to Washington and several Arab capitals. In the end the war did come, but not the feared escalation to Jordan itself. When the smoke from the Gulf War began to clear, Hussein found himself more popular at home than ever before, and he immediately used that status to achieve his long-standing goal of peace with Israel. The difference this time was the sudden solidity of his domestic base and also the 1993 Oslo Accords between Israel and the PLO. With the PLO negotiating directly with Israel, the fear of Palestinian hostility within the kingdom declined in importance. Indeed, given the sudden announcement of the Oslo Accords, the window of opportunity just as suddenly presented itself. This may explain not only Hussein's determination to achieve a peace treaty, but also the speed with which it was accomplished in 1994.

Finally, it is worth noting that King Hussein's cancer had been detected years earlier. He had returned to Jordan, after extensive medical treatments in the United States, to a triumphant welcome and a massive outpouring of popular support. But the experience underscored the king's own mortality. I argue that Jordan's rapid work toward a peace treaty, and the solidification of the kingdom's key alliances, were in large part intended to provide for a stable succession. In short, the question had for decades remained whether anyone besides King Hussein could possibly risk a peace treaty with Israel. Hussein rendered the question moot by rapidly pushing through the treaty five years (as it turned out) before he suffered a cancer relapse and died following a second round of treatments. But his goal had been achieved: to secure the state and the succession, and hence the Hashimite monarchy itself.

In February 1999, just days before his death, Hussein had returned to Jordan to make one last political move, changing the path of succession from his brother, Hasan, to his eldest son, Abdullah. Hasan had served as crown prince and designated successor for thirty-two years, but Hussein in the end determined to keep the succession within his immediate line. The sudden elevation of Abdullah as crown prince was followed almost immediately by his ascension to the throne.

For the most part, Abdullah's policy views mirror those of his father. He too is moderate and cautious and is determined to maintain close alliances with Jordan's tradition Western allies. He is even more committed to economic liberalization than his father was, although a major question remains his stance on domestic political liberalization. And, as noted above, Abdullah pushed the Jordanian shift toward rapprochement with Iraq still further by calling for an end to the UN embargo.

Interestingly, while Abdullah cannot have his father's experience and clout on the world stage, neither does he have his animosities. Abdullah, unlike the long-serving Hussein, did not come of political age in the most intense days of the Cold War and of the regional ideological conflicts of the 1950s and 1960s. He is not personally affected by the scars of the 1970–1971 Jordanian civil war, by the long rivalry between his father and President Asad of Syria, or by the many Arab-Israeli wars. Indeed, while Abdullah has managed to maintain and even strengthen each of Jordan's key external relationships (with the United States, the European Union, Israel, and Turkey), he has also achieved warm relations with Egypt and even with Syria, ending what in effect amounted to a Jordanian-Syrian Cold War. He has deepened the rapprochement with Iraq and even reestablished ties with all of the Arab GCC monarchies. In sum, Abdullah was bequeathed a stable set of international relationships, but he has managed to both broaden and deepen them. For many Jordanians, that very success presented another question: whether the King would utilize Jordan's stable international situation as an opportunity to concentrate on lingering problems of domestic reform and political change.

Conclusion

This analysis reveals the importance of the system, the state, and the individual on the policies, alliances, and maneuvers of the Hashimite Kingdom of Jordan in international relations. Jordan's policies are intended not just to ensure the security of Jordan as a state, but also to ensure the survival of Jordan as a Hashimite monarchy. And these elaborate new alignments and foreign policy arrangements may have been designed to see to it that Jordan could survive into the twenty-first century as a Hashimite monarchy even after the succession from King Hussein's rule.

This analysis has also underscored the point that it is impossible to consider Jordanian foreign policy without taking into account the kingdom's sense of its own vulnerability as a "small state." And that term can be taken at several levels of meaning. For Jordan is small in landmass and population, and it is small economically as well as militarily. Yet given its geopolitical importance from the Cold War through the regional peace process, Jordan has not only survived but also managed to play a role in regional affairs that seems to belie its "smallness." Under King Abdullah II, Jordan's international role and global activism—including its participation in UN peacekeeping operations—have increased in the early twenty-first century.

With these points in mind, Jordan's new alignments therefore cannot be seen only in the light of traditional theories of alliance, for Jordan was not really using its new alliance partners to balance against regional threats. The kingdom may have seen its Israeli, U.S., and Turkish connections as enhancing its external security vis-à-vis Syria and Iraq, but for the most part these states were not viewed as *external* threats. They were, more importantly, seen as manipulators of Jordanian domestic politics and as potential disrupters of *internal* stability in the kingdom. But even that is not new, and so balancing theory cannot explain the nature or timing of Jordan's realignment. In addition, these fears of internal subversion are not really mitigated by having powerful external allies. Indeed, the very presence of these allies might have been expected to provoke hostility from Jordan's more hard-line neighbors.

For that reason, Jordan has not restricted itself to the static definitions of alliances and balances of power that permeate much of the international relations literature. The Jordanians attempted to "have their cake and eat it too," by establishing alliances with the strongest military and economic powers available, while also attempting to mollify their critics in Baghdad and Damascus. Jordan realized that regional alignment politics are not necessarily a zero-sum game even in the often tumultuous international relations of the Middle East. Rather, Jordan tried to make it a positive-sum game so that increasing cooperation with one set of allies does not mean conflict with former allies. This has been particularly noticeable under King Abdullah, who has even managed to reestablish relatively warm relations with both Iraq and Syria.

Perhaps more importantly, Jordan's willingness to undergo repeated IMF structural adjustment programs, its signing of a peace treaty with Israel, and its increasing military cooperation with NATO ally Turkey have all combined to produce several economic rewards from the West.

In 1994 the United States and major European creditors agreed to write off $833 million of Jordan's debt. The Paris Club of official creditors similarly agreed to reschedule Jordan's remaining debt four times between 1989 and 1997. Also in 1997, Jordan signed a partnership agreement with the European Union that is intended to be the foundation for a Jordanian-EU free trade arrangement by 2010. Finally, Jordan under King Abdullah II managed to secure a free trade agreement with the United States as well as admittance to the World Trade Organization (Kiernan 1998).

The kingdom's policy of realignment must be seen as truly comprehensive. In terms of levels of analysis, domestic regime security certainly seems to be the main force driving these decisions—and the Hashimite regime shows every sign of understanding regime security in both internal and external, military and economic, terms. But of these components, the shift appears to have been toward increasing emphasis on the domestic and economic dimensions of the regime's security and survival, and even its external alliances are driven mainly by these concerns. King Abdullah II and his regime appear to see their security as best guaranteed in the twenty-first century by limited and manageable political liberalization at home, peace and enhanced relations with Israel, military cooperation with Turkey, rapprochement with Iraq and Syria, and increased economic and military links to the United States. Jordan's foreign policy strategy also includes full membership in—and compliance in the neoliberal rules of—the dominant states and institutions of the global economic regime: the United States, the European Union, the IMF, World Bank, and the WTO. Jordan has, furthermore, steadily increased its global role by active participation in UN peacekeeping operations throughout the world. After the September 2001 terrorist attacks on New York and the Pentagon, Jordan supported the U.S. war in Afghanistan and later contributed troops to the postwar UN peacekeeping operation there. Under King Abdullah, Jordan's regime survival strategy and hence its foreign policy are based ultimately on accommodating entirely to globalization, as Jordan under the Hashimite regime adjusts to—and allies with—the dominant states and institutions of a twenty-first-century new world order.

Notes

A similar version of this chapter is also found in Curtis R. Ryan, *Jordan in Transition: From Hussein to Abdullah* (Boulder: Lynne Rienner, 2003).

1. I draw on field research and interviews conducted in 1992, 1993, 1997, and 1999 with many current and former policymakers in Jordan. These interviews are not cited individually. Most interviewees, while open in their discussions of Jordanian policy, nonetheless insisted on not being quoted or even cited point for point. I have drawn on their collective points in making my own analysis and I will cite here some key officials with their permission: these include former prime ministers Mudar Badran, Ahmad al-Lawzi, Taher al-Masri, Zayd al-Rifai, and Ahmad Ubaydat, as well as former cabinet ministers or royal court officials Adnan Abu Awdah, Jawad al-Anani, and Marwan al-Qassem. The analysis also draws on interviews with necessarily anonymous sources in the Jordanian parliament, foreign ministry, and within the political opposition, in an effort to achieve a balanced accounting of causes and events.

2. The analysis in this section draws on Ryan 1998c.

9

Laos: Maintaining Power in a Highly Charged Region

Zachary Abuza

Laos is a small, landlocked country of 5.5 million people in the heart of Southeast Asia. A political anachronism, it is still ruled by some of the same communist insurgents who came to power after a two-decade guerrilla war in 1976, and is today one of only a handful of surviving communist states. Its foreign policy is seemingly inconsequential. Yet Laos is rich in natural resources and it lies in the midst of a dynamic and increasingly interdependent subregion. Moreover, Laos has always attracted the attention of outsiders. As Grant Evans notes, "Revolution in Laos did not occur as a result of internal social changes but because the war in Vietnam allowed larger countries to manipulate Lao factions for their broader interests" (1998: 183). Indeed, the great powers that surround it—China, Vietnam, and Thailand—continue to compete for influence over the "land of 10,000 elephants."

The Lao population is divided between lowland Lao, who are predominantly wet rice farmers along the Mekong River, and hill tribesmen (mainly Hmong). Nearly all are farmers and the Lao economy is based, for the most part, on subsistence agriculture with limited natural resource exploitation. It is one of the poorest and least-developed countries in the world, with per capita income approximately U.S.$300 per year, and equally low human development measures; 16 percent of its gross domestic product (GDP) is accounted for by foreign development assistance (Lintner 2001: 51). It is one of the few remaining Marxist states and the ruling Lao People's Revolutionary Party (LPRP) represses any dissent.

Laos became a French protectorate in 1893 by treaty with the Thai court, when the French were exploring the Mekong River to find a riverine route to the Chinese interior as Britain controlled much of the Chinese coast. It remained for the most part a colonial oversight for the next half century. The French angered many Lao by bringing in Vietnamese to serve as colonial administrators and by favoring the Hmong, whose opium production was an important colonial monopoly. Nonetheless, Lao political consciousness was low and there was relatively little pressure for independence. Early Lao anticolonial activists tended toward Ho Chi Minh's Indochina Communist Party, immediately subsuming the Lao revolution to the interest of the Vietnamese, or to other small nationalist groups, such as the Lao Issara. In January 1946, following World War II, French colonial forces returned to Laos, but were immediately confronted by a small force composed of Viet Minh and Lao troops, led by a radical member of the royal family, Prince Souphanouvong. Bogged down in war against the communist-led Viet Minh in Vietnam, in 1953 the French restored the monarchy and gave Laos independence, expecting that it would remain allied to France (Stuart Fox 1997: 84–89). The 1954 Geneva Accords, which saw Vietnam divided between the communist North and anticommunist South, also protected Lao neutrality and monarchy. Internal resistance to the monarchy was nascent. In 1951, Lao communists broke away from the Indochina Communist Party and on March 25, 1955, the Lao People's Party was formed. In 1956, the Lao People's Party launched a guerrilla movement, the Lao Nation (Pathet Lao), which became closely aligned with Ho Chi Minh's Democratic Republic of Vietnam. Laos was soon engulfed in the Vietnam War as North Vietnam began to infiltrate men and supplies into South Vietnam through a network of trails and roads through eastern Laos, known as the Ho Chi Minh Trail. Armed and aided by the North Vietnamese, the Pathet Lao grew in strength. Confronted with the threat of U.S. intervention, Prince Souvanna Phouma and Pathet Lao agreed to a neutralist government under the prince's direction in 1962. The coalition government broke down and, soon after, the U.S. Central Intelligence Agency (CIA) began to wage a covert war against the Vietnamese and their Lao allies, the Pathet Lao, arming an insurgent force of Hmong tribesmen (Warner 1995; Hamilton-Merritt 1993). The United States began bombing Lao portions of the Ho Chi Minh Trail as early as 1964. A second coalition government that included the communist Pathet Lao was established in 1972.

With a large degree of assistance from Vietnam, the Pathet Lao seized control in late 1975 and established a single-party socialist state that remains closely allied with Vietnam. The government detained some 40,000 members of the former government, imprisoning them in remote "reeducation camps," while the military forces, along with Vietnamese troops, waged a war in the mountainous regions to put down the lingering Hmong insurgency. The Lao king abdicated and he and several other members of the royal family died in Pathet Lao labor camps.

In 1976 the Pathet Lao imposed a communist economic system, which entailed collectivized agriculture and central planning. Collectivization led to mass shortages and the economy nearly collapsed. In 1986 the government began to experiment with market reforms, known as the New Economic Mechanism (NEM), and opened the country to foreign investment. Though Laos has experimented with economic reform, it has not enacted any political reforms, and is still ruled by a hard-line and repressive communist regime that was badly shaken by the collapse of communism in Eastern Europe and the Soviet Union between 1989 and 1991.

In that period, owing to its support of the Vietnamese occupation of Cambodia, Laos was diplomatically isolated. Since then it has gradually opened up. In July 1997, Laos, along with Burma, became a member of the Association of Southeast Asian Nations (ASEAN). The Asian economic crisis hit Laos hard, and the value of its currency declined by 900 percent. In 2000 the government had to confront a renewed Hmong insurgency and a rash of unexplained bombings in the capital. The government has been at pains to justify its continued rule, having lost most of its legitimacy in popular eyes despite celebrating its twenty-five years in power in 2001. It is increasingly illegitimate in the eyes of its people, as corruption and socioeconomic gaps continue to grow, while the market economy has eroded any ideological basis for the Communist Party's continued monopoly of power.

The Lao Economy

Lao foreign policy in many ways can be understood by the country's pressing economic needs. The Lao economy is very underdeveloped and according to the UN ranks as 140th of 178 poorest countries. By every measure of human development, Laos lags behind most of the world. Over 80 percent of the population is engaged in subsistence agriculture. In 1986 the country began to abandon its communist economy and system of central planning, and replaced it with a market system that entailed the privatization of state-owned enterprises and the decollectivization of agriculture, under the slogan *Chintanakhan Mai* (New Thinking) (Evans 1998: 2).

Since the 1990s, Laos has made some efforts to build up its textile industry and the government has placed hope in the export of hydroelectric power to Thailand (Lintner 1997; Crispin, Cohen, and Lintner 2000). Laos has received vast amounts of foreign aid, yet for the most part the aid has gone to unsustainable projects that have created severe economic distortions. Laos has little to show for the billions of dollars in aid it has received since 1976. It has become increasingly dependent on foreign aid, which shows no sign of abating. In 1985, overseas development assistance accounted for 6.25 percent of GDP, yet by 2000 it had grown to 16 percent (Lintner 2001: 51). The industrial and service sectors are dominated by debt-ridden state-owned enterprises, though there has been a commitment to expanding the role of the private sector and foreign investment. New foreign investment, which peaked in 1995 at U.S.$1.2 billion, has fled the country due to the economic crisis and the government's mishandling of the economy. By 2000 foreign direct investment had dropped to approximately U.S.$20 million. Yet that still amounts to 80 percent of public investment (Pennington 2000). Laos has chronic trade deficits with all trading partners. Imports from Thailand in 2000, for example, were U.S.$540 million, while exports were less than U.S.$323 million. The country has been unable to increase exports, even in the context of a rapidly declining currency. Since the Asian economic crisis started in 1997, the Lao kip has depreciated more than any other Asian currency, from K935 to the dollar to over K10,000 per dollar (Lintner 2001: 51). Inflation in 1998 was over 140 percent (Lintner 2000). That year, the government issued higher-denomination banknotes, K2,000 and K5,000 bills, whereas prior, K1,000 notes had been the highest denomination (Thayer 1999: 40).

Foreign Policy Behavior

There are few domestic political actors in Laos, which is ruled by the Pathet Lao, renamed the Lao People's Revolutionary Party, which came to power in 1975 after years of waging a guerrilla war against a U.S.-backed monarchy. Since then, it has maintained its monopoly of power through coercion and fear. The LPRP is an elite organization, with little turnover even by communist standards. There have been only two secretaries-general of the LPRP since its founding, and only four prime ministers since 1975. True to most communist systems, Laos is plagued by "interlocking directorates," whereby the LPRP tries to penetrate every level of the government, the military, society, and the economy through its party network. The government is dominated by the LPRP, and most senior government officials are also members of the LPRP's leading organs, the central committee and the politburo. The only other key political actor is the Lao People's Army, whose senior ranks are also well represented in the central committee and the politburo. Military representation in the LPRP's leading organs is higher than in any other communist system, evidence of the party's insecurity and the high level of threat perception that it embodies.

Authority is not "legal-rational" in the Weberian sense. Laos promulgated its first constitution in 1992, over fifteen years after coming to power. Until then, the secretive LPRP ruled by decree. Since the constitution's promulgation, laws have passed, but they closely follow LPRP directives (Johnson 1992: 84). The National Assembly serves as a rubber stamp for party decisions and almost all assembly members are party members.

Between 1975 and 1989, Laotian foreign policy was guided by the LPRP's interpretation of Marxism-Leninism, and for the most part in this period Laos had very poor relations with states outside the socialist bloc. Laos has always been closely allied to Vietnam, which condescendingly calls Laos its "little brother." Historically the two revolutions were intertwined, and to date the two governments coordinate most facets of their domestic and foreign policies. Lao officials embark on no new political, economic, or social initiative without first consulting Hanoi. Like Vietnam, Laos was also a client state of the Soviet Union and between 1976 and 1989 closely supported the USSR in its conflict with the People's Republic of China, with whom Laos had poor relations. During the Third Indochina War (1978–1991), Laos supported Vietnam's occupation of Cambodia, pitting it against both China and the ASEAN states.

Since the collapse of the Soviet Union in 1991, and the subsequent loss of Soviet development assistance, the leadership has become more divided along generational and regional lines. The younger generation of leaders, who tend to hail from the north, want to scrap Laos's alliance with Vietnam and embrace a closer relationship with China, which is able to provide greater economic assistance. The older generation, who hails from the southern city of Pakse, still sees Laos as being "as close as lips and teeth" with Vietnam, and maintains very close ties at every level of the party, state, and military. The younger generation tends to support deepened economic and market reforms and sees China as an appropriate model and partner. The more ideological older generation sees the cautious and ideological leadership in Hanoi as being the more appropriate guide and partner.

The battle between these two factions should be seen in the context of what the Lao consider to be their greatest national security and cultural threat: that posed by Thailand. The Thai threat to Laos is rooted in history and culture. The lowland Lao are an ethnic Tai people and there are more Lao people in Thailand than in Laos itself; in all, some 20 million Lao (Isan Thai) live in northeast Thailand. With the communist government's imprisonment of the Lao monarch and the exile of most other surviving members of the royal family after 1976, most Lao look to the Thai monarchy as their legitimate rulers. As Grant Evans notes, because of the Lao Revolution and the Pathet Lao's execution of the Lao king, "The Lao have been drawn into the orbit of the Thai realm" as the Thai monarch fills the void in the nation's historical and social space (1998: 179). Likewise the Buddhist Sankha in Laos now takes its lead from the Thai Sankha. Thai culture and media permeate Lao society. And with the opening of the country to foreign investment, much of its commercial assets have been acquired by Thai entrepreneurs.

In short, the "ideological" debate within the Communist Party has little to do with the pace and scope of Lao economic reform. Land has been decollectivized, private property has been restored, state-owned enterprises compose a decreasing percentage of GDP, and the market determines most prices. All pretenses of a socialist economic system are gone. The debates within the party are how to hold on to its monopoly of power and which country, China or Vietnam, is the more appropriate state to balance against greater socioeconomic pressure from Thailand, which has far more influence at the mass level.

Vietnam

Lao leaders feel a deep sense of gratitude toward the Vietnamese, who did much of the fighting in Laos in the 1960s and 1970s that allowed the LPRP to seize power in 1975. For the next fifteen years, Laos was closely allied with Hanoi and its domestic and foreign policies tended to reflect those emanating from its North Vietnamese neighbor. In 1977 the two states signed a twenty-five-year treaty of friendship and cooperation that legalized the stationing of 60,000 Vietnamese troops in the country. In 1978, Laos acceded to Hanoi's pressure and joined the Indochina Federation and implemented a three-year economic plan to coordinate economic policies with Vietnam. Likewise in 1981, Laos implemented a five-year economic plan that coincided with those in Vietnam and the Soviet Union. Since then, Laos and Vietnam have signed dozens of agreements covering aid, financial assistance, education exchange, trade, transport, and communications.

Relations with Vietnam fell into decline beginning in the late 1980s for several reasons. In December 1986 there was a seminal leadership transition in Vietnam, in which the war-era leaders were replaced by a younger generation of technocrats. The government decollectivized agriculture, implemented market-oriented reforms, and courted foreign investment. In 1988 the Vietnamese politburo issued Resolution 13, which drastically called for a reorientation of Vietnam's foreign policy. Mired with a moribund economy, Vietnam withdrew its troops from Laos and Cambodia, nearly 200,000 in total, in order to end international sanctions and improve its relations with China and the ASEAN states. In 1991 Hanoi's own economy was in shock from the sudden loss of Soviet aid, and it was unable to provide additional aid to Laos, which also lost international aid. The new Vietnamese security paradigm abandoned Hanoi's traditional concept of Indochina as a single battlefield and geographical unit, and instead focused on building up its domestic economy by integrating itself in the global marketplace (Porter 1990). Laos was thus forced to improve ties with China, made possible with Hanoi's 1991 rapprochement with Beijing, in turn made possible with the signing of the Paris Peace Accords, which ended the war in Cambodia in October 1991.

The 1986 NEM came at Hanoi's expense, and Vietnam's influence in Laos declined in the early 1990s as Chinese influence grew. China was interested in replacing Hanoi's traditional influence in Laos with its own. Moreover, China saw Laos as the gateway to Thailand, with which China was rapidly expanding economic relations in the 1990s. To that end, China financed the construction of a major highway through Laos to the Thai border.

This is not to say that ties between Laos and Vietnam broke down altogether. Throughout the decade Laos and Vietnam sent more bilateral delegations, from party, military, state, parliamentary, and cultural organs, to one another than they did to any other state. Hanoi and Vientiane are always the first foreign destinations for new members of each country's leadership. The Lao continued to view and treat the Vietnamese as their older brothers. Despite its own economic concerns, Hanoi has never stopped providing economic aid to Vientiane. In the early 1990s, Hanoi provided over U.S.$4 million annually, one-quarter of which was gratis, the remainder interest-free (*FEER* 1993).

Economic reform brought a new threat to the Lao leadership—that posed by Thailand's aggressive economic growth. By the mid-1990s, the Lao were reembracing Vietnam as a counter to the growing and dominant role of the Thais. By 1996, over half the foreign investment came from Laos, and with the opening of the Friendship Bridge in 1994 the country was awash in Thai goods. Thai television, radio, and other cultural influences dominated Laos, as Lao media and cultural programming, which were still constrained by ideology and censorship as well as poor production quality, could not compete. As a result, at the LPRP's sixth congress in March 1996, the leadership gave emphasis to the "special relationship" with Vietnam.

Increasingly the delegations between Laos and Vietnam focused on "theoretical issues," that is, how the respective communist parties continued to justify their rule in the face of marketization and a breakdown in ideological orthodoxy. Both sides sought to "study" from the other's experiences in reforming the economy, while maintaining the Communist Party's monopoly of power. The Lao are interested in how Vietnam, in fifteen years, has been able to stimulate economic growth and double per capita GDP while still maintaining a one-party system.

Vietnam has sought to wean Laos away from its economic dependence on Thailand, and has been actively constructing roads to link Lao cities with Vietnamese ports to serve as the export center for Lao raw materials. Vietnam Communist Party secretary-general Le Kha Phieu made Laos his first overseas trip in early 1998, with trade and economic cooperation at the top of his agenda. Further cooperation was agreed upon in July 1998, when the new Lao prime minister visited Hanoi and signed three agreements on transportation, energy, and drug control. In January 1999, President Khamtay Siphandon visited Hanoi, where the two sides pledged to give each other preferential economic treatment, including the waiver of all tariffs on Vietnamese goods and taxes on Vietnamese investments, to the chagrin of Thai businessmen (Lintner and Crispin 2000a). The Vietnamese president, Tran Duc Luong, returned the visit in June 1999 and agreed to upgrade another road from Laos to the port at Vung Ang.

Military ties between the two countries remain strong and Lao leaders continue to assert that the 1997 mutual defense treaty signed with Hanoi remains in force. In 1997 the two states signed a mutual assistance protocol. Military cooperation became more pressing in 1998, when the ethnic Hmong insurgency rekindled, perhaps in part after Thailand expelled some 25,000 Hmong refugees in the late 1990s (Stratfor 2000b). The Lao military made an urgent appeal to Vietnam to increase military aid to the Lao army. In May 1998, a plane carrying Lieutenant-General Dao Trong Lich, chief of staff of the Vietnamese People's Army, crashed in Xieng Khoung province in northwest Laos, killing all aboard. Xieng Khoung province is the heartland of the Hmong community and the center of the guerrilla insurgency, and there were many reports that the plane was actually shot down. Fearful that the insurgency would cross the border into Vietnam's own aggrieved ethnic minority communities, including Hmong, Hanoi introduced 10,000 troops into Laos to help quell the rebellion. Hanoi was clearly alarmed at the spate of bombings in Vientiane in 2000, which appeared to be targeting Vietnamese—including Hanoi's embassy and a bicycle bomb that exploded at the Vientiane airport ninety minutes before the arrival of the Vietnamese foreign minister in November 2000 (Barnes 2000). Following several military defeats and the loss of control over much of Xieng Khoung province, in June 2000 the Lao army commander traveled to Hanoi to secure more assistance and to strengthen the "special cooperation" between the two militaries (Associated Foreign Press 2000b). Hanoi made it clear that it wanted "the two armies to strengthen their solidarity" and "to consolidate relations and cooperation in the struggle against hostile forces" (Watkin 2000). Vietnamese assistance has not been without cost, as Vietnam has suffered casualties and at least one helicopter has been shot down.

With the February 2001 demonstrations by ethnic minorities living in the Central Highlands in Vietnam, Hanoi can be expected to be hypervigilant about unrest among its own ethnic minorities, and very fearful that rebellion in Laos could easily spread across the long and porous border (Cohen 2001). It is no coincidence that in this same month a protocol on military cooperation and mutual assistance was signed. To that end, Hanoi will likely maintain an active security role in Laos for the time to come. It is clear that the Lao government does not have the capabilities to handle the insurgency, and that it is again wed to Hanoi for maintaining its security. Both Vietnam and Laos consider this bilateral relationship their most important, and these nations' top diplomats serve in each other's capitals, despite the diplomatic opening each has enjoyed since the mid-1990s.

Thailand

In the post–Cold War era, Laos's relationship with Thailand has become its most important, if in substance and not form. Relations with Thailand have improved substantially, yet they pose the greatest challenge to Laos. No state has such an important impact, while at the same time, Thailand is perceived as also being a military threat.

Historical enmity goes back many years owing to the Kingdom of Siam's capture of the Lao kingdom in the nineteenth century and the constant threat it poses to its small neighbor. In the 1930s, the Kingdom of Siam changed its name to Thailand, a name that embodied Bangkok's irredentist claims and desire to create a single state for all ethnic Tai people. Thailand tried to reexert control over Laos as France began its process of decolonization, in an attempt to regain territory that it was forced to cede to the French in the late nineteenth century. Thailand saw France's decolonization as an attempt to reassert its traditional influence in Laos. With the emergence of the Pathet Lao, the Thai prime minister, Field Marshal Sarit, sent Thai military units to fight alongside Hmong insurgents in the CIA's secret war in Laos in the 1960s (Warner 1995: 32). Following the Pathet Lao victory, some 10 percent of the population fled to Thailand, where many continued to plot against the regime. Though Thailand established diplomatic relations with the Lao People's Democratic Republic (LPDR) regime in 1976, border disputes between the two countries broke out almost immediately, and relations were hostile throughout the 1980s, when Thailand was on the front line defending against Vietnamese aggression into Southeast Asia. In 1978–1979, following an exchange of leaders, both sides agreed to turn the Mekong River into a zone of peace and cooperation. Hostilities remained high nonetheless. Thailand accused Laos of supporting Thai Communist Party insurgents while Laos accused Thailand of "provocations" and a desire to overthrow the LPDR regime. Thailand imposed an embargo of some 273 "strategic goods," including jet fuel, cement, bicycles, and medicine, forcing Laos into a closer relationship with Vietnam (Stuart Fox 1997: 178). In 1980, to protest Hanoi's aggression in the region and Vientiane's diplomatic support, Thailand closed its border with Laos.

The closure did not last long. Trade with Thailand became Laos's main economic engine, with the Lao economy growing 2 percent in the 1980s. With Thai prime minister Chitichai Choonhaven's 1989 call to turn Indochina from "battlefields to marketplaces," coupled with the collapse of communism in Eastern Europe, bilateral relations improved markedly.

In 1989, Secretary-General Kaysone Phomvihon visited Thailand twice. In 1990, Princess Sirindhorn, the emissary from the Thai royal family, paid an official visit. Prime Minister Chitichai also visited Laos in 1990. That year the two states agreed to reestablish military attachés in each other's capitals. Following his 1991 coup, General Suchinda Kraprayoon paid his first overseas visit to Laos to assuage the leadership, and both sides agreed to pull their troops back from the border. 1992–1993 likewise saw a flurry of high-level exchanges between Thailand and Laos, culminating in the April 1994 opening of the Friendship Bridge across the Mekong. This event was especially important in that the Thai monarch, King Bhumipol Adulyadej, made his first foreign visit in several decades, indicative of the importance the Thai placed on the event. Yet it was symbolic for the Lao as well, as most consider King Bhumipol to be their legitimate ruler (Evans 1998: 108–111).

Although fighting along the border broke out again in 1994, Bangkok clamped down on the use of Thai territory by Lao exile groups trying to overthrow the LPDR, in order to restore ties. But the Lao government has repeatedly complained that Bangkok has not done enough to stop insurgent activity, indeed that many in the Thai military have turned a blind eye to it. Thailand has tried to appease Laos by closing the last refugee camps, and in the late 1990s it expelled some 25,000

Hmong refugees. In 1996, bilateral talks on the delineation of the border began, and the two sides agreed to complete the border agreement by 2003, though an August 2000 border skirmish, in which Lao militia forces seized three islands held by Thailand, slowed down the demarcation process (Stratfor 2000b).

By the mid-1990s, Vientiane had hoped that its massive dam projects would become a major source of revenue, as electricity could be sold to power-hungry Thailand, whose energy needs were growing in the early 1990s at approximately 15 percent annually. Laos had first exported electricity to Thailand in 1971 and the LPDR pinned its economic development to dam construction, and has outlined plans to construct some twenty-three dams on the Mekong and its tributaries. Four are currently completed or under construction, while eleven are undergoing environmental assessments. The original estimates of revenue earned from electricity sales were U.S.$176 million per year. This figure, however, was highly inflated, and is more likely to be around U.S.$38 million per year (Osborne 2000: 243). The estimated sales of electricity are expected to reach U.S.$350 million by 2010, accounting for 15 percent of GDP (Moreau and Ernsberger 2001).

However, two events have stymied this plan. First, with the 1997 Asian economic crisis, demand for electricity in Thailand collapsed and the Thai prime minister canceled plans to purchase additional electricity from the Nam Theun 2 dam. The second obstacle was the World Bank, which withheld funding for the Nam Theun 2 dam due to environmental and human rights concerns (Lintner 1997). Laos was forced to seek foreign investors for the U.S.$1.2 billion project. But still, with electricity sales to Thailand unlikely to increase, the project has not yet started. In 1999 the Lao prime minister traveled to Bangkok to convince it to sign an electricity purchasing agreement, which he failed to do. Lao development remains in the hands of the Thai. In 2001, sales of electricity to Thailand were only U.S.$30 million, causing many in the government to question the wisdom of the hydroelectric-oriented development program.

Thailand and Laos agreed in March 2001 to build a second Friendship Bridge by 2005 to link the two countries (*Bangkok Post* 2001). But this again will only heighten Lao fears of economic domination by its neighbor. Though increased trade will have a positive effect on some sectors of the Lao economy, the saturation of Lao markets by Thai goods and services will continue to be a strong irritant in Vientiane's dealings with Bangkok; 64 percent of Lao imports come from Thailand, though the Thais only account for 20 percent of Laos's exports (Thayer 1999: 40).

China

Following the Pathet Lao's victory in 1975, China and Laos maintained cordial relations and Beijing continued to provide aid and assist in infrastructure development in the north of the country. With the December 1978 Vietnamese invasion of Cambodia, relations between Beijing and Vientiane soured. Beijing immediately cut off aid to Laos, and Lao persecution of Chinese led to the exodus of 20,000 Chinese from Laos. Though China did not invade Laos in March 1979, as it did Vietnam in its "pedagogical war," it did amass a large number of troops along the border to challenge the Vietnamese-backed LPDR regime. Moreover, the Chinese government began to organize a small opposition guerrilla movement, the Lao Socialist Party, which was dedicated "to liberating Laos from Vietnamese domination" (Stuart Fox 1997: 181). Laos responded by purging pro-Chinese officials from the LPRP's ranks and by further consolidating relations with Vietnam. By 1993, China had cut support for the Lao Socialist Party and began to engage in cross-border trade, which grew rapidly in the 1980s.

China and Laos began to renormalize relations in 1989, though Chinese businessmen had already rushed into Laos, which was an important pathway to Thai markets. While Vietnam touted itself as the gateway and port for the landlocked provinces in China's southwest corner, Beijing looked to Thailand via Laos. Thailand had become an important trading partner and source of foreign investment to China, while Beijing deemed Laos to be a malleable partner. By 1989–1990, half of the foreign investment in Laos came from China.

By 1991 the Lao leadership had warmed to China, and Prime Minister Khamtay traveled to China in August 1992 to sign a border agreement. By 1992, Lao president and LPRP secretary-general Kaysone Phomvihon had made three visits to China, which was now a major supplier of development assistance. In 1994 a bilateral military cooperation deal was signed and China established several munitions and ordinance factories in the north of Laos in an attempt to wean the Lao from their dependence on the Vietnamese. Relations were so close as to cause angst in other Southeast Asian capitals, which had grown alarmed at Beijing's aggressiveness in the region in the early to middle 1990s (Bourdet 1996: 93). Although the primary cause for alarm was China's seizure of several islands in the South China Sea that were claimed by other ASEAN members, the ASEAN states were also concerned about the close ties—to the point of being an alliance—between Myanmar and China.

When the Asian economic crisis hit in 1997, Laos turned to China. Beijing offered millions of dollars in aid and export credits to stabilize the Lao economy. Bilateral delegations increased in 1998 and 1999, including military delegations, as Vientiane became further mired in economic crisis. In addition to aid, the Chinese accepted barter trade with Laos (McDonald 2000). In January 1999, Prime Minister Sisavit Keobounphan paid an eight-day visit to China to discuss aid programs and signed five cooperation agreements. In November 2000, Chinese president Jiang Zemin made a historic four-day trip to Laos.

One negative aspect in the Aino-Lao relationship is Chinese pressure to have Laos dynamite and dredge significant portions of the Mekong River to open it up for Chinese shipping (Osborne 2000: 234). The Lao have resisted, fearful of giving the Chinese a further means to saturate the Lao market with Chinese consumer goods. Vientiane is already angry at China's massive dam-building campaign in its portion of the river, which has reduced the fish stocks as well as the volume of water, which the Lao need for their own hydroelectric projects (Crispin, Cohen, and Lintner 2000: 22). China is in the process of constructing thirteen dams, infuriating Laos and the other downstream states, Thailand, Cambodia, and Vietnam. China has withstood pressure from Laos and the other riparian states to join the Mekong River Commission, whose collective strength gives Laos some degree of confidence in withstanding Chinese political and diplomatic pressure, as well as the threat of the cessation of development assistance (Crispin, Cohen, and Lintner 2000: 23). Laos, like the other Mekong states, has been cautious in making public its concerns about China's use of the river. As Milton Osborne notes, "For all of them, China is perceived as an impossibly large presence whose power is such that to question its actions and motives is to risk unquantifiable damage" (2000: 228).

The United States

Laos is the only Indochinese country with whom Washington did not break diplomatic relations after 1975, and became a U.S. back channel to Hanoi. However, relations were hostile at best, as the LPDR regime continued to view Washington with a high degree of mistrust. Washington cut off aid to Laos in the 1970s, and relations remained poor owing to Laos's unwillingness to cooperate with the United States over issues of prisoners of war (POWs) and soldiers missing in action (MIA), as well as the Lao role in the global drug trade. The United States first persuaded Lao leaders to cooperate on the POW/MIA issue in 1985, and by 1994 the remains of sixty servicemen had been repatriated. The Lao were less forthcoming on MIA concerns, and in 1973 they refused to provide any information on the matter. The U.S. government estimates that some 300 U.S. soldiers were taken prisoner in Laos. In treating the POW/MIA issue as a "humanitarian" concern, in April 1994 President William Clinton cleared the way for aid to Laos when the latter agreed to cooperate in a trilateral MIA commission with the United States and Vietnam (Dommen 1995: 90).

Interestingly, in the past few years the Lao government has tried to bolster its flagging legitimacy by drawing attention to its nationalist credentials. To this end, it has recently tried to downplay the role that the Vietnamese played in the LPRP's victory and ascension to power of the royal Lao government. Whereas the United States has received a high degree of cooperation from the Vietnamese government in the search for POWs/MIAs, the Lao government has resisted trilateral searches, despite the fact that most U.S. POWs/MIAs in Laos were combating Vietnamese forces (Dommen 1995: 90).

The United States has also reproved Laos for its lack of cooperation in stemming the flow of illicit drugs. In 1989, the year of peak opium production, Laos produced over 400 metric tons. The following year, the United States and Laos signed a memorandum of understanding on the suppression of narcotic production, and the United States implemented an alternative crop program for Hmong tribesmen in Houaphanh province. Since then, annual opium production has declined. Laos remains the world's third largest opium producer, behind Burma and Afghanistan, and the estimated cultivation in 1999 was 21,800 hectares, though a 16 percent decrease from 1998. In 1999, production was estimated at 140 metric tons. With the U.S. defeat of the Taliban regime in Afghanistan and the establishment of a UN-backed government in Kabul that has pledged to eradicate poppy cultivation, there will be increased demand by drug-producing syndicates for Lao opium. Moreover, Laos has become an important source of methamphetamine production.

Relations with the United States cooled in 1998 when the nephew of Hmong general Vung Pao, who led the CIA-equipped army during the Vietnam War, disappeared while in Laos. His body was later found, though the Lao government refused to comment. In early 1999, six Hmong Americans were arrested in Laos trying to smuggle in automatic weapons. Very simply, the Lao government does not believe that the Hmong insurgency, with its historical ties to the CIA, is operating independently of the U.S. government. The fact that some 100,000 Hmong refugees resettled in the United States gives Vientiane further cause for alarm (Dommen 1995: 90). There is, however, no evidence that the Hmong insurgents are still receiving support from the CIA.

Relations declined even further following an unprecedented demonstration by students in Vientiane on October 26, 1999. Although dozens of other protesters were arrested, six of the student protesters fled to Thailand, where the United States granted them asylum. The Lao government was infuriated by Washington's "interference in the internal affairs of Laos" and remained convinced that Washington was out to undermine the LPRP's monopoly of power through a strategy of "peaceful evolution" (Associated Press 2000b). The United States has raised the issue of the four known political prisoners in Laos and the 100–200 additional people who are being charged under the country's vague national security laws (Pennington 2000).

In 1997, Laos received most-favored nation (MFN) trade status from the United States for the first time. But Vientiane's dismal human and religious rights situation has angered many in the U.S. Congress, who have held up a bilateral trade agreement that would give Laos permanent normal trade relations with the United States. Until there is greater and more consistent cooperation with the United States on the POW/MIA issue and drug eradication, relations will remain poor.

ASEAN

Laos toed the Vietnamese line on ASEAN from the late 1970s through the 1980s, when ASEAN was pitted against Hanoi over the latter's occupation of Cambodia. It was not until Hanoi's September 1989 withdrawal from Cambodia that relations with ASEAN could start to improve. In July 1992, Laos became an observer in ASEAN, following its signing of the Bali Treaty of Amity and Cooperation. There was a distinct ASEAN-ization of Lao foreign policy by the mid-1990s. Much of it was oriented toward the region, and the country for the first time played host to many of the leaders of the ASEAN states, including President Suharto of Indonesia, Prime Minister Goh Chok Tong of Singapore, and President Fidel Ramos of the Philippines. In 1997 the Lao prime minister paid visits to Brunei and Malaysia and normalized relations with Myanmar. In March 1996, Laos formally applied to join ASEAN, which it did along with Myanmar on July 23, 1997. In 1997 the Lao foreign ministry opened a new division, the Office of ASEAN Affairs, to coordinate regional diplomacy (Stuart Fox 1998: 78).

Laos soon developed misgivings about ASEAN. For one thing, ASEAN membership obligated Laos to lower its tariffs on imports from other ASEAN states by 2008, inflaming fears that the country would be saturated with cheap imports. Second, Laos was concerned about increasing political interference from other member states. One of the reasons it joined, like Myanmar, was to be able to hide behind the organization's collective cloak from Western criticism of human rights violations and the lack of democratic reform. In the mid-1990s, ASEAN was self-confident and increasingly willing to stand up to the United States and European states, espousing "Asian values" as justification of its political and human rights situation. Laos believed that membership would help shield the government from such international criticism.

ASEAN adheres to two standard operating principles: noninterference in the internal affairs of other states and consensus-style decisionmaking. The first has been a cornerstone of ASEAN, and it is only through this policy that ten countries with radically different regime types have been able to work together. States like Laos, which have repressive governments and frightful human rights situations, would only join ASEAN if they had assurances that the organization would not put their domestic politics under scrutiny. The second principle, the so-called ASEAN way, is a policy of consensus building. Consensus, in the ASEAN context, means that the least common denominator, the policy or position that all can accept, no matter how diluted it is, prevails. Since 1995, when the organization grew from six to ten members, there has been a greater diversity of views on every issue, making consensus even more difficult.

With the Thai foreign minister's 1998 call for "flexible engagement," that is, greater interference in the internal affairs of other states when the issue has transborder repercussions, Laos and other states balked. Likewise, Laos, along with Myanmar, Cambodia, and Vietnam, have formed a caucus within ASEAN, and use their collective pressure to ensure that ASEAN decisions are watered down and nonthreatening. This has come at a time when the organization is already weakened and the founding members are mired in their own political and economic crises and thus unable to take on a greater leadership role.

Analyzing Lao Foreign Policy

The Individual

The Lao ruling class is elite and homogeneous. The original Pathet Lao leadership was small, with power concentrated in the hands of less than a dozen people. At the LPRP's third congress in 1975, there were only seven members on the politburo and twenty-seven members on the central committee. Twenty-five years later, there are still only eleven members on the politburo and fifty-three on the central committee. At the time of the sixth party congress in March 1996, there were only 78,000 party members, who composed only 1.7 percent of the population, making the LPRP the most elite communist party in the world. The central committee elected at the sixth congress was overwhelmingly male; only four of the forty-nine members were female. Seventy-six percent of the central committee members had joined the party before the 1975 revolution (Bourdet 1997: 73–74). At the seventh congress in March 2001, the central committee had fifty-three members, forty-five of whom joined the party before 1975 and were socialized during the revolution (LPRP 2001). By 2000 there were only some 100,000 LPRP members in the country—less than 2 percent of the population.

Since the founding of the LPDR in 1976, the leadership has been stagnant. It was not until the fifth party congress in May 1991 that a transition began to replace the ruling elite who founded the Pathet Lao. So the leadership has been remarkably stable, cohesive, and not torn by factional infighting, as occurred in Cambodia and Vietnam.

The leadership is paranoid and secretive, and it was not until December 1975 that the full rosters of the politburo and central committee were made public. The leadership lived in a heavily guarded compound, known as Kilometer Six, outside of Vientiane. There they lived in complete seclusion, with only a handful of top Vietnamese advisers. "The isolation of senior party leaders was symptomatic of the defensiveness and lack of confidence of the regime, and its distrust of its former opponents" (Stuart Fox 1997: 175). They are aloof from the citizenry, who have no input into foreign policy. Over half of the citizenry were born after 1975, have no recollection of the revolution, and tend to orient themselves toward Thailand and Thai culture.

The Lao elite's proclivity toward Vietnam can be explained in three ways. First, the Lao leadership feels very close historical, ideological, and personal ties to Vietnam. During its war for national independence, the leadership worked very closely with North Vietnam, which introduced troops into northwestern Laos to protect the Ho Chi Minh Trail. By the end of the war Vietnam had some 70,000 troops in Laos. Vietnam People's Army advisers served with every Pathet Lao unit and all battlefield operations were coordinated with North Vietnam.

The Vietnamese presence in Laos was a boon for the Pathet Lao, and it is clear that they never would have come to power as quickly as they had without Vietnamese assistance. But the ties to Vietnam are also personal at the elite level. Prince Souphanouvong, the "Red Prince," lived in Vietnam for many years and launched his anticolonial movement in 1946 with Vietnamese troops. Souphanouvong married a Vietnamese communist, while Kaysone, the leader of the Pathet Lao, was half Vietnamese. Most other Lao leaders were trained in Vietnamese party schools and military academies, and often spoke Vietnamese among themselves. Almost every member of the Lao leadership spent significant time in Vietnam and several maintained villas in Hanoi.

That most of the senior leaders spoke Vietnamese and were thoroughly socialized in Vietnamese culture clearly had a bearing on the leadership's continued willingness to follow the Vietnamese military and foreign policy line. For example, in 1976, Kaysone mimicked the words emanating from Hanoi, that ASEAN was "an organization set up by the US imperialists . . . to defend the interests of US neo-colonialism." Laos supported Hanoi's occupation of Cambodia and maintained terse relations with the People's Republic of China.

Immediately following the establishment of the LPDR, the Pathet Lao sent a delegation to Hanoi to thank their socialist brothers for their "extremely precious contributions made by Vietnamese forces in the noble spirit of proletarian internationalism." Laos immediately acquiesced to Hanoi's demands to establish an Indochina Federation and the stationing of some 60,000 troops in Laos. The Lao leaders were never confident in their own ability to hold power, despite a large domestic security apparatus, and continued to rely on the Vietnamese to ensure their political survival. To this day, they do not believe in their own ability to govern independently. Whenever there is a domestic security crisis, such as the renewed Hmong insurgency in 1999–2000, the Lao leaders immediately call on Hanoi for assistance.

Second, although the Lao government asserts that it is ruled by a collective leadership, this was true only after 1992 and was less true during the era of Lao president and LPRP secretary-general Kaysone Phomvihon. Because Kaysone was primus inter pares and ruled almost unchallenged, his foreign policy orientations held the day. And Kaysone was vehemently anti-Thai. Clashes with Thailand along the border started in 1975 and continue to this day. Under Kaysone, there could never be close ties with Thailand, which he believed still harbored irredentist designs on Laos. He personally held Thailand accountable for the sporadic anticommunist insurgency. There were thousands of Lao refugees living in camps in Thailand and the Lao government accused Thailand of allowing insurgents to organize in these refugee camps. When Thailand became serious about improving ties with Laos, it put pressure on the camps to stop all insurgent activities and expelled several Hmong émigrés. Between 1993 and 1999, Thailand repatriated more than 60,000 Hmong refugees in an attempt to improve relations, yet the Lao government still mistrusted Thai intentions.

Perhaps mistrust of Thai policy lingers because the leadership transition in Laos from the first generation of revolutionary leaders to the second is still not complete. Only with changes in leadership are changes in policy possible. The politburo elected in 2001 still has one or two first-generation members who demand that Laos follow the traditional line of maintaining close ties with Vietnam, while remaining wary of Thailand and China. The first moves in the gradual transition of leaders occurred at the LPRP's fifth congress in May 1991, when Souphanouvong and two other first-generation leaders retired. In November 1992, Kaysone died. The fact that these senior leaders who had close personal ties with Vietnam were no longer part of the decisionmaking process indicates that Laos should have reevaluated its relationship with Hanoi as new individuals with their own biases and perceptions of the security environment became top decisionmakers. Indeed, there was some attempt after 1992 to pursue a more independent foreign policy line. For instance, the "special relationship" between the two countries became "increasingly formal" (Johnson 1992: 86). Although Vientiane did not normalize relations with China until Hanoi did in November 1991, Vientiane signaled a willingness to engage Beijing in 1988, well ahead on Hanoi. In 1988, Kaysone traveled to Beijing, and in 1991 he spent his annual "vacation" in China for the first time, rather than in Vietnam. In July 1992, Laos signed the Bali Treaty of Amity and Cooperation, becoming an observer in ASEAN, and engaged in high-level exchanges with Thailand. Very clearly there were exogenous factors that forced these changes, in particular the loss of Soviet aid and Hanoi's own economic reform program, which left it less concerned about Laos. But without a change in leadership, overtures to Thailand, ASEAN, and China would not have occurred.

The third way to explain Laos's proclivity to align itself with Vietnam has to do with the high level of exchanges between the two. The relationship has been asymmetrical, with large numbers of Lao coming to Vietnam for study and training at the National Ho Chi Minh Academy of Politics and the various defense colleges. Between 1976 and 1981 alone, there were some 10,000 Lao students in Vietnam (Stuart Fox 1997: 185). Likewise, between 1978 and 1993, there were some 400 senior Lao military personnel who studied in Vietnam; indeed, most of the senior Lao officer corps has studied in Vietnamese military academies or trained with Vietnamese military personnel. This is a powerful instrument of socialization.

In short, an individual-level analysis of Lao foreign policy leads one to believe that Laos is closely aligned with Vietnam and that there would be little room for maneuver. For the most part, between 1975 and 1991, this is the best level of analysis, and indeed, Laos's foreign policy was dominated by and mirrored Vietnam's. The elite was unified, autonomous, and had close historical, ideological, and personal ties to Vietnam, as well as a shared perception of threat. After 1991, however, individual-level analysis fails to explain vacillations in Lao foreign policy. Thus one must turn to the state level of analysis.

The State

As a single-party Marxist state that exerts its dictatorship over the proletariat, denying the development of civil society, autonomous unions, a free press, nongovernmental organizations (NGOs), and opposition parties, Laos seems a poor candidate for analysis at the state level. Yet since 1991 the country's leadership has become more factionalized over the pace and scope of economic reform and foreign policy orientations. Internal politics and factional infighting have influenced foreign policy outcomes.

The fifth party congress in 1991 failed to bring about the leadership transition that the country desperately needed. Leaders were reluctant to transfer power to a new generation and much of the politburo remained on the ruling body, while those who did retire were replaced by fellow first-generation leaders (Johnson 1993: 78). For example, seventy-eight-year-old Nouhak Phoumsavanh, who had close personal ties with Vietnam, replaced Kaysone as president.

Yet with the death of strongman Kaysone Phomvihon, there was more room for debate within the LPRP over policies, and as a result, political factions emerged. The new party chief, General Khamtay Siphandone, never had the authority of Kaysone, and had to build consensus for policies, forcing him to bargain with factions and make concessions for their support. Like Kaysone, President Nouhak was conservative and pro-Vietnamese, yet his views did not carry the day. He did not have the prestige or the political capital to enforce his views and maintain Lao's foreign policy orientation toward Hanoi against the will of younger party members. As a result, after Kaysone's death in November 1992, there was an unprecedented degree of debate and factional infighting within the LPRP.

Factionalism now occurs at three separate but interconnected levels: generational, regional, and ideological. Factional infighting emerged in response to the 1997 Asian economic crisis. The split occurred between the older generation of leaders, who were clinging to power, and a younger generation, who wanted to replace them. The younger leaders were angered that there was little turnover on the politburo and central committee at recent party congresses. The younger, more reform-minded members were especially unhappy at the apparent purge at the sixth congress, when "the leading proponents of more rapid liberalization" were "dropped from the Central Committee" (Stuart Fox 1997: 207).

The younger leaders criticized the politburo's handling of the economy. They saw the septuagenarian leaders as being out of touch, too ideological, and too bound to Vietnam, which was in no position to save the Lao economy. The younger generation of leaders saw China as a more appropriate ally and were led by the relatively spry sixty-year-old foreign minister, Somsavat Lengsavad, who is also ethnic Chinese. China was already a hero to many across Southeast Asia for not devaluing its currency in the midst of the economic crisis. Somsavat traveled to Beijing to negotiate a large financial aid package that stabilized the kip, curtailed inflation at 31 percent, and allocated U.S.$7 million to build a cultural center in Vientiane. The younger leaders, who also tend to be northerners, believe that economic interdependence with the southern Chinese province of Yunnan is essential for Lao development (Lintner and Crispin 2000b: 26–27).

The factional infighting became so bad that in July and August 2000, ahead of the seventh congress, former president Nouhak Phoumsavanh held a series of crisis meetings with the leadership, warning that the country "risks disintegration" if the factional infighting did not stop (*FEER* 2000a). Yet the seventh congress not only failed to resolve the ideological and generational divide, but also exacerbated the divisions.

At the LPRP's seventh party congress in March 2001, many young party leaders hoped that Somsavat would join the politburo. He had a large following among midcareer cadres, but was not elected. Instead, Thongloun Sisoulith, the head of foreign relations in the rubber stamp National Assembly, won. Many hard-line conservatives do not like Somsavat and mistrust his policy orientation toward China. Moreover, at the seventh congress, the aging leadership, who was so ineffectual during the economic crisis, was reelected (Wong-Anan 2001).

In early 2002, Somsavat disappeared ahead of a government reshuffle indicating that he was about to lose his job in the face of continued conservative opposition to his policies (*Straits Times* 2002). In a similar case, LPRP conservatives orchestrated the dismissal of the finance minister, Khamxay Souphanouvong, who during the financial crisis had favored improving ties with China. The ouster was all the more surprising because Khamxay was the son of the "Red Prince" Souphanouvong, the former president and founder of the LPRP. Khamxay later fled the country and sought asylum in New Zealand (*FEER* 2000b).

The death of President Kaysone, the Asian economic crisis, and the fifth and sixth party congresses provided four opportunities for Laos to reorient its foreign policies away from Vietnam and closer to China or Thailand. Yet ties with Vietnam actually strengthened from the late 1990s to the present for two other domestic political reasons. First is the militarization of politics in Laos. Senior military officers have always sat on the ruling politburo. In 1991–1992, with the fifth congress and Kaysone's death, two generals took on senior positions. General Nouhak

Phoumsavanh became president while General Khamtay was promoted from prime minister to party chief of the LPRP. In all, the military controlled four of the nine politburo seats. The military's domination of political life was even more consolidated at the sixth congress in 1996. Of the nine-person politburo, six were senior military officers. At the seventh congress in 2001, seven of fifty-three central committee members (13 percent) were military, while three of eleven politburo members (27 percent) were military officers. The militarization of Lao elite politics is astounding. Comparatively speaking, the military in Laos has more political power than in other communist states. As Martin Stuart Fox notes, in Laos the "Army took control of the party. . . . All are members of the Pathet Lao revolutionary elite, all hard men determined that the party through the army, would continue to monopolize power" (1997: 207).

The result of this militarization was pressure to bring Laos back into the Vietnamese orbit beginning in 1996. The military is arguably the most conservative force in society. Ideologically the officer corps is thoroughly Marxist, and believes that its primary responsibility is to defend not the nation, but the communist regime. Vietnam has considerable leverage over the Lao military through regular exchanges, training a large number of officers, and providing the bulk of military equipment. Despite border skirmishes with Thailand, the greatest threat to the Lao regime is the lingering Hmong insurgency in the mountainous interior and the regime's perception of foreign-based opposition to communist party rule. By 1996 the regime was concerned about the pace and scope of the economic reform program and Thailand's domination of the Lao economy. The military continued to act as a break on the reform program, and to orient Lao foreign policy back toward Hanoi.

This was possible because a spate of bombings in Vientiane and a renewed Hmong insurgency starting in 1999 convinced many in the leadership that they were under attack and only one country, Vietnam, had the capability and will to defend the LPDR regime. Insurgency has always driven the government into the arms of the Vietnamese, as the Lao regime has no confidence in its own ability to contain an insurgency. There have been many outbreaks of armed defiance to the regime since its founding. Between 1975 and mid-1976 there was a rebellion under the command of a former Pathet Lao leader who opposed the "North Vietnamese annexation of Laos." In 1989 one group announced the formation of a provisional government with Prince Soulivong Savang, the son of the late king, who lives in exile in France, as its head. In January 1990 the government dispatched troops to bring an end to the rebellion. Twenty Vietnamese MiG-21s were used in the attacks, as were Vietnamese ground troops and chemical weapons (Hamilton-Merritt 1993: 550). In 1990 there was a wave of dissidence. In the spring, more than forty highland officials, calling themselves the "social democrat group," openly criticized the regime, submitted their resignations, and called for democratic elections. In October, six more officials, including two vice ministers, criticized the government and demanded multiparty elections. All were arrested and dissent was stifled throughout the 1990s (*Bangkok Post* 1990). More recently there was a brief incursion into Laos by supporters of the former ruling monarchy, and the pretender to the throne, Prince Soulivong, has traveled between Western capitals trying to build up support for a restored constitutional monarchy (Lintner and Crispin 2000d).

In the run-up to the celebrations for the twenty-fifth anniversary of the founding of the LPDR there was a wave of unexplained bombings in the capital. On the one hand, the ethnic Hmong insurgency had revived, and the fighting was on a scale large enough to warrant the reintroduction of some 10,000 Vietnamese ground troops. The chief of staff of the Vietnam People's Army, Lieutenant-General Dao Trong Lich, was killed in May 1998, when his plane was shot down over the Hmong stronghold of Xieng Khoung while on an inspection and needs assessment tour (Lintner and Crispin 2000a). The Lao minister of defense, Lieutenant-General Choummaly Sayasone, traveled to Hanoi to negotiate a military cooperation package in June 2000 (Associated Foreign Press 2000b).

The bombing campaign in 2000 strengthened the military's hands. Under the leadership of Sayasone, Laos leaned to Hanoi, and for the first time since 1989, large numbers of Vietnamese forces were based in Laos. On the other hand, the bombing campaign in Vientiane was also seen as the result of factional infighting: the targets of the bombs were often Vietnamese, or designed to embarrass the Vietnamese. As the Hmong have only a limited capability to wage a bombing campaign within the city, some ascribed the campaign to reformers in the regime protesting the reintroduction of Vietnamese troops into the country. As one Thai academic put it: "Certain elements in the pro-China northern clique are mobilizing traditional anti-Vietnamese sentiment to their political advantage" (Lintner and Crispin 2000a). Regardless of who actually perpetrated the bombings, all political factions in Laos have used the attacks to bolster their own positions.

Although the Lao leadership asserts that it operates collectively, the regime is fraught with factionalism. The LPDR leadership, however, is autonomous from the public and the various factions have made no attempt to align themselves with social forces or segments of the population. As long as factional infighting is conducted behind closed doors, it is tolerated. Nor are there independent interest groups, NGOs, or autonomous unions that can influence the regime's policy. The only organized opposition is an ethnically based and geographically isolated insurgency that is too small to threaten the regime's survival. Foreign policy is influenced at the state level—it occurs only within the elite corridors of power in Vientiane. Yet these debates, conducted since 1991, have resulted in gradual openings and shifts in foreign policy orientations.

Culture is one notable failing in the state level of analysis. Culturally, linguistically, and in terms of religion, Laos should be closely oriented toward Thailand, but it is not. At the popular level, Thai culture, symbols, and influence dominate popular society. The leadership, however, remains highly suspicious of Thai influence—both commercial and cultural. In part this is the regime's own doing. Grant Evans argues that the communist regime has fought a major war over the cultural space in the country (1998). The party has striven to erase prerevolution images, such as the royalty, from the national consciousness. The regime believes that its legitimacy is based on forging a new, socialist, collective identity. Yet these new symbols have little appeal for the vast majority of the population, over half of whom were born after 1975 and have no recollection of the revolution. Lacking traditional Lao symbols and culture, the people then turn to their dominant cultural cousins, the Thai. Thus there is a strong gravitational pull toward Thailand at the popular level. That is rejected by the government, which prefers the ideological affinity it shares with Vietnam and China.

The System

On the one hand, the Lao leadership owes its power to outside, especially Vietnamese, forces. Laos became engulfed in the Vietnam War, as the Vietnamese leadership viewed all of Indochina as a single "strategic battlefield" and used Laos as a transportation route for the war in the south. In turn, the United States waged a secret war and massive bombing campaign in the country starting in the early 1960s. Without Vietnamese support and a primary military role in Laos, the Pathet Lao would not have come to power as quickly as they did.

Because Laos is a socialist state, the international system does have some bearing on Lao foreign policy. With the Pathet Lao's 1975 victory, Laos became a firm ally of the Soviet Union and Vietnam. Laos took Moscow's side in the Sino-Soviet dispute and was a staunch supporter of Hanoi throughout the Third Indochina War. Two thousand Soviet advisers lived in Laos and two-thirds of aid came from Moscow. Yet in many ways Moscow had surprisingly little influence in Laos. The loss of aid from the Soviet Union in 1991 did force Laos to look to Beijing for assistance. And faced with the loss of aid, Laos did implement the New Economic Mechanism in 1986, by which time foreign aid and loans accounted for 51 percent of GDP (Thurlow 2000).

An interesting case study in how the international system influenced Lao foreign policy is its relationship with ASEAN. Following the Pathet Lao victory, the leadership aped the Vietnamese line that ASEAN was simply a tool of the U.S. neoimperialists. Laos was quick to acquiesce to Vietnamese pressure to join an Indochina Federation, and it had hostile relations with ASEAN throughout the 1980s. With Vietnam's 1989 withdrawal from Cambodia and Laos, the stage was set for the bettering of relations between Hanoi and ASEAN. Hanoi won observer status in the organization, which until recently it had demonized, and became a full member in 1995. Laos would never have joined ASEAN, first as an observer in 1992 and then as a full member in 1997, without Vietnam having done so first. Laos never takes a diplomatic lead that contradicts or preempts Hanoi's position.

What drove Laos to reverse its long-standing foreign policy that saw ASEAN as an enemy? On the one hand, one can look to the collapse of the Soviet Union, the loss of Soviet aid, and the decline in Hanoi's willingness to assist Laos. On the other hand, Laos did not rush to join ASEAN and was apprehensive about joining an organization about which it maintains serious misgivings. ASEAN had little to offer Laos. It would not supplant the loss of Vietnamese and Soviet aid. Nor would it serve as a security arrangement. Moreover, Thailand, Laos's historical enemy, dominated ASEAN. Membership also required Laos to abide by the ASEAN Free Trade Agreement (AFTA), lower tariffs, and stop protecting its inefficient state-owned enterprises by 2008.

Ironically, though Laos showed some interest in joining the organization, one can make the case that ASEAN courted Laos more than Laos courted ASEAN. For its part, ASEAN had misgivings about Laos. Some in ASEAN questioned whether Laos was ready to join. It is the poorest and least-developed ASEAN state. Moreover, it does not have the trained staff to handle the sheer volume of ASEAN meetings. The Lao foreign ministry established the Office of ASEAN Affairs in 1997, but with only fourteen members to attend over 100 technical meetings a year, its resources are stretched too thin (Stuart Fox 1998: 78). Yet many in ASEAN wanted to bring in the last three Southeast Asian states, Laos, Cambodia, and Myanmar, in time to celebrate the organization's thirtieth anniversary in 1997. Still, the overarching concern was security. Laos's growing closeness to China alarmed many Southeast

Asian states, which sought to limit Chinese influence and reorient Laos's foreign policy toward the region (Bourdet 1996: 93).

As Laos becomes more integrated in the region, system-level analysis will become a more interesting model. Laos is currently in the midst of a massive road-building and infrastructure program that is part of the development of a regional transportation network. Under the auspices of the UN Development Programme (UNDP) and the Asian Development Bank (ADB), this massive regional highway, road-building, and rail network seeks to link all the countries in the "Greater Mekong Subregion" to facilitate commerce and economic interdependence. Laos is the central state in this plan, linking China to Thailand and Thailand to Vietnam (Thurlow 2000). China has already funded a major highway in the north of the country, while Vietnam is upgrading many east-west roads to the Vietnamese coast. Japan has offered to fund the construction of two more bridges across the Mekong (*Bangkok Post* 2001). Very simply, the physical isolation that Laos previously enjoyed is dissipating and the country is becoming more integrated into its surroundings.

The weakness in using the system level of analysis for Laos becomes evident when one looks at the influence that the international community has, or rather does not have, to offer the pace and scope of the domestic economic and political reform (Lintner 2001; *FEER* 2001). Laos should be vulnerable, owing to its dependence on foreign aid and development assistance. Although Laos has little leverage over the international community, the international community has had little influence over the pace and scope of economic and political reforms. One ADB report complained that the moribund Lao economy was due to "inadequate government capacity and commitment . . . to pushing forward economic reforms." The World Bank likewise has linked future lending to political and economic reforms. Yet the Lao leadership has not only not implemented new reforms, but has also backtracked on some already-existing reforms (*FEER* 2001).

The international donor community has tried but usually failed in pressuring Vientiane to change. Owing to such intransigence and unwillingness to reform, there is dissatisfaction among the international community and a growing sense of donor fatigue. Yet the Lao leadership is unmoved despite its dependence on foreign aid.

Conclusion

The three different levels of analysis, individual, state, and system, can best be used to analyze Lao foreign policy at different periods. From the founding of the Lao People's Democratic Republic in 1975 to 1992, Laos's foreign policy was completely tied to Vietnam's, owing to the leadership's close personal ties, shared ideology, and shared perception of threat. The communist leadership's hatred of Thailand precluded any warming of ties between the two countries. As Hanoi leaned to the Soviet Union and confronted China over the Third Indochina War, so too did Vientiane, though China had far more to offer Laos in terms of development and security than Vietnam did. With the collapse of communism in Eastern Europe in 1989, Lao foreign policy should have changed more, according to a systems analysis. It did not. Lao policymakers react slowly and cautiously.

The state level of analysis works well in the period since 1991–1992. With the NEM implemented in 1986, Thailand came to dominate the Lao economy, reinvigorating fears among the leadership of Thai interests in its poor and vulnerable neighbor. Renewed fears of Thailand, coupled with internal debates over the pace and the scope of the economic reform program, and the death of several first-generation leaders, have led to increased factional fighting. Factional infighting has become manifest in debates over Lao foreign policy, with the older, more conservative leaders opting to lean toward the Vietnamese. Younger, more reform-minded leaders see closer ties with China, citing the failure of the Vietnamese economic model. One can also see the dominant power of the Lao military in steering Lao foreign policy. Yet the state level has its limitations. Marxism-Leninism really has no bearing on Lao foreign policy anymore, as Laos has abandoned all pretensions of being a communist state. As Grant Evans notes, "Socialism no longer represents an economic program, or a program of social and cultural transformation. Instead it is a device of political rhetoric, which proclaims, both externally and internally, that the one party state has no intention of allowing liberal democratic reforms" (1998: 2).

Likewise, if Laos's foreign policy were based more on cultural considerations, we would see a close alliance with Thailand. Yet Thailand's cultural dominance is a threat to the LPDR regime. The system level of analysis has intrinsic appeal, as it works throughout the LPDR's history. Laos's neighbors have traditionally interfered in its internal affairs, striving to compete for influence; indeed, the regime owes its position to the intervention of other states. As the region becomes more interdependent, and the Lao communications and transportation networks become more central, foreign interest will remain strong. Likewise, as Laos remains resource-rich but sparsely populated, we should expect the great powers that surround it, China, Vietnam, and Thailand, to continue to compete for influence over the "land of 10,000 elephants."

Regardless of the level of analysis used, one comes to the quick conclusion that there are policy limits for such a small, poor, and vulnerable state. At best, Laos can simply cope with its immediate security environment. It has few options, preferring to balance against its overarching threats. Which way it balances tends to reflect the domestic balance of power among the LPRP's factions. Too small to enmesh potential adversaries in an interdependent relationship, Laos has also eschewed international law and has only recently explored multilateralism.

10

Refining Our Understanding of Small State Foreign Policy

Jeanne A. K. Hey

It is useful to recall what James Rosenau (1990) anticipated about small state foreign policy behavior, now that we reach the conclusion of a volume organized around the levels of analysis employed in his "pre-theories." Size was actually less important to Rosenau than was level of development, as demonstrated by his ranking the bureaucracy as the most important explanation in all developed states, and the individual as the most important in all underdeveloped states, large or small. Size played a part in determining the importance of the global system. Rosenau ranked "system" the second most important variable for all small states, and the fourth most important for all large states. In a more detailed version of the pre-theories, Rosenau elevated the importance of systemic variables in countries that were "penetrated" by ideas, values, and goods from the exterior. In "unpenetrated" systems, he elevated the role of the individual to the top spot (Rosenau 1990: 174–175). For Rosenau's inductive theory, then, small states, especially underdeveloped ones, were more vulnerable to the vagaries of the international system and their own leaders than were their larger counterparts.

What then, do the contributors to this volume find? Each level of analysis is examined in detail below. This section describes a general ranking of the levels. Four of the eight authors (with varying degrees of intensity) ranked the individual as the most important. Two ranked the system at the top and one (Paul Luif on Austria) suggested that all the variables share roughly equal ranking. The system level ranks first or second in six of the eight cases. This leaves the domestic level of analysis as the weakest. But we shall see below that it carries a strong influence under certain conditions. It is nonetheless important at this stage to note that the two weightiest variables are exactly those that Rosenau identified over thirty-five years ago as major players in explaining small state foreign policy.

A discussion of the theory-building limits of this project is in order before conclusions are suggested. First, contributors followed an inductive approach, beginning with a description of foreign policy content and organizing policy inputs according to levels of analysis. While each level of analysis corresponds to a theoretical approach (system to realism, state to domestic politics and a "national attributes" theory, and individual to political psychology and "great man" theories), there was no guiding theory per se that grounded the empirical analyses. Our hope was to draw from the empirical content a set of conclusions. This framework afforded the project crucial benefits. It permitted contributors to focus on those areas in which they had expertise and that they considered most fruitful. It also prevented the imposition of a given theory on the chapters. In other words, contributors were not made to ensure that their research "fit" a foregone conclusion. This approach also allowed us to glean analytical conclusions from the empirical research. That said, the absence of a guiding theory makes it all the more difficult to extract specific conclusions about any particular theory. The levels-of-analysis approach was chosen as a middle ground. It organized and oriented the chapters, without dictating any findings or conclusions.

A second caveat is that this research contains no control. There are no chapters on nonsmall states with which to compare small state foreign policy behavior. The volume as a whole therefore resembles a "similar case" study approach (Ragin 1987; Hey 1995b) in which one examines a series of cases sharing crucial criteria (e.g., smallness) and draws conclusions from them. In this study, smallness is the only criterion all the cases share, as the states under study vary in terms of geography, development, and political system. This brings us to a third issue. The very diversity just mentioned accompanies diversity in foreign policy topics discussed. The behaviors examined range from the very broad (e.g., Luxembourg's foreign policy trends in the 1990s) to the very specific (Panama's canal negotiations). Such diversity allows us to hone in on smallness, but can also make comparisons difficult where other policy inputs are important.

What Patterns Emerge?[1]

The System

The chapters in this volume leave little doubt that the system level is a key explanatory factor in small state foreign policy. In a number of cases, nonsystemic factors come into play only when the system "permits" them to. In other words, the system can trump any other level for many small states. Indeed, the fact that many authors placed the system level as secondary in importance reflects the extent to which systemic constraints have been integrated into small states' foreign policy ambitions. Individual leaders or regimes often stand out as dynamic and effective, even when working within an environment in which limits on ambitions and effectiveness are taken for granted. This stems partly from the fact that most small states find themselves juxtaposed between great powers, or in the shadow of a great power. This is literally (i.e., geographically) true for a number of the cases presented here: Luxembourg between France and Germany, Austria between the Eastern and Western blocs of Europe, Paraguay between Brazil and Argentina, Jordan among Israel and three Arab powers, Panama and the Caribbean states in the shadow of the United States and Laos bordering regional powerhouses Vietnam, China, and Thailand. These states employ disparate strategies to manage their relationship with regional hegemons. Panama, after years of acquiescence, became forcefully anti-U.S. after the Cold War and during the canal treaty talks. The Caribbean states join together to increase their relative power, but mostly oppose the United States only on nonstrategic issues that could endanger their economic well-being. Luxembourg has wholly embraced European integration to ensure against future Franco-German tensions, while Austria chose the route of neutrality to manage its position between East and West. In further contrast, Paraguay has alternated its allegiance between Argentina and Brazil, and Jordan has been unpredictable, supporting Iraq during the Gulf War but also finalizing a peace with Israel only a few years later. This indicates that although small states face a common systemic challenge, operating at a disadvantage to local hegemonic powers, they respond in a myriad of ways that reflect historical circumstance, domestic political dynamics, individual choice, and of course, the behavior of the hegemonic powers.

A second systemic feature common to most small states is that they engage in international organizations and draw on global regimes, laws, and norms to enhance their political influence and economic prosperity. Luxembourg is a founding member of the EU and remains an enormously wealthy country whose skillful participation in the organization enhances its foreign policy status and effectiveness. Gambia has used international linkages to create legitimacy for a regime that lacked it. Jordan has skillfully taken advantage of the changing regional alliances to keep itself safe, protect its interests, and build a diplomatic reputation. The English-speaking Caribbean states align in a series of economic and diplomatic organizations to enhance their bargaining power and visibility. Nodding to its neutral postwar history, Austria has stayed out of the North Atlantic Treaty Organization (NATO). Unlike Switzerland, whose population has stated that neutrality should keep it out of both political and economic organizations, Austria joined the European Union (EU). All of the countries under study are active members of international governmental organizations (IGOs), many of which have a "one country, one vote" operating system that favors small states. Paraguay and Laos are to a degree exceptions to the IGO rule. Neither is known for its active participation, much less leadership, in international organizations. Both are fairly isolated, with little or no history of foreign policy activism. It can be surmised, therefore, that their failure to be active in international fora is more a reflection of their overall foreign policy inactivity than it is any reflection of their smallness.

There are two caveats to be mentioned about small states and their embrace of international organizations. First is that although global organizations on the whole benefit small states, they do not overcome or work outside of international political realities. From the United Nations to the European Union to regional trading blocs, international organizations reflect power principles. This means that the most powerful (usually larger) states are more able than small states to set agendas, weight their votes, promote their policy choices, and ignore the organization when it does not act in a favorable way. The European Union is perhaps the most equipped to keep the large countries in check. Its rules, procedures, and courts have real power. Even so, small players like Austria and Luxembourg must choose wisely the issues on which they attempt influence. Its EU brothers sanctioned small Austria for seating a coalition government whom the former thought distasteful, a reprimand they did not inflict under similar circumstances on larger Italy. Groups such as the Organization of American States, the Organization of African Unity, and even the United Nations permit small states greater voice and voting power, but regional and global hegemons ignore them when it is convenient to do so. This suggests that international organizations benefit small states best in those issue areas where powerful states are willing to take a supernational approach.

A second and related caveat is that international integration is an increasingly common global phenomenon among all states. It is difficult to say whether small states really use it more than nonsmall states do. The North American Free Trade Agreement, the proposed Free Trade Area of the Americas, and the European Union are examples of potent regional agreements in which large countries are major actors. Clearly, integration is not solely a policy instrument of small states. So while it can be said that nearly no small state is willing to eschew international organizations as a key policy alternative, this is a choice that increasingly appeals to states of all sizes in a globalized world. That said, it is fair to add that large states have greater chances of going it alone if they so choose, whereas small states have a strong incentive to join organizations to enhance their relative power to achieve foreign policy goals.

The State

The state or domestic level of analysis ranks clearly first in only one case (Jordan), second in three (Luxembourg, Panama, and Laos), and third in three (the Caribbean, Paraguay, and Gambia). As such, the analysis reveals it as the "weakest" of the three levels. Yet a domestic variable plays a sometimes overwhelming contextual role, in the same way that the system does. For example, regime security was a paramount factor in conditioning the foreign policy character in Jordan, Paraguay, and Gambia. Even though the authors of the chapters on these countries rank the state level in different ways, they make clear that concerns about the regime's survivability created the environment in which individual leaders made foreign policy decisions. A second state-level feature, regime ideology, was the dominant factor in shaping foreign policy in Laos. Zachary Abuza describes a foreign policy elite in Laos arguing over the nuances of established Marxist doctrine. That doctrine, independent of the vicissitudes of individual decisions, has given Laos its foreign policy identity over the last two decades and has contributed to the country's low international profile. Similarly, in Luxembourg, concern with maintaining wealth suffuses foreign policy decisionmaking just as much as does the concern about an eruption of Franco-German hostilities in the region. Given the variety of state types represented in this book—democratic/nondemocratic, states with and without colonial histories, developed/underdeveloped—it comes as no surprise that the specific domestic variable salient in each case differs substantially. It is nonetheless important to note that domestic variables, contrary to most conclusions of the literature on small states, can weigh heavily in explaining foreign policy behavior.

Two state-level features deserve special attention: regime type and level of development. The chapters reveal that non- and questionable democracies like Jordan and Gambia, as well as new democracies like Paraguay and Panama, use foreign policy primarily to enhance and ensure regime security. Laos is the exception here. As the regime with the firmest grip on authoritarian power in the sample, Laos has less need to legitimize itself with a constituency that is allowed no dissent. The firm democracies like Luxembourg, Austria, and the Caribbean states enjoy the legitimacy that a long tradition of democracy affords them, and therefore rarely use foreign policy for legitimacy, as opposed to popularity. This finding undermines the deep-rooted dictum that holds that democratic governments have to pay more attention to public opinion than do nondemocratic ones (Rosenau 1990). Indeed, the chapters reveal that leaders in Jordan, Panama, and Gambia worried the most about regime legitimacy. Angry populations (supporting Iraq and opposing U.S. control of the canal, respectively) concerned the Jordanian king and the Panamanian president to the extent that they developed regional foreign policy largely with those populations in mind. Because new and nondemocracies are mostly found in the "third world," the conclusion about the relationship between regime legitimacy and foreign policy behavior reinforces research that argues that third-world countries are more focused on regime interests than national interests (Thomas 1987; David 1991; Ayoob 1995). The third-world exception here is the Caribbean, which like Luxembourg is able to focus on long-term foreign policy goals the legitimacy of which are not questioned. The coalition politics of Austria's most recent national election mired the country in a European foreign policy nightmare. But even when a right-wing party that some suspect is fascist joined the Austrian government, nobody questioned whether the coalition had come about by legal and democratic means. Indeed, it was Austria's long-standing democratic credentials that enabled it to defy the European Union and retain its government.

What differences do this volume's empirical studies show relative to development and its impact on foreign policy behavior in small states? The book's case studies include only two countries clearly in the "developed world": Austria and Luxembourg. Some observations can be made about the differences between these and the less developed small states under study. First, the wealthy countries tend to have established foreign policy bureaucracies that are less vulnerable to changes in regime than the less developed countries. This is most clear in Luxembourg, where coalition politics are less hostile than in Austria, at least recently. A weak or ineffective diplomatic bureaucracy was of particular importance in explaining ineffective foreign policy in Paraguay, Panama, Gambia, and to a lesser extent, the English-speaking Caribbean. It is difficult to overstate the disadvantage at which this difference puts the underdeveloped small states. Not only are their foreign policy bureaucracies small and underfunded, but their inexperience means that most well-conceived policies designed by elected leaders become lost, diluted, or distorted at the implementation stage. Frank Mora's description of the Paraguayan foreign policy bureaucracy best illustrates this point.

Second, development and wealth help to determine differences in foreign policy content among small states. Poor countries are more likely to be dealing with life-or-death issues, such as securing loans, aid and trade, regime survival, border consolidation, and refugee crises. Wealthy Austria and Luxembourg, on the other hand, have the luxury of providing foreign aid, working on pan-European issues within the EU, managing regional diplomacy, and acting as global cultural centers. This reveals a certain class system of states, divided not by size, but by wealth. The upper class are aid donors, while the lower class are aid recipients. The former focus on maintaining and enhancing wealth, while the latter focus on economic survival. Note that economic well-being is a foreign policy goal of all these states. Indeed it figures as prominently in the foreign policy of Gambia as it does in that of Luxembourg. Yet the urgency surrounding that goal is markedly different.

In sum, the domestic level of analysis rarely emerges as the most important criterion in determining small state foreign policy. Yet a careful reading of the chapters in this volume reveals that domestic-level factors are crucial conditioners of foreign policy content. A number of domestic variables, such as bureaucratic behavior (Gambia, Luxembourg), public opinion (Panama, Jordan), government ideology (Laos), and culture (Luxembourg), emerge in some states' foreign policy profile. The two factors discussed above are even more consistently important. Regime type, and consequently regime survival, feature prominently in most of the chapters. Foreign policy becomes a tool with which to pursue regime security. Development levels similarly infuse foreign policy agendas, influencing both goals and behavior. A comparison of these chapters suggests that these state-level features are so crucial as to be assumed. Like systemic constraints, the domestic stage imposes restrictions and opportunities within which decisionmakers can operate.

The Individual

Given the long-standing notion that small states are little more than pawns on the global chessboard, with their movements decided by powers larger than themselves, it came as a surprise that so many authors ranked the individual level as the most important. Certainly this is consistent with the other long-standing notion in small state foreign policy research: that most small state foreign policy is the domain of an all-powerful, and often whimsical, leader. In some cases examined here, foreign policy truly is the domain of a single leader and his advisers. This is the case in Jordan, Gambia, Paraguay, and much of the English-speaking Caribbean. In the first three of these, leaders worried about their political survival manipulated foreign policy to boost their personal status. Individual leaders, or a small group of foreign policy elites (as in Laos), are particularly powerful in postcolonial situations that can enhance the leaders' ability to implement their foreign policy preferences. This ability often owes to weak foreign policy bureaucracies, few institutional checks on the executive, and even constitutions that provide the executive with full foreign policy powers. Not surprisingly, the individual plays a comparatively weak explanatory force in both Austria and Luxembourg.

Despite the individual level's high ranking in most countries, it remains clear that leaders rarely respond simply to idiosyncratic caprices. Rather, they implement their preferred responses to domestic and systemic circumstances and constraints. Leaders are not simply doing what global and domestic forces dictate, but neither can they overcome those pressures. It is the systemic and domestic context that allows leaders to emerge and act. But that context sets the stage. Because we take for granted that small states are under tremendous constraints and are limited in powers, the actions of often charismatic or authoritarian leaders appear all the more forceful and independent. But when we note the types of foreign policies these leaders usually implement, namely those designed to enhance their own status, as well as their countries' economic viability and regional security, we see that these leaders place their personal imprint on a set of predetermined foreign policy choices. The question is, to what extent would foreign policy differ under different leaders? While the character and style would often no doubt change, these chapters suggest that the basic content of most foreign policies would not, because leaders respond to pressures placed on the state by domestic and systemic actors. Regime and state security and economic livelihood remain the goals of small states under all leaders.

This is not to say that the personal imprint is not strong. In Luxembourg, Prime Minister Jean Claude Juncker's special foreign policy skills make him one of the most important diplomats in Europe, no small achievement. President Alfredo Stroessner for over thirty-five years personalized Paraguay's foreign policy, which nonetheless aimed to consolidate his personal power and acquire funds from abroad. Curtis Ryan explains that Jordan's diplomatic machinations, seen by some outsiders no doubt as impressive Middle East peacemaking, served King Hussein's personal power as much as anything. Throughout the English-speaking Caribbean, the Westminster style of government permits individual leaders to influence the content and character of foreign policy. Yet despite numerous changes in leadership, the region has moved toward a neoliberal economic model and toward greater integration. Indeed, in each of these cases, it can be argued that different people at the helm would have likely made similar foreign policy choices, because they would have met with similar circumstances.

Still, there are times when individuals do matter, and small states frequently enhance their influence and thus the speed and effectiveness with which that influence is felt. Peter Sanchez, for example, argues that individual leaders in Panama were crucial in determining changes in the country's attitude toward the canal treaties. In Laos, a new generation of leaders challenges the old-school doctrine, which Laos has maintained despite modernization in its region and across the globe. That determination owes to a group of elites committed to their version of the communist ideal. Hence, under unusual circumstances, or under the regime of an unusually strong leader, the individual level of analysis can defy the pressures of the global and domestic systems.

Conclusion

The analyses in this book and the above summaries permit some preliminary conclusions about explaining small state foreign policy behavior. These are based on the eight cases represented in this book.

1. Small state foreign policy is heavily constrained by systemic factors. Every country studied here, independent of development status, geography, and history, faced marked international constraints in foreign policy. Ultrawealthy Luxembourg has as its defining foreign policy element the potential hostilities between France and Germany. Austria has to contend with an angry European Union, even though Austria is unquestionably a democracy. From Panama to Laos, the less developed countries face the exigencies of poverty and therefore the demands of international financial institutions. Most of these also struggle with regional political disputes, sometimes violent, that mold and problematize their efforts at regional integration. In short, international and regional dynamics are always at the top not only of small states' foreign policy agendas, but also of the list of forces that explain those agendas and the behavior directed at them.

2. Level of development influences the impact of certain domestic and international factors. Specifically, less developed small states are more likely than developed ones to have regime security as a foreign policy goal. Similarly, they must contend with international financial institutions, on whom they rely for access to credits and aid.

3. Level of development influences the role of the leader. Again, it appears that leaders in less developed small states are more likely to put a personal imprint on foreign policy than are their counterparts in more developed countries. This seems to contradict the above conclusion that lower levels of development enhanced domestic and international variables. It is better to say that specific domestic and international determinants, regime security, and vulnerability to global financial institutions in particular come into play in less developed countries. In the more developed ones, foreign policy traditions and experienced diplomatic corps provide foreign policy behavior with a consistency not seen in less developed countries, where foreign policy style varies with changes in individual leaders.

How do these conclusions contribute to theory building in small state foreign policy? Principally, they sharpen a number of the findings and propositions previously made about small states' international behavior. For example, much of the research arguing that small states would pursue alliances and multilateral approaches, concentrate their agenda on regional issues, and have a heightened concern for physical security is here supported. On the other hand, research that argues that small states would advance neutral positions and spend little time on foreign policy is here not supported. In terms of explanatory variables, previous research argued that the system and the individual were dominant. This volume's research reveals that rather than ranking the separate levels, it is conceptually more accurate to develop an understanding of their interrelationship. In most of the cases presented here, individual leaders dominate foreign policy development and implementation, often relatively unfettered by domestic groups. But their policy choices, and their options, are severely constrained, and even molded, by domestic and international factors, such as regime security needs, culture, political ideology, geography, economic necessity, hegemonic pressure, and changes in the regional and global systems. To that extent, then, individual leaders can be seen best as the elector among a predetermined set of choices. Perhaps the most important point in this conclusion is that the domestic level, heretofore considered the least important, is quite strong in a number of small states.

This volume's conclusions also point to fruitful areas of future research. First, controlled studies will permit these conclusions to be compared with nonsmall states. Second, more comparisons of less developed and developed small states will allow researchers to fine-tune this volume's findings on their differences. Third, research designs that observe instances in which small state leaders can and cannot overcome domestic and international constraints will help us to identify the conditions under which those constraints are determinant, as opposed to simply conditional.

Note

1. In preparing these conclusions, I thank Kenneth Menkhaus for his comments at the International Studies Association meetings in Chicago in 2001.

References

abc color. 1991. "Estados Unidos: Vinculos entre legitimidad internacional y doméstica." February 4, p. 3.

———. 1993. "Buscan definición de la política exterior." September 3, p. 12.

Abente, Diego. 1988. "Constraints and Opportunities: Prospects for Democratization in Paraguay." *Journal of Interamerican Studies and World Affairs* 30, no. 1 (Spring): 82–87.

———. 1989. *Stronismo, Post-Stronismo, and the Prospects for Democratization.* Working Paper no. 119. Notre Dame: Kellogg Institute, University of Notre Dame, March.

———, ed. 1993. *Paraguay en transición.* Caracas: Editorial Nueva Sociedad.

———. 1996. "Paraguay: Transition from Caudillo Rule." In *Constructing Democratic Governance: South America in the 1990s.* Eds. Jorge I. Dominguez and Abraham Lowenthal. Baltimore: Johns Hopkins University Press, pp. 118–132.

Abu Awdah, Adnan. 1993. Former national security adviser and Jordanian representative to the United Nations. Interview by Curtis R. Ryan. February 29.

Ahtisaari, Martti, Jochen Frowein, and Marcelino Oreja. 2000. *Report.* Adopted in Paris on September 8. Mimeo.

Apple, R. W. 2002. "Luxembourg Grand Duchy: Small Treasure." *New York Times,* March 17, p. E8.

Arabuti, Khalid Ibrahim al-. 1992. *Fikr al-Husayn fi al-Mizan* (Hussein's Thought in the Balance). Amman.

Arditi, Benjamin. 1987. *Recesión y estancamiento: La economía Paraguaya durante el periodo post-boom.* Asunción: CDE.

———. 1992. *Adios a Stroessner: La reconstrucción de la política en el Paraguay.* Asunción: RP Ediciones.

Arditi, Benjamin, and Jose Carlos Rodriguez. 1987. *La sociedad a pesar del estado: Movimientos sociales y recuperación democrática en el Paraguay.* Asunción: El Lector.

Associated Foreign Press. 2000a. "Vietnam 'Joins Rebel Fight.'" June 3.

———. 2000b. "Top Laotian Commander Visits Vietnam amid Mounting Unrest." June 16.

———. 2000c. "Laos Leadership Confronting Worst Crisis in Twenty-five Years: Report." September 26.

———. 2000d. "Laotians Show Little Enthusiasm After Twenty-five Years of Communist Rule." December 3.

Associated Press. 2000a. "Bomb Found at Vietnam Embassy in Laos." August 1.

———. 2000b. "Six Lao Democracy Dissidents Seek Asylum in the United States."

Astorino-Courtois, Allison. 1996. "Transforming International Agreements into National Realities: Marketing Arab-Israeli Peace in Jordan." *Journal of Politics* 58, no. 4: 1035–1054.

Austrian Foreign Policy Yearbook 1990. 1991. Vienna–Riverside, Calif.: Austrian Ministry for Foreign Affairs–Ariadne Press.

Ayoob, Mohammed. 1991. "The Security Problematic of the Third World." *World Politics* 43, no. 3: 257–283.

———. 1995. *The Third World Security Predicament: State Making, Regional Conflict, and the International System.* Boulder: Lynne Rienner.

Azar, Edward E., and Chung-in Moon, eds. 1988. *National Security in the Third World: The Management of Internal and External Threats.* College Park: University of Maryland.

Baehr, Peter R. 1975. "Small States: A Tool for Analysis." *World Politics* 27, no. 3: 456–466.

Baer, Werner, and Melissa Birch. 1987. "The International Economic Relations of a Small Country: The Case of Paraguay." *Economic Development and Cultural Change* 35 (April): 601–627.

Bailer-Galanda, Brigitte, and Wolfgang Neugebauer. 1997. *Haider und die Freiheitlichen in Österreich.* Berlin: Elefanten Press.

Bailey, Clinton. 1984. *Jordan's Palestinian Challenge, 1948–1983: A Political History.* Boulder: Westview Press.

Baillie, Sasha. 1996. "The Seat of the European Institutions: An Example of Small State Influence in European Decisionmaking." Working Paper no. 96/28. Florence, Italy: European University Institute.

———. 1998. "A Theory of Small State Influence in the European Union." *Journal of International Relations and Development* 1A (August): 195–219.

Ball, Nicole. 1988. *Security and Economy in the Third World.* Princeton: Princeton University Press.

Bangkok Post. 1990. October 20.

———. 2001. "Thai Laos Relations: Another Bridge over Mekong." March 19.

Baram, Amatzia. 1991. "Baathi Iraq and Hashemite Jordan: From Hostility to Alignment." *Middle East Journal* 45, no. 1: 51–70.

Barnes, William. 2000. "Dissidents Pledge to Continue Fight for Freedom." October 28.

Barnett, Michael N. 1998. *Dialogues in Arab Politics: Negotiations in Regional Order.* New York: Columbia University Press.

Barnett, Michael N., and Jack S. Levy. 1991. "Domestic Sources of Alliances and Alignments: The Case of Egypt, 1962–73." *International Organization* 45, no. 3: 369–392.

Becerra Acosta, Jeanette. 1998. "Panama concede 'excesivas responsibilidades' a Washington en el CMLN: Mexico." *Excelsior,* January 27.

Becker, David G. 1984. "Development, Democracy, and Development in Latin America: A Post-Imperialist View." *Third World Quarterly* 6 (April): 411–431.

Benn, Denis. 1997. "Global and Regional Trends: Impact on Caribbean Development." In *Caribbean Public Policy: Regional, Cultural, and Socioeconomic Issues for the Twenty-first Century.* Eds. Jacqueline Anne Braveboy-Wagner and Dennis J. Gayle. Boulder: Westview Press, pp. 15–27.

Bermudez, Ricardo. 1998. "CMA: Propuesta de creación del Centro Multinacional de Lucha Contra el Narcotrafico." Facultad de Comunicación Social, Universidad de Panama, March 3.

Berns, Alphonse. 2000. Interview by Jeanne A. K. Hey. Luxembourg City, May.

Bielka, Erich, Peter Jankowitsch, and Hans Thalberg, eds. 1983. *Die Ära Kreisky: Schwerpunkte der Österreichischen Außenpolitik.* Vienna, Munich, Zurich: Europaverlag.

Birch, Melissa. 1988. "La política pendular: Política de desarrollo del Paraguay en la pos-guerra." *Revista Paraguaya de Sociología* 25, no. 73 (September–December): 73–103.

———. 1992. "Pendulum Politics: Paraguay's National Borders, 1940–1975." In *Changing Boundaries in the Americas.* Ed. Lawrence Herzog. San Diego: University of California Regents, pp. 203–228.

Black, Cyril E., Robert D. English, Jonathan E. Helmreich, Paul C. Helmreich, and A. James McAdams. 2000. *Rebirth: A Political History of Europe Since World War II.* Boulder: Westview Press.

Böhm, Wolfgang. 2000. "EU-Sanktionen gehen bereits tiefer als im Beschluß der 14." *Die Presse,* February 18.

Borda, Dionisio, and Fernando Masi. 1994. *Paraguay–Estados Unidos: Posibilidades de un acuerdo de libre comercio.* Working Paper. Asunción: Centro de Análisis y Difusion de Economía Paraguaya.

Bostrom, Mikael. 1994. "Contagion of Democracy in Latin America: The Case of Paraguay." In *Latin American Development and Public Policy.* Ed. S. Nagle. New York: St. Martin's Press, pp. 43–66.

Bourdet, Yves. 1996. "Laos in 1995." *Asian Survey* 36, no. 1: 89–94.

———. 1997. "Laos in 1996." *Asian Survey* 37, no. 1: 72–77.

Brand, Laurie A. 1991. "Liberalization and Changing Political Coalitions: The Bases of Jordan's 1990–91 Gulf Crisis Policy." *Jerusalem Journal of International Relations* 13, no. 4: 1–46.

———. 1994. *Jordan's Inter-Arab Relations: The Political Economy of Alliance Making.* New York: Columbia University Press.

Braveboy-Wagner, Jacqueline Anne. 1983. "Changes in the English-Speaking Caribbean: Implications for the International System." In *Latin America and Caribbean Contemporary Record.* Vol. 1, *1981–1982.* Ed. Jack Hopkins. New York: Holmes and Meier, pp. 101–109.

———. 1984. *The Venezuela-Guyana Border Dispute: Britain's Colonial Legacy in Latin America.* Boulder: Westview Press.

———. 1989. *The Caribbean in World Affairs: The Foreign Policies of the English-Speaking Caribbean.* Boulder: Westview Press.

———. 1992. "Winds of Change." *Hemisfile: Perspectives on Political and Economic Trends in Latin America* 3, no. 6 (November–December): 6–7.

———. 2001. *The Caribbean in International Affairs: Foreign Policies of CARICOM States.* Boulder: Westview Press.

Brynen, Rex. 1992. "Economic Crisis and Post-Rentier Democratization in the Arab World: The Case of Jordan." *Canadian Journal of Political Science* 25, no. 1: 69–97.

Caribbean Development Bank (CDB). 2000. *Annual Report 1999*. St. Michael, Barbados: CDB.

Ceesay, Jay. 1998. "Crispin Grey-Johnson Recalled from Washington." *The Point,* June, p. 3.

Cespedes, Roberto, Pablo Herken, and Jose Luis Simon. 1988. *Paraguay: Sociedad, economía y política*. Asunción: El Lector.

Ceuppens, Henry. 1971. *Paraguay año 2000*. Asunción: Artes Graficas Zamphiropolos.

Chairman's Summary of the Deliberations on Kosovo at the Informal Meeting of the Heads of State and Government of the European Union in Brussels on 14 April 1999. 1999. Press release of the German EU presidency, September 14.

Chiavenato, Julio Jose. 1980. *Stroessner: Retrato de uma ditadura*. São Paulo: Livraria Brasilense Editorial.

Christmas-Moller, Wilhelm. 1983. "Some Thoughts on the Scientific Applicability of the Small State Concept." In *Small States in Europe and Dependence*. Ed. Otmar Höll. Boulder: Westview Press, pp. 35–53.

Christophory, Jul. 1999. Interview by Jeanne A. K. Hey. Luxembourg City, November 16.

Clapham, C. 1996. *Africa in the International System: The Politics of Survival*. Cambridge: Cambridge University Press.

Clarke, Colin, and Tony Payne. 1987. *Politics, Security, and Development in Small States*. London: Allen and Unwin.

Cohen, Margot. 2001. "Thunder in the Highlands." *FEER,* March 1.

Cohen, Robin. 1987. "An Academic Perspective." In *Politics, Security, and Development in Small States*. Eds. Colin Clarke and Tony Payne. London: Allen and Unwin, pp. 203–213.

Conniff, Michael L. 1992. *Panama and the United States: The Forced Alliance*. Athens: University of Georgia Press.

Cooke, David, and Arnold Hughes. 1997. "The Politics of Economic Recovery: The Gambia's Experience of Structural Adjustment, 1985–1994." *Journal of Commonwealth and Comparative Politics* 35, no. 1 (March): 93–117.

Cordesman, Anthony. 1983. *Jordanian Arms and the Middle East Balance*. Washington, D.C.: Middle East Institute.

Crispin, Shawn W., Margot Cohen, and Bertil Lintner. 2000. "Choke Point." *FEER,* October 12, pp. 22–24.

Da Mota Menezes, Alfredo. 1990. *La herencia de Stroessner*. Asunción: Carlos Schauman Editor.

Daley, Suzanne. 2000. "Europe Lifts Sanctions on Austria, but Vows Vigilance." *New York Times,* September 13.

Dann, Uriel. 1989. *King Hussein and the Challenge of Arab Radicalism, 1955–1967*. New York: Oxford University Press.

———. 1992. *King Hussein's Strategy of Survival*. Washington, D.C.: Washington Institute for Near East Policy.

David, Steven. 1991. *Choosing Sides: Alignment and Realignment in the Third World*. Baltimore: Johns Hopkins University Press.

Day, Arthur. 1986. *East Bank/West Bank: Jordan and the Prospects for Peace*. New York: Council on Foreign Relations.

De Muyser, Guy. 1999. Interview by Jeanne A. K. Hey. Differdange, Luxembourg, November 16.

Decker, Frank. 2000. *Parteien unter Druck: Der neue Rechtspopulismus in den westlichen Demokratien.* Opladen: Leske+Budrich.
Delich, Francisco. 1981. "Estructura agraria y hegemonía en el despotismo republicano del Paraguay." *Estudios Rurales Latinoamericanos* (Bogota) 4, no. 3: 42–67.
Denton, Fatma. 1998. "Foreign Policy Formulation in the Gambia, 1965–1994." Unpublished Ph.D. diss., University of Birmingham, England.
Der Standard Aktuell. 2000. "Meinungsforscher: 'EU-Sanktionen für Regierung fast ein Glücksfall.'" May 12.
Dessouki, Ali E., and Karen Aboul-Kheir. 1991. "The Politics of Vulnerability and Survival: The Foreign Policy of Jordan." In *The Foreign Policies of Arab States: The Challenge of Change.* Eds. Bahgat Korany and Ali E. Hilal Dessouki. Boulder: Westview Press, pp. 216–232.
Diamond, Larry, Marc Plattner, Yun-han Chu, and Hung-mao Tien, eds. 1997. *Consolidating the Third Wave Democracies.* Baltimore: Johns Hopkins University Press.
Diaz de Arce, Omar. 1986. "La dictadura de Stroessner: Estado y sociedad en el Paraguay." *Cuadernos de Nuestro America* 3, no. 5 (June): 75–87.
Die Presse. 1993. "Das interne Protokoll zur Neutralität, das gestern, Dienstag, vom Ministerrat in Wien beschlossen wurde (es wird in Brüssel nicht vorgelegt)." November 10.
Dinan, Desmond. 1994. *An Ever Closer Union?* Boulder: Lynne Rienner.
Doerner, Charles. 1983. "Luxembourg: An Example of the Dependent Monetary System of a Small State." In *Small States in Europe and Dependence.* Ed. Otmar Höll. Vienna: Austrian Institute for International Affairs, pp. 140–144.
Dommen, Arthur J. 1994. "Laos in 1993." *Asian Survey* 34, no. 1: 82–86.
———. 1995. "Laos in 1994." *Asian Survey* 35, no. 1: 84–91.
Duddy, Patrick. 1998. Director of public affairs, U.S. embassy, Panama. Interview by Peter M. Sanchez. Panama City, February 7.
East, Maurice A. 1975. "Size and Foreign Policy Behavior: A Test of Two Models." In *International Events and the Comparative Analysis of Foreign Policy.* Eds. Charles W. Kegley Jr., Gregory A. Raymond, Robert M. Rood, and Richard A. Skinner. Columbia: University of South Carolina Press, pp. 159–178.
Economist Intelligence Unit (EIU). 1991. *Country Profile: Jordan.* London: EIU.
———. 1994a. 1st quarter.
———. 1994b. 4th quarter.
———. 1995a. 1st quarter.
———. 1995b. 2nd quarter.
———. 1996a. 3rd quarter.
———. 1996b. 4th quarter.
———. 1997. 1st quarter.
———. 1998a. 1st quarter.
———. 1998b. 2nd quarter.
———. 1998c. 3rd quarter.
———. 1998d. 4th quarter.
El Panama America. 1997–1999. Various issues.
Elman, Miriam Fendius. 1995. "The Foreign Policies of Small States: Challenging Neorealism in Its Own Backyard." *British Journal of Political Science* 25, no. 2 (April): 171–217.

Erklärung der Bundesregierung vor dem Nationalrat von Bundeskanzler Dr. Franz Vranitzky, 28.1.1987. 1987. Vienna: Bundespressedienst.

Espindola, Roberto. 1987. "Social Features." In *Politics, Security, and Development in Small States.* Eds. Colin Clarke and Tony Payne. London: Allen and Unwin, pp. 26–49.

Estigarribia, Jose Felix, and Jose Luis Simon. 1987. *La sociedad internacional y el estado autoritario del Paraguay.* Asunción: Aravera.

Europa: Unsere Zukunft—Eine Stellungnahme der Vereinigung Österreichischer Industrieller zur Europäischen Integration. 1987. Vienna: Vereinigung Österreichischer Industrieller.

Evans, Grant. 1998. *The Politics of Ritual and Remembrance: Laos Since 1975.* Bangkok: Silkworm Books.

Faddah, Mohammad Ibrahim. 1974. *The Middle East in Transition: A Study of Jordan's Foreign Policy.* London: Asia Publishing House.

Falcoff, Mark. 1998. *Panama's Canal: What Happens When the United States Gives a Small Country What It Wants.* Washington, D.C.: AEI Press.

FEER (Far East Economic Review). 1993. "Donations, but No Flowers." June 3.

———. 2000a. "Lao Leader Holds Crisis Meeting." August 17.

———. 2000b. "Defector to Lie Low." November 23.

———. 2001. "Lao Let-Down Threatens Foreign Aid." April 12.

Ferris, Elizabeth, and Jennie Lincoln. 1981. *Latin America Foreign Policies: Global and Regional Dimensions.* Boulder: Westview Press.

Flesch, Colette. 2000. Interview by Jeanne A. K. Hey. Luxembourg City, June 27.

Franco, Jose. 1988. *Intercambio comercial paraguayo-brasileno: Análisis de su incidencia en la economía Paraguaya.* Asunción: CPES.

Franco-British Summit: Joint Declaration on European Defense, 4.12.1998, Saint-Malo. 1998. French embassy in the United Kingdom.

Fukuyama, Francis. 1992. *The End of History and the Last Man.* New York: Free Press.

Gabriel, Jürg Martin. 1989. "Das amerikanische Exportkontroll-System." *Aussenwirtschaft* 44, no. 1: 59–74.

Galeano, Luis. 1989. *De la apertura otorgada a la transición pactada.* Working Paper. Asunción: Centro Paraguayo de Estudios Sociologicos.

Galtung, Johan. 1969. "Foreign Policy Opinion as a Function of Social Position." In *International Politics and Foreign Policy.* Ed. James N. Rosenau. New York: Free Press, pp. 551–572.

———. 1971. "A Structural Theory of Imperialism." *Journal of Peace Research* 8, no. 2: 81–117.

Gambia Daily. 1998. May 11.

Garfinkle, Adam M. 1992. *Jordan and Israel in the Shadow of War: Functional Ties and Futile Diplomacy in a Small Place.* New York: St. Martin's Press.

Garnham, David. 1991. "Explaining Middle Eastern Alignments During the Gulf War." *Jerusalem Journal of International Relations* 13, no. 3: 68–83.

Goebbels, Robert. 2000. Interview by Jeanne A. K. Hey. Luxembourg City, June 13.

Goetschel, Laurent. 1998. "The Foreign and Security Policy Interests of Small States in Today's Europe." In *Small States Inside and Outside the European Union: Interests and Policies.* Ed. Laurent Goetschel. Dordrecht, Netherlands: Kluwer Academic, pp. 13–31.

Gomez, S. 1978. "The Gambia's External Relations: A Study of the Internal and External Factors That Influenced Foreign Policy Positions, 1965–1975." Unpublished Ph.D. diss., Baltimore: Johns Hopkins University.

Gonzalez, Luis. 1990. *Paraguay: Prisonero geopolítico*. Asunción: Instituto de Estudios Geopolíticos e Internacionales.

Gonzalez Alsina, Ezequiel. 1988. *Paraguay ante el mundo: Verdad, democracia y derechos humanos*. Asunción: Colección Biblioteca Republicana.

Goodwin, Paul B., Jr., comp. 2000. *Global Studies: Latin America*. 9th ed. Guilford, Conn.: Dushkin/McGraw-Hill.

Gray, Simon. 2000. Interview by Jeanne A. K. Hey. Luxembourg City, June 30.

Green, Peter S. 2000. "Backlash Grows in Eastern Europe Against EU." *International Herald Tribune*, June 29, pp. 1, 6.

Griffith, Ivelaw L. 1997. *Drugs and Security in the Caribbean: Sovereignty Under Siege*. University Park: Pennsylvania State University Press.

Guevara Mann, Carlos. 1994. *Ilegitimidad y hegemonía: Una interpretación histórica del militarismo panameño*. Panama City: Editorial La Prensa.

Gurdian Guerra, Reymundo. 1998. *La presencia militar de los Estados Unidos en Panama: Antecedentes, evolución y perspectivas*. Panama City: Universidad de Panama.

Haag, Emil. 2000. Interview by Jeanne A. K. Hey. Luxembourg City, May 22.

Hamilton-Merritt, Jane. 1993. *Tragic Mountains: The Hmong, the Americans, and the Secret Wars for Laos, 1942–1992*. Bloomington: University of Indiana Press.

Harknett, Richard, and Jeffrey Vandenberg. 1997. "Alignment Theory and Interrelated Threats: Jordan and the Persian Gulf Crisis." *Security Studies* 6, no. 3: 112–153.

Henderson, John. 1991. "New Zealand and the Foreign Policy of Small States." In *Beyond New Zealand II: Foreign Policy into the 1990s*. Eds. Richard Kennaway and John Henderson. Auckland: Longman Paul, pp. 3–16.

Hermann, Charles F., and Gregory Peacock. 1987. "The Evolution and Future of Theoretical Research in the Comparative Study of Foreign Policy." In *New Directions in the Study of Foreign Policy*. Eds. Charles F. Hermann, Charles W. Kegley Jr., and James N. Rosenau. Boston: Allen and Unwin, pp. 13–32.

Hersh, Seymour. 1986. "Panamanian Strongman Said to Trade in Drugs, Arms, and Illicit Money." *New York Times*, June 12.

Hey, Jeanne A. K. 1995a. "Foreign Policy in Dependent States." In *Foreign Policy Analysis: Continuity and Change in Its Second Generation*. Eds. Laura Neack, Jeanne A. K. Hey, and Patrick J. Haney. Englewood Cliffs, N.J.: Prentice Hall.

———. 1995b. *Theories of Foreign Policy and the Case of Ecuador in the 1980s*. Athens: Ohio University Press.

———. 1998. "Is There a Latin American Foreign Policy?" *Mershon International Studies Review* 42 (May): 106–116.

Hicks, Frederick. 1971. "Interpersonal Relationships and Caudillismo in Paraguay." *Journal of Interamerican Studies and World Affairs* 13 (January): 89–111.

Höll, Otmar, ed. 1983. *Small States in Europe and Dependence*. Vienna: Austrian Institute for International Affairs.

———. 1994. "The Foreign Policy of the Kreisky Era." In *The Kreisky Era in Austria*. Vol. 2 of *Contemporary Austrian Studies*. Eds. Günter Bischof and Anton Pelinka. New Brunswick, N.J.: Transaction, pp. 32–77.

Hoyer, Hans. 1975. "Paraguay." In *Latin American Foreign Policy: An Analysis*. Eds. Harold E. Davis and Larman C. Wilson. Baltimore: Johns Hopkins University Press, pp. 294–305.

Hughes, A. 1991. "The Attempted Gambian Coup d'État of 30 July 1981." In *The Gambia: Studies in Society and Politics*. Ed. A. Hughes. Birmingham, England: University of Birmingham Press, pp. 92–106.

———. 1992. "The Collapse of the Senegambian Confederation." *Journal of Political and Comparative Politics* 30, no. 2: 202–222.

———. 2000. "'Democratization' Under the Military in the Gambia: 1994–2000." *Commonwealth and Comparative Politics* 38, no. 3: 35–52.

Hughes, William. 1998. U.S. ambassador to Panama. Interview by Peter M. Sanchez. Panama City, May 21.

Hummer, Waldemar, and Michael Schweitzer. 1987. *Österreich und die EWG: Neutralitätsrechtliche Beurteilung der Möglichkeit der Dynamisierung des Verhältnisses zur EWG*. Vienna: Signum Verlag.

Hussein, King. 1962. *Uneasy Lies the Head*. London: Heinemann.

Jagan, Janet, ed. 1999. *A New Global Human Order (Speeches by Cheddi Jagan)*. Ontario: Happy.

Janson Perez, Brittmarie. 1997. *Golpes y tratados: Piezas para el rompecabezas de nuestra historia*. Panama City: Litho Editorial Chen, S.A.

Jervis, Robert. 1976. *Perceptions and Misperceptions in International Politics*. Princeton: Princeton University Press.

Job, Brian L., ed. 1992. *The Insecurity Dilemma: National Security of Third World States*. Boulder: Lynne Rienner.

Johnson, Stephen T. 1992. "Laos in 1991." *Asian Survey* 32, no. 1: 82–87.

———. 1993. "Laos in 1992." *Asian Survey* 33, no. 1: 75–82.

Jorden, William J. 1984. *Panama Odyssey*. Austin: University of Texas Press.

Kamal, Sana. 1997. "Election Boycott Widens." *Middle East International*, August 29, p. 10.

Katzenstein, Peter. 1985. *Small States in World Markets*. Ithaca: Cornell University Press.

Kaufman, Edy. 1984. "Authoritarianism in Paraguay: The Lesser Evil?" *Latin American Research Review* 19, no. 2: 193–207.

Kelly, Philip, and Thomas Whigham. 1990. "Geopolítica del Paraguay: Vulnerabilidades regionales y propuestas nacionales." *Perspectiva Internacional Paraguaya* 2, no. 1 (January–June): 41–77.

Kemble, John H. 1943. *The Panama Route, 1848–1869*. Los Angeles: University of California Press.

Kempe, Frederick. 1990. *Divorcing the Dictator: America's Bungled Affair with Noriega*. New York: G. P. Putnam's Sons.

Keohane, Robert. 1969. "Lilliputians' Dilemmas: Small States in International Politics." *International Organization* 23, no. 2 (Spring): 210–291.

Kerr, Malcolm. 1970. *The Arab Cold War: Gamal Abd al-Nasir and His Rivals, 1958–70*. London: Oxford University Press.

Kiernan. 1998. "Special Report: Jordan." *Middle East* (London), September, pp. 29–31.

Kissinger, Henry. 1979. *White House Years*. Boston: Little, Brown.

Kitschelt, Herbert, and Anthony J. McGann. 1997 (originally 1995). *The Radical Right in Western Europe: A Comparative Analysis*. Ann Arbor: University of Michigan Press.

Klieman, Aharon. 1998. "Israel's 'Jordanian Option': A Post-Oslo Reassessment." In *The Middle East Peace Process*. Ed. Ilan Peleg. Albany: State University of New York Press, pp. 179–195.

Korany, Baghat, Rex Brynen, and Paul Noble. 1993. *The Many Faces of National Security in the Arab World*. New York: St. Martin's Press.

Koster, Richard. 1998. Interview by Peter M. Sanchez. Panama City, June 11.

Koster, R. M., and Guillermo Sánchez. 1990. *In the Time of the Tyrants: Panama, 1968–1990*. New York: W. W. Norton.

Kramer, Helmut. 1988. "'Wende' in der Österreichischen Außenpolitik? Zur Außenpolitik der SPÖ-ÖVP-Koalition." *Österreichische Zeitschrift für Politikwissenschaft* 17, no. 2: 117–131.

———. 1996. "Foreign Policy." In *Contemporary Austrian Politics*. Ed. Volkmar Lauber. Boulder: Westview Press, pp. 151–200.

Kurier Online. 2000. "Van der Bellen: Schelte für Joschka Fischer." August 21.

La Prensa. 1997–1999. Various issues.

Labra, Fernando. 1990. "Paraguay: Nuevo perfil internacional." *Perspectiva Internacional Paraguaya* 2, no. 4: 7–33.

LaFeber, Walter. 1989. *The Panama Canal: The Crisis in Historical Perspective*. Updated ed. New York: Oxford University Press.

Lambert, Peter. 1996. "Mechanisms of Control: The Stroessner Regime in Paraguay." In *Authoritarianism in Latin America Since Independence*. Ed. William Fowler. Westport, Conn.: Greenwood, pp. 93–108.

———. 1997. "The Regime of Alfredo Stroessner." In *The Transition to Democracy in Paraguay*. Eds. Peter Lambert and Andrew Nickson. New York: St. Martin's Press, pp. 3–23.

Lambert, Peter, and Andrew Nickson, eds. 1997. *The Transition to Democracy in Paraguay*. New York: St. Martin's Press.

Latin America Weekly Report. 1990–1999. Various issues. London: Latin America Ltd.

Le Rider, Jacques. 2000. "Quand l'Autriche haidérisée sanctionne l'Europe." *Le Monde*, September 17.

Leis, Raul. 1985. *Comando sur: Poder hostil*. 2d ed. Panama City: Centro de Estudios y Acción Social Panameño.

Lewis, Paul. 1980. *Paraguay Under Stroessner*. Chapel Hill: University of North Carolina Press.

Lezcano, Carlos Maria. 1989. "El régimen militar de Alfredo Stroessner: Fuerzas armadas y política en el Paraguay (1954–1988)." *Revista Paraguaya de Sociología* 26, no. 74 (January–April): 426–438.

———. 1990. "Relaciones exteriores del Paraguay y percepciones de amenaza: La política pendular del régimen de Stroessner y las perspectivas de cambio despues del golpe de febrero de 1989." In *Política exterior y relaciones internacionales del Paraguay contemporaneo*. Ed. Jose Luis Simon. Asunción: CPES, pp. 369–392.

Lezcano Claude, Luis. 1989. *El poder ejecutivo en el Paraguay*. Asunción: Intercontinental Editora.

Lincoln, Jennie, and Elizabeth Ferris, eds. 1984. *The Dynamics of Latin American Foreign Policies: Challenges for the 1980s*. Boulder: Westview Press.

Lindmark, Sture. 1985. "Den amerikanska embargopolitiken mot öststaterna: Dess följder för svensk utrikeshandel." *Nordic Journal of Soviet and East European Studies* 2, no. 2: 39–50.

Lintner, Bertil. 1997. "Before the Flood." *FEER,* February 13.

———. 2001. "Laos: Gifts from Above." *FEER,* August 30.

Lintner, Bertil, and Shawn Crispin. 2000a. "Brothers in Arms." *FEER,* May 11.

———. 2000b. "Behind the Bombings." *FEER,* July 27, pp. 26–27.

———. 2000c. "Living on the Edge." *FEER,* July 27.

———. 2000d. "Kingdom Come?" *FEER,* August 17.

Linz, Juan. 1975. "Authoritarian and Totalitarian Regimes." In *Handbook of Political Science.* Eds. Fred Greenstein and N. Polsby. Reading, Mass.: Addison-Wesley, pp. 259–293.

LPRP (Lao People's Revolutionary Party). "Report on the Results of the Election of the Seventh Central Committee of the Lao People's Revolutionary Party." March.

Luif, Paul. 1982. "Österreich zwischen den Blöcken: Bemerkungen zur Außenpolitik des neutralen Österreich." *Österreichische Zeitschrift für Politikwissenschaft* 11, no. 2: 209–220.

———. 1987. "Strategic Embargoes and European Neutrals: The Cases of Austria and Sweden." In *Challenges and Responses in European Security: TAPRI Yearbook 1986.* Ed. Vilho Harle. Aldershot: Avebury, pp. 174–188.

———. 1988. *Neutrale in die EG? Die westeuropäische Integration und die neutralen Staaten.* Informationen zur Weltpolitik no. 11. Vienna: Braumüller.

———. 1995. *On the Road to Brussels: The Political Dimension of Austria's, Finland's, and Sweden's Accession to the European Union.* Laxenburg Papers no. 11. Vienna: Braumüller.

———. 1999. "The Austrian EU Presidency: Analysis and Comment." In *Austria, Finland, and Sweden: The Initial Years of EU Membership.* Eds. Paul Luif and Karin Oberegelsbacher. Vienna: Federal Academy of Public Administration, pp. 219–238.

Luif, Paul, and Karin Oberegelsbacher, eds. 1999. *Austria, Finland, and Sweden: The Initial Years of EU Membership.* Vienna: Federal Academy of Public Administration.

Lukacs, Yehuda. 1997. *Israel, Jordan, and the Peace Process.* Syracuse, N.Y.: Syracuse University Press.

Lunt, James. 1989. *Hussein of Jordan.* London: Macmillan.

Luxembourg News. 1999. "Reding and Kinnock Say EU Officials Will Stay." June 5, p. 9.

———. 2000a. "Juncker in the UK." March 9, p. 14.

———. 2000b. "Council Praise for Luxembourg Stability Program." March 16, p. 4.

———. 2000c. "European Celebration: Fiftieth Anniversary of Schuman Plan." May 11, pp. 8–10.

———. 2000d. "Juncker Issues Veto Warning on Banking Secrecy Deal Hedged with Ifs and Buts." June 29, p. 4.

Lynch, Marc. 1999. *State Interests and Public Spheres: The International Politics of Jordan's Identity.* New York: Columbia University Press.

Madfai, Madiha. 1993. *Jordan, the United States, and the Middle East Peace Process, 1974–1991.* New York: Cambridge University Press.

Maier, Michael. 2000. "Haiders Schatten über Europa: Lehren aus dem EU-Boykott gegen Österreich." *Internationale Politik* no. 4: 19–34.

Major, John. 1993. *Prize Possession: The United States and the Panama Canal, 1903–1979*. Cambridge: Cambridge University Press.

Maniruzzaman, T. 1982. *The Security of Small States in the Third World*. Canberra: Australian National University Press.

Manners, Ian. 2000. "Small States and the Internal Balance of the European Union: Institutional Issues." In *Enlarging the European Union: The Way Forward*. Eds. Jackie Gower and John Redmond. Burlington, Vt.: Ashgate, pp. 123–135.

Manning, Patrick A. M. 1997. "A Policy Vision for the Region." In *Caribbean Public Policy: Regional, Cultural, and Socioeconomic Issues for the Twenty-first Century*. Eds. Jacqueline Anne Braveboy-Wagner and Dennis J. Gayle. Boulder: Westview Press, pp. 223–228.

Marques, Jaime G. 1989. *Panama en la encrucijada: Colonia o nación?* Panama City: Editorial Renvación Comercial, S.A.

Marquis, Christopher, and Glenn Garvin. 1999. "U.S. Spied on Panamanians to Uncover Smuggling Ring." *Miami Herald*, September 1.

Martin, Pascal. 2000. "L'Art et la science autrichiens, victimes collatérales." *Le Soir* (Brussels), May 23.

Masi, Fernando. 1989. *Stroessner: La extinción de un modelo político en Paraguay*. Asunción: Intercontinental Editora.

———. 1990. *Paraguay en el proceso de integración del Cono Sur: Discusión y análisis, IDIAL*. Asunción: IDIAL.

———. 1991a. "Paraguay: Hasta cuando la diplomacia presidencialista?" *Perspectiva Internacional Paraguaya* 3, no. 5 (January–June): 7–21.

———. 1991b. *Relaciones internacionales del Paraguay con Stroessner y sin Stroessner*. Working Paper no. 3. Asunción: Instituto Paraguayo para la Integración de America Latina, March.

———. 1993. "El contexto internacional en la transición a la democracia." In *Paraguay en transición*. Ed. Diego Abente. Caracas: Editorial Nueva Sociedad, pp. 131–146.

———. 1997. "Foreign Policy." In *The Transition to Democracy in Paraguay*. Eds. Peter Lambert and Andrew Nickson. New York: St. Martin's Press, pp. 174–182.

Masi, Fernando, and Jose Luis Simon. 1993. *Lineamientos estratégicos y programáticos para la política exterior del Paraguay de la consolidación democrática*. Document prepared at the request of Foreign Minister Diogenes Martinez, Asunción, December.

Masri, Tahir al-. 1993. Former Jordanian prime minister. Interview by Curtis R. Ryan. Amman, March 2, 1993, and July 14, 2001.

Mayrzedt, Hans, and Waldemar Hummer. 1976. *20 Jahre österreichische Neutralitäts- und Europapolitik (1955–1975): Dokumentation, Part I*. Vienna: Braumüller.

McDonald, Mark. 2000. "Tug of War for Laos." *San Jose Mercury News*, October 8.

McGraw, David J. 1994. "New Zealand's Foreign Policy Under National and Labour Governments: Variations on the 'Small State' Theme?" *Pacific Affairs* 67, no. 1: 7–25.

Melvern, Linda, Nick Anning, and David Hebditch. 1984. *Techno-Bandits.* Boston: Houghton Mifflin.
Mendez, Roberto N. 1999. *Panama, 9 de Enero de 1964: Que paso y por que.* Panama City: Imprenta Universitaria.
Mendy, Lamin. 1998. "Form Council of Muslim Elders." *Gambia Daily,* May 11, pp. 1–2.
Mény, Yves, and Yves Surel. 2000. *Par le peuple, pour le peuple: Le Populisme et les démocraties.* Paris: Fayard.
Miami Herald. 1997–1999. Various issues.
Michel, Louis. 2000. "'Je veux faire tomber l'actuel gouvernement autrichien, en tout humilité.' L'Interview de Pascal Vrebos." *Le Journal du Mardi* 40 (February 29–March 6): 4–5.
Ministry of Foreign Affairs and Foreign Trade of Barbados. 2000. *Statement of Objectives.*
Ministry of Foreign Affairs of the Republic of Guyana. 2000. *Mission Statement.*
Miranda, Anibal. 1987. *EEUU y el régimen militar Paraguayo, 1954–1958.* Asunción: El Lector.
Miranda, Carlos. 1990. *The Stroessner Era: Authoritarian Rule in Paraguay.* Boulder: Westview Press.
Momem, W. 1978. "The Foreign Policy and Relations of The Gambia." Unpublished Ph.D. diss., London School of Economics and Political Science.
Moon, Bruce. 1983. "The Foreign Policy of the Dependent State." *International Studies Quarterly* 27, no. 3 (September): 315–340.
———. 1985. "Consensus or Compliance: Foreign Policy Change and External Dependence." *International Organization* 39, no. 2 (Spring): 297–330.
Mora, Frank O. 1988. "Política exterior del Paraguay: A la busqueda de la independencia y el desarrollo." *Revista Paraguaya de Sociología* 25, no. 73 (September–December): 253–273.
———. 1993. *Politica exterior del Paraguay, 1811–1989.* Asunción: CPES.
———. 1995. "Poder duro y poder blando: La influencia en las relaciones Estados Unidos–Paraguay." *Foro Internacional* 35, no. 2 (April–June): 219–261.
———. 1997. "From Dictatorship to Democracy: The US and Regime Change in Paraguay, 1954–1994." *Bulletin of Latin American Research* 17, no. 1: 59–79.
———. 1998. "The Forgotten Relationship: United States–Paraguay, 1937–1989." *Journal of Contemporary History* 33, no. 3 (July): 451–473.
———. 2000. "Paraguay and the Inter-American System: From Authoritarianism and Paralysis to Democracy and the Application of Resolution 1080." In *The Inter-American System and the Promotion of Democracy in Latin America.* Eds. Arlene Tickner and Ruben Perina. Washington, D.C., and Bogota: OAS and Universidad de los Andes.
Moreau, Ron, and Richard Ernsberger Jr. 2001. "Strangling the Mekong." *Newsweek,* March 19.
Morgenthau, Hans J., and Kenneth W. Thompson. 1985. *Politics Among Nations: The Struggle for Power and Peace.* 6th ed. New York: Alfred A. Knopf.
Mörth, Ulrika, and Bengt Sundelius. 1993. "Dealing with a High Technology Vulnerability Trap: The USA, Sweden, and Industry." *Cooperation and Conflict* 28, no. 3 (September): 303–328.
Muñoz, Heraldo, and Joseph Tulchin, eds. 1996. *Latin American Nations in World Politics.* Boulder: Westview Press.

Mutawi, Samir. 1987. *Jordan in the 1967 War.* Cambridge: Cambridge University Press.

Neack, Laura, Jeanne A. K. Hey, and Patrick J. Haney, eds. 1995. *Foreign Policy Analysis: Continuity and Change in Its Second Generation.* Englewood Cliffs, N.J.: Prentice Hall.

Neue Zürcher Zeitung. 2000a. "Konfusion über die Sanktionen gegen Österreich: Mögliches Ausstiegsszenario der EU-Vierzehn als Totgeburt?" June 29, p. 1.

———. 2000b. "'Österreich'-Sanktionen für Prodi künftig undenkbar: Klage Wiens gegen andere EU-Staaten?" September 18, p. 3.

Nickson, Andrew. 1989. "The Overthrow of the Stroessner Regime: Reestablishing the Status Quo?" *Bulletin of Latin American Research* 8, no. 2: 185–209.

———. 1993. *Historical Dictionary of Paraguay.* Metuchen: Scarecrow Press.

———. 1997. "The Wasmosy Government." In *The Transition to Democracy in Paraguay.* Eds. Peter Lambert and Andrew Nickson. New York: St. Martin's Press, pp. 185–199.

Nimri Aziz, Barbara. 1997. "Iraq and Jordan: A Partnership Restored." *Middle East International,* May 2, pp. 18–19.

North, Andrew. 1996. "Confusion on Iraq." *Middle East International,* March 15, p. 13.

Nyang, S. 1975a. "Gambia: In Search of Viability." *Africana Marbugensia* 8: 15–28.

———. 1975b. "Ten Years of Gambia's Independence." *Presence Africaine* 94: 96–105.

OECD (Organization for Economic Cooperation and Development). 1999. *OECD National Accounts.* Vol. 1. www.oecd.org.

Ortner, Christian. 2000. "Joschka Fischer, Haiders williger Helfer." *Format* 34, August 21, p. 15.

Osborne, Milton. 2000. *The Mekong: Turbulent Past, Uncertain Future.* New York: Atlantic Monthly Press.

Pace, Roderick. 2000. "Small States and the Internal Balance of the European Union: The Perspective of Small States." In *Enlarging the European Union: The Way Forward.* Eds. Jackie Gower and John Redmond. Burlington, Vt.: Ashgate, pp. 107–119.

Pennington, Mathew. 2000. "After Twenty-five Years, Communists in Laos Show No Signs of Yielding Power." Associated Press, December 1.

Perez Balladares, Ernesto. 1999. President of Panama 1994–1999. Interview by Peter M. Sanchez. Panama City, June 10.

Perez-Venero, Alex. 1978. *Before the Five Frontiers: Panama from 1821–1903.* New York: AMS Press.

Petitpierre, Max. 1980. *Seize ans de neutralité active: Aspects de la politique étrangère de la Suisse (1945–1961).* Neuchâtel: Éditions de la Baconnière.

Pincus, Joseph. 1968. *The Economy of Paraguay.* New York: Praeger.

Porter, Gareth. 1990. "The Transformation of Vietnam's World View: From Two Camps to Interdependence." *Contemporary Southeast Asia* 12: 1–19.

Purnell, R. 1973. *The Society of States: An Introduction to International Politics.* London: Weidenfeld and Nicolson.

Qassem, Marwan al-. 1993. Former Jordanian foreign minister. Interview by Curtis R. Ryan. April 6, 1993.

Ragin, Charles C. 1987. *The Comparative Method: Moving Beyond Qualitative and Quantitative Strategies*. Berkeley: University of California Press.

Ramirez Boettner, Luis Maria. 1995. "La política exterior de la administración Wasmosy." In *Politica exterior y democracia en el Paraguay y sus vecinos*. Ed. Jose Luis Simon. Asunción: Fundación Hanns Seidel, Universidad Nacional de Asunción, pp. 89–98.

Ray, David. 1983. "The Dependency Model of Latin American Underdevelopment: Three Basic Fallacies." *Journal of Inter-American Studies and World Affairs* 15 (February): 4–20.

Rehren, Alfredo. 1994. "Wasmosy frente al Estado prebendario-clientelista: Desafios del liderazgo presidencial democrático." In *La democracia en Paraguay: Cinco años despues*. Ed. Jose Luis Simon. Asunción: Fundación Hanns Seidel, Universidad Católica, pp. 93–127.

Rifai, Zayd al-. 1993. Former Jordanian prime minister. Interview by Curtis R. Ryan. Amman, March 29, 1993.

Riquelme, Marcial Antonio. 1992. *Stronismo, golpe militar y apertura titulada*. Asunción: RP Ediciones.

———. 1994. "Toward a Weberian Characterization of the Stroessner Regime, 1954–1989." *European Review of Latin American and Caribbean Studies* no. 57: 5–31.

Ritter, Jorge. 1999. Minister of canal affairs and chief Panama CMA negotiator. Interview by Peter M. Sanchez. Panama City, June 23.

Rivarola, Domingo. 1988. "Política y sociedad en el Paraguay contemporaneo: El autoritarismo y la democracia." *Revista Paraguaya de Sociología* 25, no. 73 (September–December): 141–183.

———, ed. 1990a. *Civiles y militares en una transición atípica*. Asunción: CPES.

———, ed. 1990b. *Estado, partidos políticos y sociedad: Análisis de la transición política paraguaya*. Asunción: CPES.

Roberts, Duncan. 2000. Interview by Jeanne A. K. Hey. Luxembourg City, May 31.

Robinson, Glenn E. 1998. "Defensive Democratization in Jordan." *International Journal of Middle East Studies* 30, no. 3: 387–410.

Rodriguez Alcala, Guido. 1987. *Ideología autoritaria*. Asunción: RP Ediciones.

Rodriguez Silvero, Ricardo. 1986. *Las mayores empresas alemanas, brasilenas, norteamericanas*. Asunción: El Lector.

———. 1987. *La integración economico del Paraguay en el Brasil*. Asunción: Editorial Histórica Fundación Friedrich Nauman.

Roett, Riordan. 1991. "Paraguay Without Stroessner." In *Friendly Tyrants*. Eds. Daniel Pipes and Adam Garfinkle. New York: St. Martin's Press, pp. 285–306.

Roett, Riordan, and Richard Scott Sacks. 1991. *Paraguay: The Personalist Legacy*. Boulder: Westview Press.

Roodbeen, Hendrik. 1992. *Trading the Jewel of Great Value: The Participation of the Netherlands, Belgium, Switzerland, and Austria in the Western Strategic Embargo*. Leiden: Proefschrift.

Ropp, Steve C. 1982. *Panamanian Politics: From Guarded Nation to National Guard*. New York: Praeger.

Rosenau, James N. 1966. "Pre-Theories and Theories of Foreign Policy." In *Approaches to Comparative and International Politics*. Ed. R. Barry Farrell. Evanston, Ill.: Northwestern University, pp. 27–93.

———. 1980a. "The Adaptation of National Societies: A Theory of Political Behavior and Transformation." In *The Scientific Study of Foreign Policy.* Ed. James N. Rosenau. New York: Nichols, pp. 501–534.
———. 1980b. "Pre-Theories and Theories of Foreign Policy." In *The Scientific Study of Foreign Policy.* Ed. James N. Rosenau. New York: Nichols, pp. 115–170.
———. 1990 (originally 1966). "Pre-Theories and Theories of Foreign Policy." In *Classics of International Relations.* 2d ed. Ed. John A. Vasquez. Englewood Cliffs, N.J.: Prentice Hall, pp. 164–175.
Rothstein, Robert L. 1968. *Alliances and Small Powers.* New York: Columbia University Press.
———. 1977. *The Weak in World of the Strong.* New York: Columbia University Press.
Ruoho, Seppo. 1985. "Finnish-Soviet Trade and Technology Transfer." *Nordic Journal of Soviet and East European Studies* 2, no. 2: 23–38.
Russett, Bruce, and Harvey Starr. 1996. *World Politics: The Menu for Choice.* 5th ed. New York: W. H. Freeman.
Ryan, Curtis R. 1998a. "Elections and Parliamentary Democratization in Jordan." *Democratization* 5, no. 4: 194–214.
———. 1998b. "Jordan and the Rise and Fall of the Arab Cooperation Council." *Middle East Journal* 52, no. 3: 386–401.
———. 1998c. "Jordan in the Middle East Peace Process: From War to Peace with Israel." In *The Middle East Peace Process.* Ed. Ilan Peleg. Albany: State University of New York Press.
———. 2000a. "Between Iraq and a Hard Place: Jordanian-Iraqi Relations." *Middle East Report* no. 215 (Summer): 40–42.
———. 2000b. "Jordan's Changing Relations." *Middle East Insight* 15, no. 6 (November–December): 83–87.
Ryan, Curtis R., and David L. Downie. 1993. "From Crisis to War: Origins and Aftermath Effects of the 1990–91 Persian Gulf Crisis." *Southeastern Political Review* 21, no. 3: 491–510.
Sackx, Annemarie. 2000. "Professional Secrecy." *Luxembourg Business* 131 (June): 52–61.
Saine, A. 1996. "The Coup d'État in the Gambia, 1994: The End of the First Republic." *Armed Forces & Society* 23, no. 1: 97–111.
———. 1997. "Vision 20/20: The Gambia's Neoliberal Strategy for Social and Economic Development." *Western Journal of Black Studies* 21, no. 2 (Summer): 92–98.
———. 1998. "The Military's Managed Transition to 'Civilian' Rule." *Journal of Political and Military Sociology* 26, no. 2 (Winter): 157–168.
———. 2000. "The Soldier–Turned–Presidential Candidate: A Comparison of Flawed Democratic Transitions in Ghana and Gambia." *Journal of Political and Military Sociology* 28, no. 2 (Winter): 192–209.
Salibi, Kamal. 1998. *The Modern History of Jordan.* New York: I. B. Tauris.
Salum Flecha, Antonio. 1989. "Nueva proyección de la política internacional del Paraguay." *Perspectiva Internacional Paraguaya* 1, nos. 1–2: 157–161.
Sanders, Ron. 1989. "The Relevance and Function of Diplomacy in International Politics for Small Caribbean States." *The Round Table* no. 312: 413–424.
Sannemann, Martin. 1995. "Reflexiones sobre los desafios internacionales que enfrenta el Paraguay." In *Politica exterior y democracia en el Paraguay y*

sus vecinos. Ed. Jose Luis Simon. Asunción: Fundación Hanns Seidel, Universidad Nacional de Asunción, pp. 109–114.

Satloff, Robert. 1994. *From Abdullah to Hussein: Jordan in Transition*. Oxford: Oxford University Press.

Scranton, Margaret E. 1991. *The Noriega Years: U.S.-Panamanian Relations, 1981–1990*. Boulder: Lynne Rienner.

———. 1995. "Panama's First Post-Transition Election." *Journal of Interamerican Studies and World Affairs* 37 (Spring): 69–100.

Seiferheld, Alfredo, and Jose Luis De Tone. 1988. *El asilo a Peron y la caída de Epifanio Mendez*. Asunción: Editorial Histórica.

Senghore, Jeggan. 1982. "SeneGambia: The Logical Bases for Integration." *African Quarterly* 22: 95–110.

Sharp, Paul. 1987. "Small State Foreign Policy and International Regimes: The Case of Ireland and the European Monetary System and the Common Fisheries Policy." *Millennium* 16, no. 1: 55–72.

Shaw, Timothy. 1988. "Southern Africa in Comparative Perspective." In *Foreign Policy in Small States*. Eds. David Black, Josuha Mugyenyi, and Larry Swatuk. Halifax: Centre for Foreign Policy Studies, Dalhousie University, pp. 1–7.

Sheinin, David, ed. 2000. *Beyond the Ideal: Pan-Americanism in Inter-American Affairs*. Westport, Conn.: Greenwood.

Shlaim, Avi. 1988. *Collusion Across the Jordan: King Abdullah, the Zionist Movement, and the Partition of Palestine*. New York: Columbia University Press.

Simon, Jose Luis. 1988. "Aislamiento político internacional y desconcertación: El Paraguay de Stroessner de espaldas a America Latina." *Revista Paraguaya de Sociología* 25, no. 73 (September–December): 185–236.

———. 1989. "Del aislamiento a la reinserción internacional: El Paraguay de la inmediata transición post-stronista." *Perspectiva Internacional Paraguaya* 1, nos. 1–2: 163–200.

———. 1990a. "Integración y democracia: Una aproximación al factor externo subregional en la crisis terminal del autoritarismo stronista." *Perspectiva Internacional Paraguaya* 2, no. 4 (July–December): 139–171.

———. 1990b. *La dictadura de Stroessner y los derechos humanos*. Asunción: Comite de Iglesias.

———, ed. 1990c. *Política exterior y las relaciones internacionales del Paraguay contemporaneo*. Asunción: CPES.

———. 1990d. "Transición política pero inmovilismo e improvisación en relaciones exteriores." In *Estado, partidos políticos y sociedad: Análisis de la transición política*. Ed. Domingo Rivarola. Asunción: CPES, pp. 7–12.

———. 1990e. "Una política exterior de automarginamiento: El Paraguay en la crisis terminal del autoritarismo de Stroessner y America Latina la decada de los ochenta." In *Política exterior y relaciones internacionales del Paraguay contemporaneo*. Ed. Jose Luis Simon. Asunción: CPES, pp. 323–368.

———. 1991. *Modernización insuficiente, carencia de una vision global y condicionamientos de un estado prebendario en crisis*. Asunción: Mimeo.

———. 1993. *Propuestas para las relaciones exteriores del Paraguay de la consolidación democrática*. Asunción: UNDP.

———, ed. 1994. *La democracia en Paraguay: Cinco años despues*. Asunción: Fundación Hanns Seidel, Universidad Católica.

———. 1995a. "Las pesadillas de Wasmosy y del canciller." *Hoy,* February 18, p. 10.

———. 1995b. "Los deficits de la actual politica exterior paraguaya frente a los avances de las democracias vecinas." In *Politica exterior y democracia en el Paraguay y sus vecinos.* Ed. Jose Luis Simon. Asunción: Fundación Hanns Seidel, Universidad Nacional de Asunción, pp. 201–216.

Simon, Maron J. 1971. *The Panama Affair.* New York: Charles Scribner's Sons.

Singer, Marshall. 1972. *Weak States in a World of Powers.* New York: Free Press.

Smith, Peter H. 2000. *Talons of the Eagle: Dynamics of U.S.–Latin American Relations.* 2d ed. New York: Oxford University Press.

Sondrol, Paul. 1990. "Authoritarianism in Paraguay: An Analysis of Three Contending Paradigms." *Review of Latin American Studies* 3, no. 1: 83–105.

———. 1992a. "The Emerging New Politics of Liberalizing Paraguay: Sustained Civil-Military Control Without Democratization." *Journal of Interamerican Studies and World Affairs* 34, no. 2 (Summer): 127–163.

———. 1992b. "The Paraguayan Military in Transition and the Implications for Civil-Military Relations." *Armed Forces and Society* 19, no. 1 (Fall): 105–122.

Speech by George C. R. Moe, minister of external affairs. 1975. *Barbados Bulletin* 1, no. 3 (October–December).

Stephens, Robert. 1983. "Jordan and the Powers." In *The Shaping of an Arab Statesman: Abd al-Hamid Sharaf and the Modern Arab World.* Ed. Patrick Seale. London: Quartet Books, pp. 39–60.

Stolz, Joëlle. 2000a. "Wolfgang Schüssel triomphe, mais se prépare à une nouvelle partie de poker." *Le Monde,* September 14.

———. 2000b. "Face au succès du chancelier Schüssel, Jörg Haider lance des initiatives tous azimuts." *Le Monde,* September 15.

Stourzh, Gerald. 1985. *Geschichte des Staatsvertrages, 1945–1955: Österreichs Weg zur Neutralität—Studienausgabe.* 3d ed. Graz, Vienna, Cologne: Styria.

———. 1998. *Um Einheit und Freiheit: Staatsvertrag, Neutralität und das Ende der Ost-West-Besetzung Österreichs, 1945–1955.* 4th ed. Vol. 62 of *Studien zu Politik und Verwaltung.* Vienna, Cologne, Graz: Böhlau.

Straits Times. 2002. "Laos Minister Missing Ahead of Govt. Reshuffle." February 18.

Stratfor. 2000a. "Vietnamese Troops in Laos Due to China, Not Militants." June 21.

———. 2000b. "Continued Border Tensions Between Thailand and Laos." September 7.

Streitenberger, Wolfgang. 2000. "Die Kommission und die 'Sanktionen.'" *Die Presse,* September 1.

Stroessner, Alfredo. 1977. *Política y estrategía del desarrollo.* Asunción: Biblioteca Colorado Contemporaneo.

Stuart Fox, Martin. 1997. *Laos: A History.* New York: Cambridge University Press.

———. 1998. "Laos in 1997." *Asian Survey* 38, no. 1: 75–79.

Sutton, Paul. 1987. "Political Aspects." In *Politics, Security, and Development in Small States.* Eds. Colin Clarke and Tony Payne. London: Allen and Unwin, pp. 3–25.

Taylor, Alan R. 1982. *The Arab Balance of Power.* Syracuse: Syracuse University Press.

Telefonumfrage (telephone survey). 2000. Nr. A38 der Sozialwissenschaftlichen Studiengesellschaft, March 17–25, 2000 (998 people called).

Terrill, W. Andrew. 1985. "Saddam's Closest Ally: Jordan and the Gulf War." *Journal of South Asian and Middle Eastern Studies* 9, no. 2: 43–54.

Thayer, Carlyle A. 1994. *The Vietnam People's Army Under Doi Moi*. Singapore: Singapore Institute of Southeast Asian Studies.

———. 1999. "Laos in 1998." *Asian Survey* 39, no. 1: 38–42.

Thomas, Caroline 1987. *In Search of Security: The Third World in International Relations*. Boulder: Lynne Rienner.

Thurer, Daniel. 1998. "The Perception of Small States: Myth and Reality." In *Small States Inside and Outside the European Union: Interests and Policies*. Ed. Laurent Goetschel. Dordrecht, Netherlands: Kluwer Academic, pp. 33–42.

Thurlow, Fred. 2000. "Laos Takes Long and Winding Market Road." *Asia Times,* November 28.

Touray, Omar. 1994. "The Foreign Policy Problems of Developing Microstates: The Case of the Gambia: 1975–1990." Unpublished Ph.D. diss., University of Geneva.

———. 2000. *The Gambia and the World: A History of the Foreign Policy of Africa's Smallest State, 1965–1995*. Hamburg, Germany: Institute of African Studies.

Ulram, Peter A. 1999. "Public Opinion About the EU in Austria." In *Austria, Finland, and Sweden: The Initial Years of EU Membership*. Eds. Paul Luif and Karin Oberegelsbacher. Vienna: Federal Academy of Public Administration, pp. 139–156.

Ultima Hora. 1993. "Cancilleria diseñera nueva política exterior paraguaya." September 2, p. 12.

United Nations. 2000. *Report on the Global HIV/AIDS Epidemic*. New York: UNAIDS, June.

U.S. Southern Command. 1997. "Profile of the United States Southern Command." Fact sheet. Headquarters, U.S. Southern Command, Quarry Heights, Panama, August 19.

USIS (U.S. Information Service). 1998. Press release.

Valenzuela, Arturo. 1999. *The Collective Defense of Democracy: Lessons from the Paraguayan Crisis of 1996—A Report of the Carnegie Commission on Preventing Deadly Conflict*. New York: Carnegie Corporation of New York.

Vayrynen, Raimo. 1983. "Small States in Different Theoretical Traditions of International Relations Research." In *Small States in Europe and Dependence*. Ed. Otmar Höll. Boulder: Westview Press, pp. 83–104.

Verdross, Alfred. 1978. *The Permanent Neutrality of Austria*. Vienna: Verlag für Geschichte und Politik.

Vital, David. 1967. *The Inequality of States: A Study of the Small Power in International Relations*. Oxford: Clarendon Press.

———. 1971. *The Survival of Small States*. London: Oxford University Press.

Von Daniken, Franz. 1998. "Is the Notion of Small State Still Relevant?" In *Small States Inside and Outside the European Union: Interests and Policies*. Ed. Laurent Goetschel. Dordrecht, Netherlands: Kluwer Academic, pp. 43–48.

Voogt, Fabrice. 2000. "Louis Michel n'ira pas skier dans le Tyrol . . ." *Le Soir,* February 3.

Wahby, Mohammad. 1989. "The Arab Cooperation Council and the Arab Political Order." *American-Arab Affairs* 28, no. 2: 61–66.

Walt, Stephen M. 1987. *The Origins of Alliances.* Ithaca: Cornell University Press.

Waltz, Kenneth N. 1959. *Man, the State, and War.* New York: Columbia University Press.

———. 1979. *Theory of International Politics.* Reading, Mass.: Addison-Wesley.

Warner, Roger. 1995. *Backfire: The CIA's Secret War in Laos and Its Link to the War in Vietnam.* New York: Simon and Schuster.

Watkin, Huw. 2000. "Allies May Join to Fight Border Rebels." *South China Morning Post,* June 21.

Webster, Philip. 1998. "Britain to Back Defence Role for Europe." *The Times,* October 21.

Wendt, Alexander. 1992. "Anarchy Is What States Make of It: The Social Construction of Power Politics." *International Organization* 46, no. 2: 391–425.

———. 2000. *Social Theory of International Politics.* New York: Cambridge University Press.

West Africa. 1995a. "Sanctioning the Future." January 9–15.

———. 1995b. "Living in Crisis." February 13–19.

———. 1996a. "At Home and Abroad." October 14–20.

———. 1996b. "The Gambia: Libya Backs Jammeh." October 28–November 3.

———. 1996c. "Gambia: 'Big Four' Penalized." December 9–15.

Whitehead, Laurence. 1986. "International Aspects of Democratization." In *Transitions from Authoritarian Rule: A Comparative Perspective.* Eds. Guillermo O'Donnell, Philippe Schmitter, and Laurence Whitehead. Baltimore: Johns Hopkins University Press, pp. 3–46.

Wilson, Mary. 1987. *King Abdullah, Britain, and the Making of Jordan.* New York: Cambridge University Press.

Winestock, Geoff. 2000. "If Diplomacy Is Poker, Austria Knows How to Play the IMF Card—State Uses Nomination to Snag Bilateral Chat with Germany." *Wall Street Journal Europe,* March 14, pp. 1, 12.

Wiseman, J. A. 1996. "Military Rule in the Gambia: An Interim Assessment." *Third World Quarterly* 17: 917–940.

Wiseman, J. A., and E. Vidler. 1995. "The July 1994 Coup d'État in the Gambia: The End of an Era?" *The Roundtable* 333: 291–310.

Wong-Anan, Nopporn. 2001. "Old Guard in Charge After Laos Communist Meet." Reuters, March 14.

Wood, D. P. J. 1967. "The Smaller Territories: Some Political Considerations." In *Problems of Smaller Territories.* Ed. G. Benedict. London: Athlone Press, pp. 23–24.

Yeebo, Z. 1995. *State of Fear in Paradise: The Military Coup in the Gambia.* London: Africa Research and Information Bureau.

Yopo, Mladen. 1985. "La política exterior del Paraguay: Continuidad y cambio en el aislamiento." In *America Latina y el Caribe: Políticas exteriores para sobrevivir.* Ed. Heraldo Muñoz. Santiago: PROSPEL, pp. 447–467.

———. 1991. *Paraguay-Stroessner: La política exterior del régimen autoritario.* Santiago: PROSPEL.

Yore, Fatima Myriam. 1992. *La dominación stronista: Origenes y consolidación.* Asunción: BASE-IS.

Young, Alma H., and Dion E. Phillips, eds. 1986. *Militarization in the Non-Hispanic Caribbean.* Boulder: Lynne Rienner.

Zahariadis, Nikolaos. 1994. "Nationalism and Small-State Foreign Policy: The Greek Response to the Macedonian Issue." *Political Science Quarterly* 109, no. 4: 647–667.

Zemanek, Karl. 1959. "Wirtschaftliche Neutralität." *Juristische Blätter* 81, nos. 10–11: 249–251.

The Contributors

Zachary Abuza is assistant professor of political science and international relations at Simmons College, where he teaches Southeast Asian politics and security issues. He is the author of *Renovating Politics in Contemporary Vietnam* (Boulder: Lynne Rienner, 2002), a study of intra–communist party dissent in Vietnam. He is currently completing a study of the Al-Qaeda network in Southeast Asia.

Jacqueline Anne Braveboy-Wagner is professor of political science at the Graduate School and University Center of the City University of New York, and director of the master's program in international relations at the City College of New York. She is a former president of the Caribbean Studies Association (CSA) and is the NGO-UN representative for the International Studies Association. Her books include *Caribbean Public Policy: Regional, Cultural, and Socioeconomic Issues for the Twenty-first Century* (coeditor with Dennis Gayle; Boulder: Westview Press, 1997); *The Caribbean in the Pacific Century* (with W. Marvin Will, Dennis G. Gayle, and I. Griffith; Boulder: Lynne Rienner, 1993); *The Caribbean in World Affairs: The Foreign Policies of the English-Speaking Caribbean* (Boulder: Westview Press, 1989; rev. ed. forthcoming); *Interpreting the Third World: Politics, Economics, and Social Issues* (New York: CBS/Praeger, 1986); and *The Venezuela-Guyana Border Dispute: A Study in Conflict Resolution* (Boulder: Westview Press, 1984). She has also published numerous articles and analytical pieces in books and journals.

Jeanne A. K. Hey is associate professor of political science and director of international studies at Miami University in Oxford, Ohio. She has published in the area of foreign policy analysis, especially concerning

Latin American and small states. She is the author of *Theories of Dependent Foreign Policy and the Case of Ecuador in the 1980s* (Athens: Ohio University Press, 1995) and has published in numerous scholarly journals, including *Comparative Political Studies, The Journal of Latin American Studies, Third World Quarterly,* and *International Interactions.*

Paul Luif is a member of the scientific staff at the Austrian Institute for International Affairs in Vienna. His research focuses on media in Austria, causes of war, foreign policy of neutral countries, neutrality and nonalignment, neutral countries and European integration, European political integration, the Common Foreign and Security Policy (CFSP) of the European Union, and enlargement of the European Union.

Frank O. Mora is associate professor and chair of international studies at Rhodes College, Memphis, Tennessee. He also holds the Latin American Studies Research Fellowship at Rhodes College. Professor Mora is the author of several articles and monographs on Paraguayan politics and foreign policy, including *Política Exterior del Paraguay, 1811–1989* (Asunción: CPES). He also has published studies on civil-military relations, democratization, and U.S.–Latin American relations.

Curtis R. Ryan is assistant professor of political science at Appalachian State University in North Carolina. He was a Fulbright Scholar to the Hashimite Kingdom of Jordan in 1992–1993, working as a guest researcher at the Center for Strategic Studies at the University of Jordan. Parts of his chapter also draw on his new book, *Jordan in Transition: From Hussein to Abdullah* (Boulder: Lynne Rienner, 2003).

Abdoulaye Saine teaches African studies and international political economy in Miami University's Department of Political Science. He has published numerous articles and book chapters on the military, democracy and democratization, elections, and human rights in Gambia, Africa, and black America. Journals in which his work has appeared include *Armed Forces & Society, Electoral Studies, Journal of Democracy, Journal of Modern African Studies,* and *International Politics.*

Peter M. Sanchez is associate professor of political science at Loyola University, Chicago. He was a Senior Fulbright Scholar at the University of Panama during 1997–1998, where he taught U.S.–Latin American relations and researched the final disposition of the Panama Canal treaties and the U.S.-Panama negotiations over a continued U.S. military presence on the isthmus.

Index

About the Book

Have the changes of the past decade made this an easier or a more difficult world for small states as they pursue their foreign policy goals? To understand the foreign policies of small states, are new explanatory factors needed? Does the concept of the "small state" still have utility at all? *Small States in World Politics* addresses these questions, deftly analyzing the impact of new economic and political realities. Offering empirical richness within a consistent theoretical framework, the authors provide a comprehensive examination of small state foreign policy.

Jeanne A. K. Hey is associate professor of political science and director of international studies at Miami University, Ohio. She is coeditor of *Foreign Policy Analysis: Continuity and Change in Its Second Generation* and author of *Theories of Dependent Foreign Policy and the Case of Ecuador in the 1980s.*